TREME™

STORIES AND RECIPES
from the
HEART OF NEW ORLEANS

CHRONICLE BOOKS

SAN FRANCISCO

LOLIS ERIC ELIE

Foreword by **ANTHONY BOURDAIN**
Preface by **DAVID SIMON**
Recipe photographs by **ED ANDERSON**

www.hbo.com

Copyright © 2013 by Home Box Office, Inc. All rights reserved. HBO and related trademarks are the property of Home Box Office, Inc.

All rights reserved. No part of this book may be reproduced in any form without written permission from the publisher.

Library of Congress Cataloging-in-Publication Data:

Elie, Lolis Eric.

  Treme : stories and recipes from the heart of New Orleans / Lolis Eric Elie ; recipe photographs by Ed Anderson.

    pages cm

  Includes index.

  ISBN 978-1-4521-0969-5 (alk. paper)

  1. Cooking, American—Louisiana style. 2. Treme (Television program) 3. Cooking—Louisiana—New Orleans. I. Simon, David, 1960- II. Bourdain, Anthony. III. Title. IV. Title: Stories and recipes from the heart of New Orleans.

  TX715.2.L68E45 2013

  641.59763—dc23

                                    2012044421

Manufactured in China

Pages 18–19, Emeril's Tuna and Butter Lettuce Wraps: Recipe reproduced courtesy of Emeril Lagasse, copyright MSLO, Inc., all rights reserved.

Pages 42–43, Momofuku's Poached Eggs with Caviar: from *Momofuku* by David Chang and Peter Meehan, Photographs by Gabriele Stabile, copyright © 2009 by David Chang and Peter Meehan. Photographs copyright © 2009 by Gabriele Stabile. Used by permission of Clarkson Potter/Publishers, an imprint of the Crown Publishing Group, a division of Random House, Inc. Any third party use of this material, outside of this publication, is prohibited. Interested parties must apply directly to Random House, Inc. for permission.

Pages 54–55, Le Bernardin's Pounded Tuna with Foie Gras: from *Le Bernardin Cookbook* by Maguy Le Coze and Eric Ripert, copyright © 1998 by Maguy Le Coze and Eric Ripert. Used by permission of Doubleday, a division of Random House, Inc. Any third party use of this material, outside of this publication, is prohibited. Interested parties must apply directly to Random House, Inc. for permission.

Pages 156–57, Dooky Chase's Gumbo Z'Herbes: adapted from *The Dooky Chase Cookbook* by Leah Chase © 1990 used by permission of the publisher, Pelican Publishing Company, Inc., www.pelicanpub.com

Pages 181, 182, and 185, Rodekool met Appels and Hachee Met Leffe Bier: adapted with permission from *The Dutchman's Kitchen* by Dirk-Jan Zonneveld. Courtesy of Dirk-Jan Zonneveld.

Pages 17, 27, 34, 45, 47, 49, 50, 53, 67, 68, and 229: recipes from Soa Davies. Page 20: recipe from Chef Anne Kearney. Page 24: recipe from Chef André Daguin. Pages 28, 32, 65, and 126: recipes from Chef Jacqueline Blanchard. Page 30: recipe from Chef Aaron Burgau. Pages 36 and 160: recipes from Chef Dana Logsdon. Pages 38, 73, and 114: recipes from Chef Susan Spicer. Page 39: recipe from Chef Alon Shaya. Page 40: recipe from Chef Anne Churchill. Page 46: recipe from Chef Donald Link. Page 56: recipe from Chef Myung Hee Lee. Page 58: recipe from Chef John Besh. Page 60: recipe from Chefs Allison Vines-Rushing and Slade Rushing. Page 62: recipe from Chef Greg Sonnier. Page 70: recipe from Chef Sue Zemanick. Page 82: recipe from Dutch Morial. Page 83: recipe from Althea Pierce. Pages 84 and 87: recipes from Phyllis Montana-LeBlanc. Page 88: recipe from Kermit Ruffins. Pages 96, 99, 166, and 175: recipes from Chef Poppy Tooker. Page 98: recipe from Chef Ken Smith. Pages 102, 103, and 104: recipes from Chef Tory McPhail. Page 105: recipe from Chef Paulette Rittenberg. Page 106: recipe from Chef Frank Brigtsen. Pages 112, 122, 128, 146, 149, and 153: recipes from Gerri Elie. Page 113: recipe from Chef Austin Leslie. Page 119: recipe from Chef Sue Wespy Ceravolo. Page 133: recipe from Carmen Owens. Page 137: recipe from Chef Darin Nesbit. Page 138: recipe from Chef Nathaniel Zimet. Page 140: recipe from Chef Joe Segreto. Page 142: recipe from Chef Wayne Baquet. Page 143: recipe from Prejean's Restaurant. Page 155: recipe from Chef Frances Chauvin. Page 167: recipe from Chef Christina Quackenbush. Page 172: recipe from Chef Scott Boswell. Page 174: recipe from Chef Philipe La Mancusa. Page 189: recipe from Chef Ruth Fertel. Page 191: recipe from Chef Alfred Singleton. Page 194: recipe from Chef Tenney Flynn. Page 197: recipe from Chef Stephen Stryjewski. Page 205: recipe from Ralph Brennan. Page 206: recipe from Chef Mary Jo Mosca. Page 209: recipe from Chef Jared Tees. Pages 213 and 214: recipes from Chris Hannah. Page 215: recipe from Chris McMillian. Pages 216 (top) and 222 (top): recipes from Lucinda Weed. Pages 216 (bottom) and 222 (bottom): recipes from Marvin Allen. Pages 217 and 221 (bottom): recipes from Rhiannon Enlil. Page 218: recipe from Lu Brow. Page 220: recipe from Kimberly Patton Bragg. Page 221 (top): recipe from Wayne Curtis. Page 223: recipes from Star Hodgson. Page 224 (top): recipe from Martin Sawyer. Page 224 (bottom): recipe from Geoffrey Wilson. Page 225: recipe from Ian Julian.

Page 10, Ellis Marsalis's quote: reprinted with permission of Ellis Marsalis.

Page 141, Martin Brothers' letter to striking Streetcar Workers: Clovis J. and Bennie Martin to the Striking Carmen of Division 194, August 6, 1929, New Orleans Street Railway Union records, Louisiana Research Collection, Tulane University.

Page 141, Bennie Martin's quote: from http://www.poboyfest.com/history

Page 150, Joe Logdson quote: from oral history, given by Dana Logsdon on 9/3/2012.

Page 211, Ella Brennan's quote: reprinted with permission from Ella Brennan.

Page 226, origin of the term "cocktail": from http://www.museumoftheamericancocktail.org/museum/thebalance.html

TRADEMARKS

Page 27: Sriracha Hot Chili Sauce is a registered trademark of Huy Fong Foods, Inc.

Pages 30, 35, 47, 98, 166, and 191: Crystal is a registered trademark of Baumer Foods, Inc.

Page 30: Pernod is a registered trademark of Pernod Ricard.

Page 30: Wondra is a registered trademark of General Mills Marketing, Inc.

Page 65: Bob's Red Mill is a registered trademark of Bob's Red Mill Natural Foods, Inc.

Pages 65, 67, and 126: Steen's is a registered trademark of C. S. Steen Syrup Mill, Inc.

Page 68: Huy Fong is a registered trademark of Huy Fong Foods, Inc.

Pages 70 and 111: Grand Marnier is a registered trademark of Societe des Produits Marnier-Lapostolle.

Pages 98, 138, 143, and 189: Tabasco is a registered trademark of McIlhenny Company.

Pages 102 and 103: Chef Paul Prudhomme's Poultry Magic Seasoning Blend is a registered trademark of Magic Seasoning Blends, LLC.

Pages 102 and 189: Zatarain's is a registered trademark of Zatarain's Brands, Inc.

Page 111: Mandarine Napoleon is a registered trademark of Koninklijke De Kuyper B.V.

Page 111: St-Germain is a registered trademark of Cooper Spirits, International.

Pages 116, 213, 216, 222, and 224: Angostura is a registered trademark of Angostura International Limited.

Page 143: Kitchen Bouquet is a registered trademark of The HV Food Products Company.

Page 155: McCormick is a registered trademark of McCormick & Company, Inc.

Page 182: Guinness is a registered trademark of Diageo Ireland.

Page 189: Hellmann's is a registered trademark of CPC International, Inc.

Page 194: Chef Paul Prudhomme's Shrimp Magic Seasoning Blend is a registered trademark of Magic Seasoning Blends, LLC.

Page 198: Matouk's West Indian is a registered trademark of Highgate Investment Corp.

Pages 213 and 224: Maraschino Originale Luxardo is a registered trademark of Girolamo Luxardo S.P.A.

Pages 214 and 215: Herbsaint is a registered trademark of The Sazerac Company, Inc.

Page 215: Legendre is a registered trademark of The Sazerac Company, Inc.

Pages 215 and 216: Peychaud's is a registered trademark of The Sazerac Company, Inc.

Page 216: Hayman's Old Tom Gin is a registered trademark of Hayman Distillers.

Pages 216, 221 and 224: Benedictine is a registered trademark of Bacardi & Company Limited.

Page 222: Chambord is a registered trademark of Brown-Forman Corporation.

Page 222: Domaine de Canton is a registered trademark of 750 ML, LLC.

Page 223: Bulleit is a registered trademark of Diageo North America, Inc.

Page 224: Maker's Mark is a registered trademark of Maker's Mark Distillery, Inc.

Page 224: Rittenhouse is a registered trademark of Heaven Hill Distilleries, Inc.

Page 225: Hendrick's Gin is a registered trademark of William Grant & Sons Limited.

Designed by Public
Series photographs by Paul Schiraldi
Food styling by Lillian Kang
Prop styling by Christine Wolheim

10 9 8 7 6 5 4 3 2

Chronicle Books LLC
680 Second Street
San Francisco, CA 94107
www.chroniclebooks.com

DEDICATION

To the cooks of New Orleans, the women and men who tend the home fires; who shuck the oysters and stir the stock pots; who peel the potatoes and the shrimp before the chef arrives; who sell their pralines and calas and hot sausage sandwiches at second-line parades and church suppers; who tend the little patches of mustard greens and Creole tomatoes and fence-buttressed vines of mirlitons; who share their food with family and friends and neighbors and strangers and the members on the sick and shut-in list; who understood and taught us that red beans and rice is a taste of home, a sacramental dish, a statement of what is good and necessary about New Orleans, and a full-throated declaration about why rebuilding this city and its culture was and remains a matter of great urgency.

CONTENTS

Foreword..6

Preface...8

Introduction by Janette Desautel.................10

JANETTE DESAUTEL

Oysters on the Half Shell with Yuzu Mignonette.............. 17

Emeril's Tuna and Butter Lettuce Wraps 18

Peristyle's Jumbo Lump Crabmeat and Herb Salad
over Chilled Roasted Beets and Pickled Onions.................20

L'Hôtel de France's Foie Gras in a Pumpkin Terrine.......24

Seared Duck Breast on Green Onion Pancakes
with Daikon Salad...27

Creole Crab-and-Corn Bisque.....................................28

Patois Oyster Stew with Pan-Fried Grouper
and Fried Parsnips 30

Yaka Mein..32

Ajan Étouffée...34

La Spiga's Sweet Potato Turnovers.............................. 36

Bayona's Sweet Potato Brioche.................................... 38

Domenica's Crispy Kale... 39

Karma Kitchen's Husk-Wrapped Mushroom
Boudin Tamales 40

Momofuku's Poached Eggs with Caviar...................... 42

Soa's Garden Vegetable "Fettuccine"
with Fresh Tomato Sauce..45

Herbsaint's Shrimp and Louisiana
Brown Rice Risotto 46

Crawfish Ravioli with Sea Urchin Butter Sauce
and Mississippi Paddlefish Roe...................................47

Clemenceau'd Shrimp... 49

Peppy Lobsters..50

Listen-to-Your-Fish Fish..53

Le Bernardin's Pounded Tuna with Foie Gras..............54

Genghis Khan's Whole Fried Fish...............................56

Grandmother Besh's Braised Rabbit with Cavatelli 58

MiLa's Chicory Coffee–Glazed Quail
with Swiss Chard and Creamy Grits 60

Gabrielle's Slow-Roasted Duck with Cracklin' Skin 62

Paper-Skin Chicken and Rice-Flour Waffles
with Asian-Cajun Red Pepper Syrup............................65

Bacon-Wrapped Pork Loin with Smothered Greens,
Butternut Squash, and Cane Syrup Jus.......................67

Peppered Hanger Steak with Crispy Rice Cakes............ 68

Gautreau's Citrus–Olive Oil Cake
with Kumquat Marmalade and Almonds......................70

Bayona's Café au Lait Pots de Crème
with Mudslide Cookies... 73

Thyme-Satsuma–Black Pepper Ice...............................75

The Food of the Streets..76

ANTOINE BATISTE AND DESIREE

Dutch Morial's Oyster Dressing....................................82

Tee's Smothered Okra..83

Creole Stuffed Bell Peppers...84

Smothered Cabbage with Onion and Bacon 85

Creole Succotash..87

Kermit Ruffins's Butter Beans 88

White Beans and Shrimp 89

Kermit Ruffins: Life is a Picnic Every Day...................... 90

TONI AND CREIGHTON BERNETTE

Pecan Pancakes 94

Crawfish Calas with Green Garlic Mayonnaise................ 96

Upperline's Oysters St. Claude 98

Trout Farci..99

Pasta with Shrimp, Garlic, and Parsley....................... 101

Commander's Palace Thanksgiving Dinner....................102

Chunky Peanut Butter and
Chocolaty Banana Cake..105

Brigtsen's Banana Bread Pudding 106

A Brief History of Bread Pudding................................107

JACQUES JHONI

Oatmeal and Fresh Berry Parfaits
with Chantilly Cream 111

Uptown Egg and Rice..112

Black Beans and Rum à la Austin Leslie 113

Bayona's Roasted Duck with Bourbon-Molasses Sauce
and Sweet Potato Fries..114

Habanero-Laced Lamb Shanks
with Spiced Couscous 116

The Great Gumbo Controversy 117

Pie Four Nuts... 118

Pound Cake Paul Trevigne...119

LADONNA BATISTE-WILLIAMS

Creole Gumbo 122

Smothered Turnip Soup...125

Jalapeño Cornbread...126

Yeast Calas...127

Potato Salad 128

Oven-Braised Turkey Necks..129

Cajun v. Creole (v. Alan Richman)...............................130

Microwave Pralines..133

DAVIS MCALARY

Waffles (or Pancakes) Lafon 136

Bourbon House Trio of Oyster Shooters 137

Boucherie's Collard Greens
with French Fried Grits 138

Eleven 79's Pasta Bolognese 140

Signature Sandwiches:
Po-Boys, Poor Boys, and Muffalettas 141

Li'l Dizzy's Trout Baquet 142

Prejean's Pheasant-Quail-Andouille Gumbo 143

ALBERT LAMBREAUX

Carrot Casserole 146

Vegetarian Mustard Greens 147

Lambreaux's Cornbread 148

Cornbread–French Bread Dressing 149

How Do You Explain New Orleans' "French" Bread? 150

Stuffed Mirliton 153

Cushaw Pie 155

Dooky Chase's Gumbo Z'herbes 156

ANNIE TALARICO

La Spiga's Buttermilk Biscuits 160

Beignets and Calas 163

Salad without Papers 164

Shrimp Bisque 166

Chicken Adobo 167

TERRY COLSON

Beignets 171

Restaurant Stanley's Chili-Prawn Po-Boy
with Asian Slaw 172

Kitchen Witch's Hot and Cold Redfish Salad 174

Chicken Étouffée 175

Oyster Farmers: Croatian, Black, Vietnamese,
and Cambodian 176

SONNY SCHILDER

Rodekool met Appels
(Braised Red Cabbage with Apples) 181

Hachee met Leffe Bier
(Beef Onion Stew with Dark Beer) 182

Bun (Vietnamese Vermicelli Salad with Beef) 183

Madame Bégué and the Invention of Brunch 184

Appeltaart (Dutch Apple Pie) 185

DELMOND LAMBREAUX

Muscadine Wine Lemonade 188

Ruth's Garlicky White Shrimp Remoulade 189

Dickie Brennan's Steakhouse Tomato Napoleon 191

Zucchini and Shrimp Semplice 192

GW Fin's Grilled Lemon Fish with Thai-Style
Mirliton Slaw, Blue Crab Fritters, and Chile Oil 194

Cochon's Braised Pig
with Stewed Turnips and Cabbage 197

Red Beans and Rice with Smoked Turkey Wings 198

Pork and Beans with Bacon and Onions 199

The Mirliton Missionary 200

NELSON HIDALGO

Ralph's on the Park's Crabmeat Lasagna 205

Mosca's Chicken à la Grande 206

Cousin Kami's Carne Guisada 207

New Orleans Cuisine: Caribbean or Southern? 208

Besh Steakhouse's Cowboy Steak with
Wild Mushrooms, Root Vegetables,
and Bordelaise Sauce 209

AUNT MIMI

Brandy Crusta 213

French 75 214

Absinthe Suissesse 214

Sazerac 215

Ramos Gin Fizz 216

Vieux Carré 216

Hurricane 217

The Casserole Cocktail 218

Congo Square Cooler 220

Ginger-Peach Julep 221

The Neutral Ground 221

Bittersweet Sour 222

Second Line Swizzler 222

N'awlins Nectar 223

Creole Sno-Ball 223

The Marsaw 224

McMillian 224

Hot-or-Cold Hendrick's #1 225

New Orleans and the Invention of the Cocktail 226

Basics

Basic Creole Seasoning Blend 228

Fish Stock 228

Shrimp Stock 229

Rich Shrimp Stock 229

Basic Chicken Stock 230

Veal Stock 230

Postscript 231

Acknowledgments 233

Index 234

Table of Equivalents 240

FOREWORD

The city of New Orleans has, rather famously over time, attracted a diverse, some might even say crazy-ass, mix of characters. It's one of the things we all love about the place: it's black, it's white, it's Spanish, Indian, French, Canadian, Italian, African—who the hell knows? Whatever it is today, it's a strange and wonderful mutation, a hell broth of colors, flavors, and influences that could only have happened here. It is the most uniquely American of cities because, let's face it, what came out of New Orleans, what started there, jazz, for instance, could have happened nowhere else.

Like very few other great cities around the world, the price of admission to New Orleans—what qualifies one for citizenship, so to speak—is simply a deep and abiding love for the place: a need to live there no matter what. What unites the characters on the show *Treme* is that same love for a place; an attitude, a culture where delicious food and great music are birthrights.

You could, I suggest, say similar things about professional cooks—also a subculture with a tendency to attract misfits, the mad, the passionate, refugees, fugitives, seekers, and sensualists. They could survive in no other industry.

Unique for television, this is a show about people making things—and not just thing things, but intangible things. It's about the creative process, about what it takes and how it happens that certain people make beautiful music or delicious food and others can't. It's about the cost of trying to do those things, the difficulty and the obstacles, how undervalued a thing like "culture" can be in a world where an entire city is allowed to drown in slow motion on national television while its leaders do nothing.

My responsibilities on the show have largely revolved around the chef character, Janette Desautel, someone whose trials and tribulations I like to think I understand. In the process

of working on her story, I found a curious and wonderful thing: that just about every real-life, hot-shot, big-time chef I mentioned the show to was already passionate about it. They loved the show, they loved the music, they loved who worked on it. When I called up friends like Dave Chang, Eric Ripert, Tom Colicchio, and Wylie Dufresne and asked if they'd care to appear as themselves, every one of them immediately said yes. These are busy guys for whom it usually takes six months to schedule a cup of coffee. Dave Chang, these days juggling a restaurant fleet of half a dozen (and growing) and constantly in motion between New York, Sydney, Japan, Canada, and elsewhere, has repeatedly put down the phone and instantly cleared an otherwise unclearable schedule for what has turned out to be a continuing role.

The show's creators built a kitchen replica for Chang, a hybrid of his groundbreaking, multistarred Momofuku Ko and the more casual Momofuku Ssäm in New Orleans, that he has described as better designed than the originals. He has had to create, and re-create, dishes for the show, and—more painfully, I believe—learn to act, as himself. Not known for being the most agreeable guy on the planet, he has done all these things enthusiastically and with aplomb.

These days, Eric Ripert, chef/owner of Le Bernardin in New York, can sometimes be seen walking slowly to work across Central Park, practicing his lines in a thick French accent. He, too, has had to play himself on the show, as one of Desautel's three mentors during her season-long odyssey in New York. I know that the prospect of reciting lines on television fills him with mortal dread, yet he perseveres. The scenes set in the kitchen at Le Bernardin were in fact shot there, using a great number of its actual staff. At least as significantly, Eric's trusted lieutenant and enforcer, the iron fist inside his velvet glove, Soa Davies, has been dispatched on numerous occasions to attend to the details of 2006-era David Bouley-esque food; or, more recently, a mammoth, classically old-school chef-only feast that included *lièvre à la royale*— "an Escoffier-era preparation of wild hare, carefully boned, stuffed with foie gras and truffles, served with a sauce made from its own blood."

Local heroes like Susan Spicer have been with the show since the beginning, working on and off camera to make the food and all that goes on around the food look and sound right.

So, the involvement of all of the above, and the fierce love that chefs everywhere seem to have for the show, helps, I think, to explain why you will see recipes from Spicer, Ripert, Dave Chang, John Besh, and Donald Link in the pages that follow—along with other real-life cooks and artists whose food I've enjoyed over the years, like Kermit Ruffins and Austin Leslie.

The on-camera talent, both chefs and otherwise, may be already ridiculously overqualified, but what surprised me on my first visit to the writers' room (and many subsequent meals with its occupants) was how seriously food-obsessed the show's creators are. David Simon is, I have found, a complete slut when it comes to a good meal. Lolis Eric Elie has been writing about food (and eating it) expertly for years. George Pelecanos comes from the restaurant business, having pretty much grown up under a broiler— and the rest seem all too happy to follow a day's work with many hours of multicourse adventures in food. In fact, I have serious suspicions about Simon's actual motivation for dragooning all these great chefs onto the show: I think he does it so he can eat in their restaurants.

Food, music, and New Orleans are all passions about which—it seems to me—all reasonable persons of substance should be vocal. *Treme* does that week after week. This book gives voice to characters, both real and imaginary, whose love and deep attachments to a great but deeply wounded city should be immediately understandable with one bite.

Anthony Bourdain
Writer, HBO's *Treme*

PREFACE

Unless arrested, I tend toward pounds. And they tend toward me. And because my metabolism begins falling to the canvas in the first and second rounds of any bout with anything fried, fatty, or flavorful, I have long been wary of New Orleans and all that it offers.

This is not to say that I have avoided the Crescent City and its fare. On the contrary, I have taken a home in the belly of that beast, gone to work there, embraced the very idea of New Orleans in the same way that all pilgrims do.

Moth to flame, sure. But always, I flutter toward the light with a certain self-awareness, even self-loathing. The town is lethal in so many ways. Its decadence is legendary; its very physicality, a romantic argument for gluttony and sloth and debauch. From ruined shotguns to crumbling French Creole cottages to vacant business district warehouses, New Orleans actually manages to fall apart more beautifully than any other place on earth.

To live in such a place, you have two choices: One is to live life in measured, compartmentalized moments. Overdo it, then repent. Then overdo it a little more, then repent a little more—a careful balance of joy and regret that makes the annual Carnival-Lent ritual an everyday narrative. New Orleans, after all, can burn ordinary human life down to its embers with food, with drink, with music, with sex, and with all possible combinations of those things. To reside for any length of time in the city is to walk gingerly through an alluring minefield, blowing a leg off one night, then limping around for a few days, walking off the hurt, then going back out to blow the other leg to shards in similar fashion. The other choice, to paraphrase our greatest warrior-poet of excess, Shane MacGowan, is to take your entire life as you would a whore. Which is to say, throw all restraint to the wind and immerse yourself in the New Orleans street parade without the slightest self-restraint, self-regard, or hope of salvation.

It is hard to argue against the merits of the latter, I admit. But given that most of us would last about fourteen months before being carted off and entombed at the foot of Canal Street, one must acknowledge that it is, alas, a choice with some fixed costs. But again, we are talking about fourteen very good months.

By the time we started the second season of *Treme*, I weighed 200 pounds, at least 15 more than said frame has any right to carry. By the time that season of filming ended six months later, I was up to 218 and approaching the planetary realm. And this, despite the fact that I had tried not to eat extra meals on the film set; to hunt down a bowl of Vietnamese *pho* once or twice a week, omitting noodles; to restrict myself to no more than two or three batter-fortified po-boys a month.

I retreated to Baltimore for a Lenten period of four months. When I returned for Season 3 filming, I weighed a crisp, clean 190 pounds and the wardrobe department had to punch fresh holes high in my leather belts. And then, of course, it began again.

Now, as I write this, from Baltimore—or inpatient rehab, as others might legitimately term it—I am obliged to reflect on how much affection I have for a place that wreaks so much havoc on the human condition, while at the same time exalting the human spirit.

For its part, New Orleans is unrepentant. My producing partner in *Treme*, Eric Overmyer, recalls a morning when he was greeted by a New Orleans *Times-Picayune* account of a public health study that had calculated the city to be the fattest in these United States. The front-page photograph accompanying news of the study was that of an enormous human midsection navigating Canal Street. The bold kicker above the headline offered only one syllable: "Duh." I confess I haven't gone to the *Times-Pic* library to confirm Eric's memory. It is, in the parlance of old newspapermen, too good a story to check out.

Is the food really that good? Does the absinthe tempt because of its actual effect, or because we know it is absinthe and therefore fraught? Is New Orleans a wonder because of its grandiose carnival of culture and street theater, or because it requires one to be, well, something of a happy fool to live there?

The crime is epic and appalling. The schools, problematic at best, catastrophic at worst. Government, when it is not inert, is hilariously, shamelessly corrupt. Nothing works quite as it should. Levees collapse. Pumping stations fail. Potholes become sinkholes and, eventually, geologic phenomena. When the road collapsed a block from my home, the city was good enough, after a couple weeks, to half-bury a plastic, orange-and-white barrel in the gaping void. So it remained for months, until Mardi Gras, when neighbors rallied, festooning the civic totem with beads and a boa.

And that which is great to New Orleans—that which is, frankly, the only engine that powers the town from day to day, is not very good for people when experienced day to day. I did not make the grave mistake of coming here in my teens or early twenties, of enrolling, say, at Tulane or Loyola as an undergraduate. I would be dead now. Or if not dead, then spent up and rode hard and put away somewhere down in the Bywater with the other too-long-at-the-fair wraiths.

All in all, not a bad life, but a definite choice.

So here, in such context, we have an assemblage of classic and nouveau New Orleans cuisine. Some might innocently call it a cookbook. And if used in careful, Presbyterian moderation, it can be considered no worse than that. If you love New Orleans, if you love food, if you savor the great banquet of life, you could—once a week, perhaps—pull it down from a shelf and wallow in some joy. And then you could replace it on that shelf, perhaps a higher one, and leave it be for a fortnight or two. No problem.

Or you can read and learn and cook and eat to your heart's content. In which case, this is not a cookbook. It seems so as you stand in a sunlit bookstore and glance at its contents, I know. On page after page, you are greeted by recipes from not only the culinary canon of New Orleans, but from some of America's finest chefs working in homage to Southern, Creole, or Cajun fare. What could be more benign, more reasoned than a fresh new taste, a new challenge every now and then. Yet if consulted and used daily and without sufficient self-reflection, this compendium is the work of Mephistopheles. He will own you. He will own more of you with every meal, and, of course, there will be more of you to own with every meal. You will be transfigured. And soon, too soon, you will die. And when you do, when Doc Minyard's men come with the litter to haul you to Metairie or Greenwood or St. Roch or wherever you are to moulder, they will first pry the last shard of chili-prawn po-boy from your rigored clutches, wipe the remoulade from your weirdly grinning mouth with a rag, and then proceed to knock a larger hole where your front door once sufficed, so that they might actually be able to egress your epic remains into the great and knowing gape of the waiting morgue wagon.

There now. If that last paragraph doesn't sell some copies, well, hey, I guess I don't know what will.

David Simon
Writer and Executive Producer, HBO's *Treme*

INTRODUCTION
by **Janette Desautel**

New Orleans food has always been magical for me.

A couple of times a year my parents would drive my sister and me down from Huntsville to spend a weekend in the Crescent City. We'd go to Saints games or the museum or Carnival parades. Then we'd eat. I didn't care if it was po-boys from Parasol's, buttermilk drops from McKenzie's, Lucky Dogs on Royal Street, or brunch at Commander's Palace. I loved it all. I looked forward to those trips like I looked forward to Christmas.

New Orleans has always been a tourist town, and the waiters never failed to put on a fiery show for two little girls from Alabama. At Antoine's it was flaming Baked Alaska. At Brennan's it was flaming Bananas Foster. At Galatoire's, Daddy always finished the meal with *café brûlot*, and the waiters made a show of telling us girls to move our elbows off the table. By the time the *café brûlot* was lit, our elbows were right back where they weren't supposed to be. So the waiter would drizzle some of the flaming coffee on the tablecloth inches from the offending arms.

Nobody believes me, but I swear this is how it happened:

We were in Café Du Monde. Mama always taught us that, if our food was hot, we should blow on it so it wouldn't burn our tongues. When the beignets got to the table, they were really hot. So I took a deep breath and blew on them as hard as I could. Some of the powdered sugar blew all over my sister's face. And in her hair. And on her Frank Warren jersey. Call it magic. Call it an accident. Call it little sister's revenge for a certain doll that remains missing to this day.

Eating in New Orleans made me want to cook. It's not just the food. It's the passion of the people about their food. You succumb to it. If you're standing in line at the supermarket, the lady in front of you will look at the items in your basket and ask you how you're going to cook them. If you're at the fish market, they'll give you a couple of just-boiled crawfish to munch on while you wait your turn. And don't mention the word roux. You'll get a dissertation from everybody within earshot on the proper color and proportions to strive for when you heat your flour and oil.

This book is designed to put you in the middle of one of those roux conversations. Reading it, you'll get a sense of the various peoples and backgrounds and philosophies that make New Orleans one of the world's food capitals. As the great pianist Ellis Marsalis famously put it, "In New Orleans, culture doesn't come down from on high, it bubbles up from the street." That's what distinguishes this place.

Let's face it: these days, every 'burg or 'ville worth its salt has one or two restaurants with a Wine Spectator Award of Excellence and a CIA graduate promising fresh, local ingredients cooked to perfection. What New Orleans has that most of these other places don't is a real dialog between fine dining and traditional home cooking. Sure, this book contains recipes from James Beard Award–winners like John Besh and Susan Spicer and Donald Link. But we also have recipes from LaDonna Batiste-Williams, whose neighborhood barroom cooks up some mean specials; and her mother, Odella Brooks, whose Creole gumbo is not like anything you'll find at a white-tablecloth place. We have recipes from some of the famous chefs I've cooked with in New York, like Eric Ripert, David Chang, and the inimitable Enrico Brulard. But I'm just as excited about the fact that we have recipes from Kermit Ruffins, a trumpet player.

This book is like a picture of the real New Orleans I've come to know. It's multiracial. It's formal and fanciful, planned and improvised, and above all soulful.

JANETTE DESAUTEL

My parents didn't discourage me from being a cook, but they didn't encourage me either. They are wonderful, practical, conservative people. And when I enrolled at the University of Alabama, they couldn't have been happier. (My father went to Alabama. The Saints' quarterback Ken Stabler went to Alabama. The Saints' defensive lineman, Frank Warren, and my sister, went to Auburn. Roll damn Tide!) After a year, I knew college wasn't for me. I didn't do badly; I just didn't like it.

So I made a deal with my parents: I could move to Birmingham and work for one year with Frank Stitt at his restaurant, Highlands Bar and Grill. He and Daddy are both originally from Cullman, AL, and Frank's the dean of Alabama fine dining. If Frank said I had talent, I could leave college permanently to become a chef.

Me walking into the kitchen at Highlands was like a kid walking into F.A.O. Schwarz. It seemed to me that the kitchen was large and gleaming, and had every gadget an aspiring cook could ask for. (When I told Frank's wife and business partner, Pardis, about this memory, she laughed. "No one would ever describe the Highlands kitchen as 'large and gleaming.' It is cramped and dark and a wonder that we are able to produce what we do every day.") Frank combines Alabama ingredients with French techniques and inspiration he got cooking at Chez Panisse in Berkeley and with Richard Olney in France. I couldn't have explained it to you then, but once I saw his approach, I knew something immediately. I wanted to combine New Orleans, Alabama, and France in my restaurant. After three years, Frank kicked me out of the nest. "Either you need to go to France or to cooking school," he told me.

My parents weren't ready to see their little girl go to a far-off foreign country. I was ready for the adventure, but just a little scared at the prospect of a French chef yelling at me in a language I couldn't understand. So I enrolled at the CIA—the Culinary Institute of America, that is. Hyde Park, New York.

Things might be different now with all this food and cooking on television, but when I was in college, if you were obsessed with food and cooking the way I was, you didn't have a whole lot of people to talk to. Being at the CIA, I felt like the Muslim who finally makes it to Mecca, or the ballerina who finally makes it to the Bolshoi. I had found my people. It was hard; everybody was competitive, and there were more than a few backstabbers in the bunch. But the thing I really remember is being around a bunch of people you could talk to about food, really talk to, and not only not have them look at you like you were crazy, but also have them contribute to the conversation.

Everybody had their ideas about what they wanted to do when they left the CIA, which famous chef they wanted to work for in New York or in France. As much as I liked the idea of the bright lights, I knew I ultimately wanted to cook in the kitchens of the Crescent City. But first I had to go to France. It's a rite of passage.

I had this great idea that, using the CIA network, I would cook my way across the country. Various regions, various styles, various experiences. Then I found Chef André Daguin at l'Hôtel de France in Auch. Chef Daguin played a major role in putting the food of Gascony on the international culinary map. Foie gras, cassoulet, duck confit—these are signature dishes of the region that are now on almost every Frenchified menu in the United States. If you don't know the Michelin system, it's hard to explain that even one star is almost impossible to get. The standards of food and service exceed those of almost all the restaurants most of us have ever been to. Two stars is even impossibler to get, and three stars is the impossiblest. L'Hôtel de France had two Michelin stars. Auch is not Paris. No one comes there to see the Louvre and stay for dinner. Many of the diners have traveled specifically to eat at the restaurant. That experience taught me to imagine that every diner has come a long way and gone through a lot of trouble just to eat your food. You have to make every meal count.

Chef used to tell us all the time, *"Va chercher le goût là ou il est et ramène le dans les assiettes sans l'abimer,"* or "Go get the taste where it is and bring it back to the plates without damaging it." His other favorite saying was, *"Vous êtes ici pour apprendre où et quand le gout est le meilleur"*: "You are here to learn where and when taste is at its best." Chef's daughter, Ariane, founded D'Artagnan, the great purveyor of foie gras and other items that have gradually become less rare on American restaurant menus, thanks in part to her. She reminded me of another of chef's adages. "A chef is not judged by how he cooks with luxurious items—foie gras, caviar, truffles, lobster. A chef is judged by his ability to use and do something tasty with all the different cuts of any animal."

By the time I returned to New Orleans in the mid-1990s, the dining scene had changed. No one talked about the oysters Rockefeller at Antoine's, or the blackened redfish at K-Paul's, or the gumbo at Dooky Chase, or the soufflé potatoes at Arnaud's. It was all about the barbecued shrimp and banana cream pie at Emeril's, the red pepper–brioche bread pudding at Mike's on the Avenue, the slow-roasted duck at Gabrielle, the conch with risotto and Scotch Bonnet sauce at Dominique's, the butternut-shrimp bisque and pecan pie at Brigtsen's, and the crabmeat cheesecake and the white chocolate bread pudding at Palace Café. It didn't have to be fancy. The Trout Muddy Water at Uglesich's was a big hit with all the chefs, as was the fried chicken at Willie Mae's, the roast beef po-boy at Parasol's, and the sweet potato turnovers at La Spiga. And by then New Orleans had discovered Vietnamese food. Nine Roses, Pho Tau Bay, Dong Phuong, and Kim Son—we went to all of them.

A lot of the men act like women are only in the kitchen as some sort of affirmative action experiment. They're pulling for us to quit. They forget about all those mothers and grandmothers and maids and church ladies who cooked the first good food they ever ate! I'd seen some of that at CIA. Don't get me started. There were two women in New Orleans that all the women chefs and many of the men wanted to work for: Susan Spicer and Anne Kearney. Bayona was hot then. Susan had just won a James Beard Award a few years earlier. Everybody loved her food. She could not have been a better teacher. She knew how to take traditional, home-cooking recipes and make them at home in a white tablecloth

restaurant. Sure, you grew up on peanut butter and jelly, but did you ever think to put smoked duck, cashew nut butter, and pepper jelly between your slices of whole-grain bread? Even if your father hunted quail, like mine did, and your mother cooked them, did either of them ever think of cold smoking quail, then frying it, then putting it on a pear salad with a bourbon dressing?

For a young chef, moving around is an essential part of the education process. So after two years with Susan, it was time for me to move a few blocks away to Peristyle, where Anne Kearney was doing a totally different style of food. Anne had cooked at Emeril's, then moved to Peristyle. But when chef John Neal died, she bought the restaurant.

Anne describes her food as "American bistro fare," and she sticks far closer to the French classics than Susan does. Dishes like oysters poached in a Pernod-infused velouté, trout amandine, or mussels *bourride* might taste different when Anne cooks them, but they still would be at home on a French bistro menu. And Anne was intense. Looking back on those days, and having been through the Brulard boot camp, I sometimes forget that Anne could be just as exacting and just as demanding. Well, almost as exacting and demanding.

Recently, I ran into Kamili Magee (now Hemphill), a young chef from Jackson, Mississippi, who used to work with me at Peristyle. This is what she remembers about working for Anne: "We were always thinking about the diner. Not only would we think of the food, but we had to constantly think of how someone eating the food would experience it. I felt that nearly every plate going out of that kitchen was perfection because of what [Anne] demanded of us. I am still filled with pride when I think of it."

When Greg and Mary Sonnier decided to expand beyond Gabrielle and open Gamay in the French Quarter, Mary convinced me to help them open the restaurant. She's a trained chef, just like her husband. In fact, they met while working together at K-Paul's. But Mary mostly ran the front of the house and the pastry operations. I had never worked at a restaurant *before* it opened. But that was the inspiration I needed. Watching Greg and Mary work on their new menu and create their vision made me want to do the same.

It was at Gamay that I met Jacques Jhoni and fell in love, culinarily speaking. Two things I have to have in a sous chef: dependability and coolness under pressure. Jacques is soft spoken and works as if he expects something to go wrong. So he never gets rattled when the produce man delivers only half of the onions in our order or the gas burners suddenly stop working because the federal flood put water in the gas lines. Jacques has a magic touch with seasoning. He knows how to get to the edge of spicy without going over into the burn region. He knows that salt can make or break a dish more than any other single ingredient. I knew he would be my sous chef when I opened my own place.

Though I had spent my entire New Orleans restaurant career in the French Quarter, when Nardo's Trattoria closed Uptown, it was time to make my move. The place was practically around the corner from Clancy's, a mainstay of traditional New Orleans cooking where common dishes like the pan-roasted chicken and smoked duck are excellent. I figured a lot of people would see our sign en route to Clancy's. If a few of them stopped to taste our food, and if we blew them away the way I knew we could, word of mouth would be better than advertising. Advertising that I couldn't afford, anyway.

Speaking of couldn't afford, I can't go any further without thanking my parents. The only reason I could "afford" to open a restaurant is that they loaned me some cash and cosigned a loan. (My sister refers to this as an advance on my share of the inheritance.) Almost exactly two years before Hurricane Katrina and the levee failures did us in, Desautel's was launched.

These days, cooks of every stripe are writing cookbooks. I may write my own cookbook one day. But until then, let's be clear: this is not that book. I might be the one who pulled this all together. But it's really a collective book encompassing the recipes, ideas, and spirits of the many fine cooks I've met since I moved down here.

I'll let you in on a little secret. This book was really my excuse to peek into the pots of some of my favorite cooks and chefs. And it's your excuse to join me on the tour.

OYSTERS ON THE HALF SHELL WITH YUZU MIGNONETTE

Before Hurricane Katrina, Louisiana produced more oysters off its coast than any other state. Oysters are pretty common on menus here, and they're cheap compared to what they cost in other places. So finding something different to do with them isn't easy. Instead of the usual ketchup and horseradish sauce that's the standard here, or the onion mignonette that's more common up North, I decided to go Asian. *Yuzu* is a citrus fruit you seldom see in the United States, and its flavor is different from any citrus you ever tasted. Getting the fruit on this side of the Pacific is difficult, but getting the juice at a good Asian market isn't so hard anymore.

If you're not confident about shucking oysters, or don't have time, or just aren't in the mood, your fishmonger will almost certainly do it for you (usually for a small surcharge, and be sure to ask ahead of time). Keep the oysters well chilled in the refrigerator until ready to serve.

6 tablespoons yuzu juice

2 tablespoons rice wine vinegar

1 small shallot, minced

2 teaspoons freshly ground pepper

2 dozen fresh oysters on the half shell, well chilled

Crushed ice for serving (optional)

In a bowl, stir together the yuzu juice, vinegar, shallot, and pepper until well mixed. Transfer the mignonette sauce to a small serving bowl.

Arrange the oysters on a platter. Nestle them in a bed of crushed ice, if you like, for a pretty presentation and to keep them perfectly cold. Tuck the bowl of mignonette on the platter or place alongside at the table. Serve right away.

Makes 4 appetizer servings

EMERIL'S TUNA AND BUTTER LETTUCE WRAPS

Marinated Red Cabbage

½ pound red cabbage, cored and thinly sliced

1½ teaspoons kosher salt

½ cup fresh orange juice

½ cup white wine vinegar

¼ cup sugar

Bagna Cauda Drizzle

1 cup olive oil

5 tablespoons minced garlic (about 1 large head)

8 to 10 anchovy fillets, chopped

Kosher salt and freshly ground black pepper

2 pinches of cayenne pepper

2 tablespoons extra-virgin olive oil, plus more for frying

8 ounces sushi-grade yellowfin tuna fillet

Kosher salt and freshly ground black pepper

3 corn tortillas, halved and then cut crosswise into ⅛-inch strips

16 equal-size (small to medium) attractive whole butter lettuce leaves (from 1 to 2 small heads)

Sriracha hot chili sauce or other spicy chile-garlic sauce for garnish

1 large jalapeño chile, very thinly sliced (with seeds)

Makes 4 large appetizer servings

Emeril Lagasse is an inspiration. He's brought New Orleans food to the widest stage it has ever had; he's taught a generation of Americans that cooking good food doesn't have to be hard; his foundation is helping underprivileged kids learn to grow, cook, and appreciate food; and his restaurants are consistently among the best in town. He's done so much outside of the kitchen that people sometimes forget his immense impact in it. His recipe for barbecued shrimp rivals the classic version from Pascal's Manale Restaurant.

This recipe is typical Emeril in that it takes a traditional dish, in this case the warm dip of northeast Italy called *bagna cauda* (meaning "hot bath"), and uses it in a delicious new way. Note: The cabbage recipe yields up to 3 cups of delicious sweet-and-sour slaw, but you will only need 1 to 2 cups to top the lettuce wraps. This gives you some leeway to overstuff any wraps for the particular cabbage lovers in your crowd, or pass the remaining cabbage at the table. It will also keep, covered in the refrigerator, for a couple of days, so you can snack on it or toss it into another salad or side dish. You can also make a whole meal for two out of this dish; just reduce the number of lettuce leaves and pile extra cabbage and tuna on each.

To make the cabbage: Put the cabbage in a large nonreactive bowl and sprinkle with the salt. Toss to combine. Set aside at room temperature to marinate for about 1 hour, tossing occasionally.

In a small saucepan, combine the orange juice, vinegar, and sugar and bring to a boil over medium-high heat. Cook until reduced to ½ cup, about 6 minutes. Remove from the heat and set aside to cool.

Rinse and drain the cabbage in a colander set in the sink, then squeeze out as much liquid as possible and return it to the bowl. When the orange juice mixture has cooled, pour it over the cabbage and toss to combine. Let stand at room temperature for at least 1 hour, or covered in the refrigerator overnight.

To make the drizzle: In a small saucepan, heat ¼ cup of the olive oil over medium heat. When the oil is hot but not quite smoking, add the garlic and cook until aromatic, about 1 minute. Add the remaining ¾ cup olive oil and the anchovies to taste. Reduce the heat to low and cook, stirring occasionally and mashing the anchovies with a fork to help them dissolve, about 10 minutes. Season with salt, about ¼ teaspoon black pepper, and the cayenne. Remove from the heat and set aside to cool. Transfer to a blender and process to a smooth purée. Cover the blender jar and place in the refrigerator until ready to assemble the wraps.

In a 12-inch sauté pan or skillet, heat the 2 tablespoons olive oil over high heat. Season the tuna on all sides with 1 teaspoon salt and ¼ teaspoon black pepper. Quickly sear the tuna on all sides, 10 to 15 seconds per side, or until there is just a ¼-inch-thick band of raw fish visible in the middle of the fillet. Transfer to a cutting board. When cool enough to handle, carve the tuna into slices about ¼ inch thick (you should end up with 16 slices). Set aside until ready to serve.

Wipe the pan you used to cook the tuna clean with a paper towel. Add enough olive oil to come about ¼ inch up the sides of the pan. Heat over medium-high heat. When the oil is hot but not quite smoking, cook the tortilla strips in batches until golden brown, 30 to 45 seconds per batch, stirring and tossing to get both sides of the strips in the oil as needed. Using a slotted spoon, transfer the cooked strips to a paper towel–lined plate to drain. Sprinkle each batch with a pinch or two of salt while still hot. Set aside.

Arrange 4 lettuce leaves on each of four plates, patting them dry thoroughly with paper towels if necessary. Place an equal amount of the crispy tortilla strips in the center of each leaf, and mound 1 to 2 tablespoons of the marinated cabbage on top. Place a slice of tuna over the cabbage, sprinkling each with a pinch of salt, and place a dot of Sriracha on the tuna. Follow with the jalapeño slices and drizzle with the Bagna Cauda Drizzle (see Note). Serve at once.

Note: Any unused drizzle can be stored in an airtight container in the refrigerator for up to 2 weeks. Bring to room temperature before using.

PERISTYLE'S JUMBO LUMP CRABMEAT AND HERB SALAD OVER CHILLED ROASTED BEETS AND PICKLED ONIONS

Pickled Red Onions

1 pound small red onions, julienned

2 tablespoons kosher salt

¾ cup water

⅔ cup rice vinegar

3 thick strips orange zest, removed with a vegetable peeler

8 whole coriander seeds

8 whole white peppercorns

Roasted Beets

1 pound small beets of uniform size

2 tablespoons rice wine vinegar

¾ cup light olive oil

Kosher salt

Freshly ground white pepper

Herb Salad

½ cup fresh flat-leaf parsley leaves

½ cup fresh chervil leaves

¼ cup fresh tarragon leaves

¼ cup snipped fresh chives (½-inch pieces)

1 large egg yolk

1 tablespoon fresh lemon juice

¾ cup vegetable oil

Salt

Freshly ground white pepper

½ cup sour cream

2 tablespoons freshly grated horseradish, or as much as you dare

¼ cup minced fresh chives

1 pound fresh jumbo lump crabmeat, carefully picked over for shell fragments and cartilage and well chilled

Makes 8 servings

I remember three things about this dish from my days at Peristyle: It was very popular. It was quite delicious. And Anne was always telling pantry to cut the chives in precise lengths and only pick the perfect leaves of tarragon, parsley, and chervil. I can remember how intently she would stare at the dish every time it was made, making sure it was just right, before placing it in the hands of a waiter. No bruises—no nothing! The herb salad would crown the tower of crabmeat and it had to be tossed very carefully and placed just right. The station would need about two cups of these herb leaves a night. It doesn't sound like a lot until you have to do it. EVERY DAY! And before the pantry cook had even clocked in for his or her shift, the sous chef would have already had a fight with the delivery person about shitty chervil—many times it would come in yellow—and she might have the produce truck come back to the restaurant three times until they got it right.

When I asked Anne for the recipe, she gave me a far more prosaic backstory. "Here I was in New Orleans. I had just bought Peristyle from my mentor's estate. September 1995. I was riding shotgun in Felicia Willets's car (I didn't own a car yet). As we drove around town, I began to write the first menu, readying myself to go public with the news of the purchase. My mother kept a jar of pickled beets and hard-boiled eggs in the fridge when I was growing up, I came to appreciate them. I wanted my roots and my new culture to marry. Horseradish and beets work well together, horseradish and crab do, too. Herb salad to brighten the palate, pickled red onion to add a crunchy acid."

Note that the pickled onions should be made the night before.

To make the pickled onions: In a bowl, toss the onions with 1 tablespoon of the salt and let stand for 20 minutes. Meanwhile, in a small saucepan, combine the water, vinegar, orange zest, coriander seeds, peppercorns, and remaining 1 tablespoon salt and bring to a boil over medium-high heat. Simmer for 2 minutes, then remove from the heat and let cool for 10 minutes. Transfer the onions to a colander and place under cold running water for 2 minutes to rinse off the salt, then drain well. Place the onions in a small plastic container. Strain the brine into the container with the onions. Let cool to room temperature, then cover and refrigerate overnight or for up to 3 days.

To make the beets: Preheat the oven to 350°F. Rinse any soil from the beets. Slice off the top of each beet to make a flat surface and trim the root ends. Place in a shallow baking pan, cut side down. Fill the pan with water about one-third of the way up the sides of the beets. Cover tightly with aluminum foil and roast until tender when pierced with the tip of a sharp knife, about 30 minutes. Remove from the water and set aside until cool enough to handle. Strain the beet roasting liquid and reserve 1 cup. When the beets are cool enough to handle, using your hands, gently rub the skins off. Where the skin does not come off easily, gently work it free with a paring knife. Place a mandoline over a large stainless-steel mixing bowl and very thinly slice the beets into the bowl. (Alternatively, use a large, sharp knife to cut the beets into very thin slices and add them

continued

to the bowl.) Add the reserved beet roasting liquid, vinegar, and olive oil, season with salt and white pepper, and stir gently. Cover and refrigerate until well chilled, at least 2 hours. Pour off the excess vinaigrette from the bowl and transfer to a squirt bottle; set aside.

To make the Herb Salad: In a medium bowl, toss all the herbs together until well combined. Cover with a damp towel and refrigerate until ready to dress.

In a food processor, combine the egg yolk and lemon juice and process until frothy. With the machine running, slowly drizzle in the vegetable oil until a thick emulsion forms. Season with salt and white pepper, add the sour cream, and process for 1 minute. Add the 2 tablespoons horseradish and pulse to mix. Taste and add more horseradish, if you like. Transfer the sauce to a bowl. Add the chives and crabmeat and fold gently to mix. Taste and adjust the seasoning.

To assemble, place 6 thin beet slices in a tight overlapping circle in the center of each plate. Mound 2 tablespoons of the red onions in the center of the beets. Shake the reserved beet vinaigrette well and drizzle 1 tablespoon directly onto the onions, allowing it to disperse around the plate. Place 2 to 3 tablespoons of the dressed crabmeat in the center of the onions and beets, forming a tight, high mound and dividing the crab mixture equally among the eight plates. Place 1 tablespoon of herb salad on top of the crab. Serve at once.

L'Hôtel de France's Foie Gras in a Pumpkin Terrine

One 1½-pound whole grade-A foie gras, at room temperature

One 3- to 4-pound pumpkin, any variety, about 12 inches in diameter

Coarse salt

Freshly ground white pepper

1 cup Banyuls or tawny port

Crusty French bread for serving

You won't find an easier, or better, recipe for foie gras terrine than this one. (But be aware that you need to start this dish a day ahead.) It's classic Chef André. When all the foie gras has been scooped out and served, he recommends using the roasted pumpkin container left behind to make a soup.

Ariane, Chef André's daughter and the founder of D'Artagnan, says, "The terrine is very forgiving, as long as the oven temperature is no hotter than 275 degrees Fahrenheit. The foie gras will reach at least 120 degrees within 2 hours. If the temperature of the foie gras rises up to 150 degrees Fahrenheit, the terrine will still be fine—again, as long as the oven never goes over 275 degrees.

"This recipe is perfect for autumn because a pumpkin is an ideal container for foie gras. The most important thing for this recipe is the size rather than the type of pumpkin. A pumpkin with a diameter around 12 inches will snugly fit the whole foie gras. To keep all of the flavors of the foie gras in the terrine, the pumpkin is wrapped in aluminum foil. This makes it airtight and prevents outside flavors from mingling with the liver."

Banyuls is a fortified sweet red wine from the Languedoc-Roussillon region of France. If it is unavailable, use a tawny port. Banyuls would also be the ideal wine to pair with this dish.

Prepare the foie gras: Fill a large bowl with water and ice. Put the foie gras in the ice water bath and push to submerge. Refrigerate overnight.

The next day, remove the foie gras from the ice water and pat dry with paper towels. Cover loosely with plastic wrap and let stand at room temperature for 1 hour. Using a small, sharp knife, carefully trim away any green spots (these are caused by contact with the gall bladder). You'll see the foie gras has two distinct lobes, one large and one smaller. Using your hands, gently pull the two lobes apart, just enough to see the vein that runs into the center of each. Using the small knife or your fingers, sever the vein, then gently finish pulling the lobes apart completely.

Cover the smaller lobe loosely with a dish towel while you devein the larger lobe. Locate the main vein on the underside of the lobe. Carefully run the tip of the small, sharp knife along the main vein to expose it. Gently open the lobe; you will need to split it almost, but not completely, apart. Carefully remove the primary vein and then the small veins throughout the lobe; while working, keep the lobe from breaking apart as much as possible (though it will eventually be

squeezed back together). Cover the larger lobe with the dish towel and repeat the process to clean and devein the smaller lobe.

Preheat the oven to 275°F.

Place the pumpkin on a work surface. Using a sharp knife and cutting straight downward with the point, carefully cut a circular opening in the pumpkin shell, centering the hole around the stem on top, as you would for a jack-o'-lantern. Wiggle the top out gently, trim off any membrane or flesh clinging to the underside, and set aside. Scrape out and discard the seeds and membranes.

Make a bed of crumpled aluminum foil on a baking sheet. Nestle the pumpkin securely in the foil, adjusting it so it sits level.

Season the foie gras with salt and white pepper. Pour the wine into the pumpkin shell and sprinkle with more salt and pepper. Carefully place the foie gras inside the pumpkin, with the large lobe beneath the smaller lobe. Replace the pumpkin top snugly and wrap the whole pumpkin securely in aluminum foil to make it mostly airtight. (Leave the seams of the aluminum wrapping on top of the pumpkin to make it easier to check the foie gras for doneness.)

Makes 8 to 10 appetizer servings

Bake, without disturbing, for 2 hours and 30 minutes. Remove from the oven and unwrap the top edges of the foil to expose the pumpkin stem "handle." Wearing an oven mitt, carefully lift off the top. Insert an instant-read thermometer into the thickest part of the foie gras. It should register 120°F. If it's not done, replace the top, reseal the foil, and return to the oven. Check again every 10 minutes or so. When the terrine is done, unwrap and discard the aluminum foil, fit the top back onto the pumpkin snugly again, and let the whole thing cool to room temperature. Refrigerate overnight.

Remove the terrine from the refrigerator about 30 minutes before serving. Serve at the table, using a hot spoon to scoop out the foie gras onto warmed small plates and passing the crusty bread.

SEARED DUCK BREAST ON GREEN ONION PANCAKES WITH DAIKON SALAD

This is my twist on David Chang's famous pork buns. Duck breast has almost as much fatty flavor as pork belly. The green onion pancakes here don't provide a pillowy plain canvas like the steamed buns at Momofuku, but they complement the composition: the crunch of the crispy duck skin goes perfectly with the savory onion filling. It's not really Asian, but at the restaurant we'd fry the pancakes in a little butter. It enhances the browning.

Remember to take the duck breasts out of the refrigerator 30 minutes to 1 hour before you sear them to take the chill off.

To make the pancakes: In a large bowl, combine the flour, egg, water, sliced green onions, season with the salt and some pepper, and stir to mix well. Set the batter aside and let rest at room temperature for about 30 minutes.

Place a large nonstick skillet over medium heat. Add 1 teaspoon of butter. Working in batches, spoon tablespoonfuls of the pancake batter into the skillet and spread evenly to make thin pancakes 3 to 4 inches in diameter and spacing them about 1 inch apart. Do not crowd the pancakes in the pan. Gently press the cilantro leaves into the pancake batter. Cook until golden brown on the bottom, about 2 minutes. Flip and cook until browned on the second side, about 1 minute longer. Add a little butter to the pan between each batch. Transfer to a plate. Repeat with the remaining batter to make a total of 12 pancakes. Cover the plate with aluminum foil and place in a low oven to keep warm while you cook the duck breast (see Note).

Score the skin of the duck breasts in a ½-inch diamond pattern, being careful not to cut into the flesh, and season generously all over with salt and pepper. In a large heavy skillet over medium heat, melt the butter. Brush or swirl the butter to coat the pan bottom. Place the duck breasts, skin-side down, in the hot pan and sear until the skin is golden brown and crispy, 5 to 7 minutes.

Turn the breasts and cook for 2 to 3 minutes longer for medium-rare. (Note: There will be a lot of duck fat left in the pan. Strain it into a glass jar and store in the refrigerator for another use.) Transfer the duck to a cutting board and let rest for 5 to 10 minutes.

While the duck is resting, in a small bowl, stir together the hoisin sauce, soy sauce, vinegar, Sriracha, and 3 tablespoons oil. In a medium bowl, combine the radish, carrot, and julienned green onion and toss to mix well. Season with salt and pepper. Dress the vegetables with 2 tablespoons of the hoisin-soy vinaigrette.

Arrange two green onion pancakes on each of six small plates. Cut the duck breasts crosswise into slices about ¼ inch thick and place 2 slices in the center of each pancake. Top each with a generous pinch of the vegetable salad, dividing it equally. Garnish with the cilantro leaves and duck sauce. Serve at once, passing the remaining sauce at the table.

Note: The pancakes can be made earlier in the day and kept covered at room temperature. Just before you are ready to serve, reheat gently in a low oven.

Green Onion Pancakes

1 cup all-purpose flour

1 large egg, beaten

¾ cup water

½ cup plus 1½ tablespoons thinly sliced green onions, white and tender green parts

½ teaspoon salt

Freshly ground pepper

Butter for frying

1 tablespoon whole cilantro leaves

2 duck breast halves (about 6 ounces each)

Salt and pepper

1 teaspoon unsalted butter

2 tablespoons hoisin sauce

2 tablespoons soy sauce

2 tablespoons rice wine vinegar

1 teaspoon Sriracha Hot Chili Sauce

3 tablespoons canola oil

½ cup peeled and julienned daikon radish or regular radishes

½ cup peeled and julienned carrot

¼ cup julienned green onion

Fine sea salt and freshly ground pepper

¼ cup fresh cilantro leaves

¼ cup duck sauce (available in Asian markets)

Makes 6 servings

CREOLE CRAB-AND-CORN BISQUE

¼ cup (½ stick) unsalted butter

2½ ounces smoked slab bacon, cut into ½- to 1-inch cubes, or thick-cut bacon, diced, or andouille or other smoked pure pork sausage, chopped

2 fresh or thawed frozen raw gumbo crabs (about 6 ounces total weight) (see Note)

½ large white or yellow onion, finely chopped

2 celery stalks, finely chopped (about ½ cup)

1 red bell pepper, seeded and finely chopped

1 green bell pepper, seeded and finely chopped

½ fennel bulb, trimmed and finely chopped (about ½ cup)

5 to 6 cloves garlic, very thinly sliced (about ¼ cup)

1½ teaspoons kosher salt, plus 1 tablespoon

¼ teaspoon freshly ground black pepper

3 ears corn, husks and silk removed

2 tablespoons tomato paste

1½ teaspoons red pepper flakes

¼ cup all-purpose flour

¼ cup good-quality brandy

1 quart Fish Stock (page 228) or good-quality store-bought fish or seafood stock

1 cup water

12 ounces red potatoes, scrubbed but not peeled, coarsely chopped

1½ large ripe tomatoes, chopped

2½ teaspoons finely chopped fresh thyme

3½ ounces (half of a 7-ounce bag) frozen baby lima beans, thawed, or about 4 ounces shelled field peas of your choice

8 to 12 ounces large shrimp, peeled and deveined

8 ounces fresh lump crabmeat, picked over for cartilage and shell fragments

½ bunch green onions, tender green parts only, cut on the diagonal into ¼-inch slices (about ¾ cup)

2½ teaspoons finely chopped fresh tarragon

Jackie Blanchard is a true Louisiana chef, and destined to be a star. She grew up in south Louisiana, went to Chef John Folse's Culinary Institute at Nicholls State, and then worked her way into the sort of great kitchens that culinary school graduates would kill to get into. After an internship at the French Laundry, she worked at Frasca in Boulder, Colorado, and Blue Hill in New York before coming home and joining John Besh at Restaurant August. She's now a sous chef there. Her version of crab-and-corn bisque reflects both her south Louisiana roots and her fine-dining education. Take note: as is the case with most Cajun "bisques," there is no cream here. Instead of a proper roux, flour is added to the vegetables as they simmer.

Making your own fish stock is quick and very rewarding. But you can also find good-quality boxed fish stock at better supermarkets, or ask your fishmonger, who may have fresh or fresh frozen stock on hand.

Heat a heavy-bottomed soup pot or Dutch oven over high heat for 1 minute. Add the butter and let it melt. When the butter is melted, stir in the bacon and cook, stirring occasionally, until most of the bacon fat is rendered, about 5 minutes. Reduce the heat to low and continue cooking, still stirring occasionally and using the spoon to scrape the pan bottom clean, until the bacon is browned around the edges, about 4 minutes longer. Using a slotted spoon, transfer the bacon to a plate, leaving the butter and fat mixture behind. Set the bacon aside.

Raise the heat to medium. Add the gumbo crabs to the pan of fat and cook, stirring occasionally and turning the crab halves as needed, until evenly browned, about 6 minutes. Transfer the crabs to a bowl and set aside.

Add the onion, celery, red and green bell peppers, fennel, and garlic to the pot and stir to coat nicely with the fat. Add 1½ teaspoons salt and the black pepper and stir well. Raise the heat to high and cook, stirring constantly, for 5 minutes. Reduce the heat to medium-high and cook, stirring occasionally, until the vegetables are golden, about 15 minutes longer.

Meanwhile, cut the corn kernels from the cobs. You should have about 2 cups of kernels. Put the kernels in a bowl, cover, and refrigerate until ready to use. Take up a corncob and hold it upright in a large shallow bowl. Using a butter knife or paring knife, scrape the cob to extract the juice and any remaining pulp. Repeat with the remaining cobs. You should get about ¼ cup mixed juice and pulp; set aside.

Once the vegetables are golden, return the bacon to the pot. Add the tomato paste and red pepper flakes and stir for a few minutes to cook the tomato paste. Stir in the flour and cook, stirring often and scraping the pan bottom clean, for about 3 minutes. Stir in the reserved corn juice mixture and the brandy, and cook and stir for 1 minute. Return the gumbo crabs to the pot and add the fish stock and water, stirring well and scraping the pan bottom clean. Cover the pot and bring to a boil, still over medium-high heat, then reduce the heat to low and stir in the 1 tablespoon salt. Add the potatoes, tomatoes, and thyme to the pot. Reduce the heat to low, cover partially, and simmer, stirring occasionally, for 10 minutes. Add the corn kernels and lima beans and cook until all the vegetables are tender, about 5 minutes longer. Remove the gumbo crabs from the bisque and discard.

Add the shrimp to the bisque, stir well, and cook, uncovered, for 5 minutes. Gently stir in the lump crabmeat, being careful not to break up the chunks of crab. Add the green onions and tarragon, reduce the heat to very low, and simmer gently to allow the flavors to blend, about 10 minutes, gently stirring occasionally. Remove from the heat and serve hot in large, shallow gumbo or soup bowls, ladling out about 1½ cups for each person.

Notes: Crabs designated for gumbo are uncooked larger hard-shell blues that have been specially prepared, that is, cleaned of all the nonedible portions except for the shell and then broken in half. They are used more for flavor than for meat, like a ham hock. If "gumbo crabs" are not available in your area, you may substitute other raw hard-shell crabs that are cleaned and cut in half.

You can make the bisque up to 2 days ahead. In fact, it may be better that way. Reheat gently over medium-low heat before serving.

Makes about 3½ quarts, or about 8 generous main-course servings

PATOIS OYSTER STEW WITH PAN-FRIED GROUPER AND FRIED PARSNIPS

Oyster Stew

4 tablespoons unsalted butter

2 small leeks, white parts only, chopped and rinsed well

½ fennel bulb, cored and finely chopped

2 stalks celery, finely chopped

1 clove garlic, minced

½ cup all-purpose flour

¾ cup dry white wine

½ teaspoon red pepper flakes

2 bay leaves

1 teaspoon fresh thyme leaves

3 cups oyster liquor (see Note) or bottled clam juice

1¾ cup heavy (whipping) cream

¼ cup Pernod liqueur (substitute ouzo or pastis, if you like)

1 teaspoon Crystal or other hot sauce

Salt and freshly ground black pepper

24 medium-to-large fresh raw oysters, with their liquor

Fried Parsnips

Canola oil for deep-frying

2 parsnips

Salt

¼ cup plus 2 tablespoons canola oil

8 snowy, yellow edge, or scamp grouper fillets (about 5 ounces each)

2 tablespoons Wondra flour

2 tablespoons unsalted butter

7 ounces fresh spinach, stems removed, rinsed and patted dry thoroughly

Salt and freshly ground black pepper

Less than a year after Desautel's closed, Patois opened up in our old location. Driving along Annunciation Street, seeing all the full tables at Patois felt kind of like seeing an old boyfriend with his new girlfriend. You know that feeling? You don't necessarily think things could have worked out any better, but some part of you wishes that they had. I closed Desautel's because, at the time, I didn't have any real options. I was broke and in debt and the business wasn't paying for itself. Every time I came home from New York, my car drove itself to Desautel's/Patois. I couldn't help myself. Finally, I had dinner there.

Aaron Burgau is doing great food. This was my favorite dish from that night. The oyster stew is so good, you don't necessarily need the grouper. But, like my father says, "if it's worth doing, it's worth overdoing."

To make the stew: In a soup pot over low heat, melt the 4 tablespoons butter. Add the leeks, fennel, celery, and garlic and let the vegetables sweat until soft, about 10 minutes, stirring once or twice. Add the flour and cook for about 3 minutes, stirring constantly and making sure the flour does not stick to the pan bottom. Raise the heat to medium and add the wine, red pepper flakes, bay leaves, and thyme, stirring well. Cook for about 3 more minutes. Add the oyster liquor, bring to a simmer, and cook until reduced by one-fourth, about 15 minutes. Reduce the heat to low and stir in the cream, then the Pernod and hot sauce. Season with salt and pepper. Set aside and cover to keep warm while you make the other parts of the stew.

To make the parsnips: Pour oil into a deep-fryer to a depth of 2 inches, or a deep 12-inch skillet or sauté pan to a depth of 1 inch. Place over medium heat and heat the oil to 325°F.

Meanwhile, peel the parsnips. Using the vegetable peeler, create parsnip ribbons, turning the parsnip after each strip is cut so the parsnip is cut evenly on all sides.

Once the oil reaches 325°F, ease the parsnip ribbons into the hot oil, working in small batches if necessary so the pan is not crowded. Fry the strips until they start to brown and the oil stops bubbling around them, about 4 minutes, constantly moving the strips around with metal tongs while they cook. Remove each strip as it starts to brown and transfer to a plate lined with paper towels to drain. Sprinkle the fried parsnips with salt and keep warm while you cook the fish.

In a heavy 12-inch skillet, heat the ¼ cup plus 2 tablespoons oil over high heat until almost smoking, about 2 minutes. Meanwhile, dredge the fish in the flour, shaking off the excess. Working in batches so the skillet isn't crowded, ease the fish into the hot oil and reduce the heat to medium-high. Cook the fillets on each side until golden brown, 3 to 4 minutes per side. Transfer the fish to a plate lined with paper towels to drain and keep warm while you finish cooking the remaining fish.

When the fish is all fried, quickly cook the spinach. In a large sauté pan, melt the 2 tablespoons butter over medium-high heat. Add the spinach and season with salt and pepper. Toss the spinach with metal tongs or a spoon until wilted and completely cooked, about 2 minutes.

Makes 8 servings

Just before serving, return the stew to a very gentle simmer over medium-low heat. Add the oysters and their liquor and simmer just until the oysters' edges curl, about 3 minutes.

Ladle about ¼ cup of the stew and 3 oysters into each of eight shallow bowls. Divide the wilted spinach on top of the stew, then place the cooked fish atop the spinach and garnish with the fried parsnips. Serve at once.

Note: You may be able to buy oyster liquor from the same fishmonger that sells you raw oysters. If oyster liquor is not available, reserve as much liquor as you can from the oysters you have and add fish stock to total 3 cups.

YAKA MEIN

Broth

2 quarts Basic Chicken Stock (page 230) or store-bought chicken broth

1½ ounces dried shiitake mushrooms

1 ounce dashi kombu (available in Asian markets) (see Notes)

3 ounces smoky bacon, cut into 1-inch cubes (see Notes)

9 green onions, each trimmed to a 3-inch-long piece starting at the root end (save the tender green tops for garnishing the dish (see below)

Cloves from ½ head garlic, unpeeled, lightly smashed

1 tablespoon kosher salt

Noodles (see Notes)

½ teaspoon baking soda

2 ⅓ cups all-purpose flour

⅔ cup warm water

4 tablespoons hoisin sauce

1 pound jumbo shrimp, peeled and deveined

2 tablespoons soy sauce

Freshly ground pepper

Kosher salt

6 eggs (see Notes)

6 tablespoons vegetable oil

6 green onions, tender green parts only (from above), cut on the diagonal into ¼-inch slices (about 6 tablespoons)

6 tablespoons fresh cilantro leaves

Makes 6 servings

Yaka mein is a strange dish. While it has obvious Asian elements, in New Orleans it's served almost exclusively at black po-boy shops and from the makeshift food concessions that pop up along the routes of the "second line" parades, the moving phalanx of friends and fans that join in with the official procession. Writer Sara Roahen, a Wisconsin transplant who ate her way across New Orleans, details two major theories about how yaka mein got to New Orleans in her book *Gumbo Tales: Finding My Place at the New Orleans Table*. One speculates that black Korean War veterans came home with a taste for the noodle soup they'd had in Korea; an earlier possibility she cites is that Chinese railroad workers, who came to the South in the 1800s, taught the dish to the locals. There was a Chinatown in downtown New Orleans in the early 1900s, and Louis Armstrong himself relates tales of eating Chinese food there as a boy. Whatever the genealogy of yaka mein, it is clear that the Afro-Asian cross-culinary connection has been evolving in New Orleans for years.

Recently, Linda Green has emerged as a champion of yaka mein, keeping it in the forefront of this city's idiosyncratic, iconic dishes; she sells her version at Jazz Fest. Noting how David Chang's menu mixes his Korean and Southern heritages at his restaurant Lucky Peach in midtown Manhattan, I immediately thought of yaka mein. This version is far more Asian than Creole. I'm not sure if Linda would approve of it, but they lapped it up in New York.

In an interesting step for the homemade noodles, the baking soda is baked first, which transforms it from bicarbonate of soda (which is what it is in the box) into a simple carbonate. This improves the flavor of the noodles and gives them a pleasantly chewy texture.

To make the broth: In a heavy 3-quart saucepan, combine the stock, shiitake mushroms, dashi kombu, and bacon without stirring. (Stirring can make the broth cloudy.) Place the pan over low heat and add the 9 green onion pieces and the garlic, again without stirring. Let the mixture slowly come to a simmer, still never stirring; it should take about 10 minutes. Remove the broth from heat and add the salt, *still* without stirring. Set aside.

While the broth is cooking, make the noodle dough: Position a rack in the middle of the oven and preheat to 300°F. Place the baking soda on a 3-inch square of aluminum foil and fold up the sides of the foil to make a little bowl to contain the baking soda. Place on a baking sheet or directly on the oven rack and bake for 30 minutes. Remove from the oven and set aside for 5 minutes to cool.

In the bowl of a stand mixer fitted with the pastry hook, combine the flour and cooled baking soda and beat on medium speed until blended, about 30 seconds. With the mixer still on, slowly add the warm water. Reduce the speed to low and beat until a rough dough just starts to form, about 2 minutes. Stop the mixer, remove any moist dough stuck to the hook, and knead the whole mass by hand in the bowl for about 30 seconds. Turn the mixer on low again and beat until the dough comes together in a ball, about 5 minutes longer. Transfer the dough to a clean, unfloured work surface and knead just until it starts to smooth out, about 3 minutes. (This will take some elbow grease; it is a dense dough that yields dense, chewy noodles.) Form the dough into a 5-inch disk, wrap well in plastic wrap, and let stand at room temperature for 1 hour.

Note: There are no difficult techniques ahead, but the timing for this dish gets a little tricky as you approach assembly. Read the recipe over before you proceed. Then just stay focused and you will deliver eye-popping, piping hot bowls of soup. Have ready six very large individual soup bowls.

About halfway through the dough's resting time, strain the reserved broth through a large colander into a heatproof bowl; discard all the solids. Return the broth to the saucepan. Gently stir in 2 tablespoons of the hoisin sauce. Set aside.

Put the shrimp in a small bowl. Add the remaining 2 tablespoons hoisin sauce, the soy sauce, and 8 grinds of a pepper mill and stir to coat and mix well. Cover, refrigerate, and let marinate for about 30 minutes.

When the dough has finished resting and the shrimp is toward the end of its marinating time, bring a 4-quart saucepan three-fourths full of water to a boil for the noodles and a medium saucepan halfway filled with water to a boil for the eggs. Fill a large, deep bowl with water and ice cubes to make an ice water bath.

While the water is heating, roll out the noodles. Unwrap the dough and place on a lightly floured work surface. Dust a rolling pin with flour and use long strokes away from you to roll the dough out into a rough rectangle about 1/16 inch thick, rotating it as needed. Lightly flour both sides of the dough sheet again. Fold the dough sheet into thirds, like you're folding a letter. Using a large, sharp knife, cut the folded dough crosswise into noodles 1/8 inch thick. Fluff the cut noodles so they don't stick together.

Stir 1 tablespoon salt into the large pan of boiling water and add the noodles all at once. As soon as the noodles are in, gently lower the eggs, in their shells, into the medium pan of boiling water with a slotted spoon or spider. (Some may crack, though they should still be usable even if they're not beautiful.) Set a kitchen timer for 5 minutes and 10 seconds from the moment the eggs go into the water.

Cook the noodles, stirring gently once or twice, until tender but still chewy, about 4 minutes. When the timer rings, use the spoon or spider to transfer the eggs to the ice water. When the noodles are done, remove from the heat, drain quickly, and divide among the soup bowls.

Place the reserved broth on a vacant burner and begin to reheat gently over medium-low heat. Simultaneously, heat a medium, heavy skillet over medium-low heat until hot, about 2 minutes.

By now the eggs should be cool enough to handle. Crack them open on a cutting board and peel them underwater, in the bowl.

Add the oil and then the shrimp with its marinade to the hot skillet. Cook the shrimp, turning once, just until cooked through, about 1½ minutes per side. Remove from the heat and divide equally among the bowls, arranging the shrimp on top of the noodles. Garnish each serving with 1 tablespoon of the sliced green onions and 1 tablespoon of the cilantro leaves.

Finally, add a poached egg to the center of each bowl and ladle 1 cup of the hot broth around each egg. Serve at once.

Notes: Dashi kombu is dried edible kelp, a staple of the Asian pantry used for making flavorful (and vegetarian) broths.

For this recipe, choose a bacon that's heavy on smoke. Two brands I love are Benton's and Nueske's.

You can substitute four 3½-ounce packages of ramen noodles, cooked per the package directions but without the seasoning packet, for the handmade noodles.

The egg poaching method here is from David Chang (see Momofuku's Poached Eggs with Caviar, page 42). You can poach the eggs any way you like, of course. But in addition to being practically foolproof, David Chang's method of poaching eggs has the advantage of a make-ahead trick, up to 8 hours ahead, which you might well want to use for this recipe. It takes a little pressure off the orchestration in the timing of the finale.

AJAN ÉTOUFFÉE

Sesame Rice Cakes

1 cup sushi rice

1½ cups water

1 teaspoon fine sea salt

3 tablespoons canola oil

¼ cup untoasted white sesame seeds

4 tablespoons unsalted butter

¼ cup all-purpose flour

1 tablespoon canola oil

3 cloves garlic, minced

1 yellow onion, diced

½ green bell pepper, seeded and diced

1 large celery stalk, diced

¼ cup dry white wine

3 cups Rich Shrimp Stock (page 229) or store-bought shrimp or seafood stock

Charred Green Onions

1 bunch green onions, trimmed

Fine sea salt and freshly ground pepper

1 tablespoon canola oil

1 pound peeled fresh Louisiana crawfish tails (if unavailable, substitute frozen and thawed)

2 tablespoons soy sauce

1 tablespoon Crystal hot sauce, or to taste

Fine sea salt and freshly ground pepper

Makes 4 servings

The middle of Carnival season and there I was, on the levee, trying to get a dead fire to come alive and trying to get some live crawfish to behave and get cooked. I guess I learned that cooking outside on live television is not for me. Give me an indoor kitchen any day.

As a chef in New Orleans, the challenge is to respect tradition but not be bound by it. This dish takes all the old-school elements of crawfish étouffée but mixes them up and adds an Eastern spin. Instead of steamed rice, you get rice cakes. Instead of chopped green onion as a garnish, you get the whole plant, with beautifully charred stalks. I've altered the dish slightly since my television fiasco. Now there is a little roux in the dish, a nod to the étouffée tradition. And in addition to all the usual seasonings, you get a little soy sauce. Hence, *Ajan*.

To make the rice cakes: Thoroughly rinse the sushi rice in a sieve until the water runs clear. Place the rinsed rice in a small saucepan with the water and salt. Bring the rice to a boil, uncovered, over medium-high heat. Reduce the heat to medium and simmer until most of the water has been absorbed by the rice, about 5 minutes. Cover the rice, reduce the heat to low, and continue cooking for another 5 minutes. Remove from the heat and let steam, covered tightly, for 15 minutes. Line a small baking sheet with plastic wrap. Scoop the rice onto the prepared pan and pat into an even rectangle ½ inch thick. Refrigerate until cold and set, at least 4 hours and up to overnight. When the rice has set, make 2 diagonal cuts between opposite corners to make 4 equal-size triangular rice cakes. Set aside until ready to serve. (You will finish the cakes with the sesame seeds and a quick toasting when you are ready to assemble the dish.)

In a medium skillet, melt the butter over medium heat. Using a wooden spoon or whisk, stir in the flour to make a roux. Reduce the heat to medium-low and cook the roux, stirring often, until deep golden brown, about 15 minutes. Remove from the heat and set aside.

In a saucepan over medium-low heat, heat 1 tablespoon canola oil. Add the garlic, onion, bell pepper, and celery and stir to coat with the oil. Sweat the vegetables (this means cook them gently; you don't want to hear any sizzle), stirring often, until they release their liquid and turn tender and translucent in the juices without taking on color, about 5 minutes. Stir in the wine, scraping up any bits stuck to the pan bottom. Cook until the liquid has almost completely evaporated, about 5 minutes longer. Add the roux and the stock, bring to a simmer, and reduce the heat to low. Simmer the sauce gently until thickened, about 20 minutes.

While the sauce is cooking, make the green onions: Put the green onions in a large bowl. Sprinkle with salt and pepper, drizzle with the oil, and toss to coat. Heat a large, heavy skillet over high heat until it begins to smoke. Add the green onions to the very hot pan and cook, using tongs to turn each as needed, until golden or blackened in spots on all sides, 30 to 45 seconds total. Transfer the onions to a plate as they are finished.

When all of the onions are nicely charred, set them aside and wipe the skillet clean. To finish the rice cakes, place the skillet over medium heat and add the 3 tablespoons oil.

While the oil is heating, spread the sesame seeds on a wide plate. Press each rice cake into the sesame seeds to coat evenly on both sides. Carefully add the rice cakes to the hot oil. Fry until the sesame seeds on the first side are golden brown and toasty, 3 to 4 minutes. Turn the rice cakes and fry until golden brown on the second side, another 3 to 4 minutes. Transfer to a plate and cover with aluminum foil to keep warm.

Add the crawfish tails to the sauce and return to a simmer. Once the tiny shellfish heat through, they're done. Stir well and season with the soy sauce, hot sauce, and salt and pepper. Place a toasted rice cake in the center of each plate. Spoon the étouffée on top and around the rice cakes, dividing the crawfish equally. Garnish each plate with a couple of charred green onions and serve at once.

LA SPIGA'S
SWEET POTATO TURNOVERS

Pastry Dough

1¾ cups (3½ sticks) cold unsalted butter

6 tablespoons ice water

1¼ teaspoons vanilla extract

3 cups unbleached all-purpose flour, plus more for dusting

¾ cup cake flour

¼ cup plus 1 teaspoon granulated sugar

¾ teaspoon salt

Sweet Potato Filling

4 to 6 medium sweet potatoes (3 to 4 pounds total weight)

¾ cup packed light brown sugar

¼ cup granulated sugar

½ teaspoon salt

½ teaspoon ground cinnamon

¼ teaspoon ground allspice

¼ teaspoon freshly grated nutmeg

1 large whole egg and 1 large egg yolk, lightly beaten together

2½ tablespoons unsalted butter, melted and cooled

2 tablespoons heavy (whipping) cream

1 tablespoon vanilla extract

1 large egg beaten with 1 teaspoon water to make an egg wash

Raw or granulated sugar for sprinkling (optional)

Makes 20 to 24 turnovers

When we reopened right after the flood, there was one night when all I had to serve for dessert was one Hubig's pie and some house-made lemon ice. Hubig's is an institution, but Hubig's pies are not the same as made from scratch. I made my share of fried apple pies when I was cooking with Frank Stitt up in Birmingham, and after growing up on the fast-food versions at chain restaurants, Frank's were a revelation of how good the real thing can be. That experience prepared me for the wonders of La Spiga. This bakery and café used to be just a few blocks up from the Hubig's pie plant. Dana Logsdon, the chef and co-owner along with her mother, Mary, make sweet potato turnovers of such flaky, buttery perfection, you might think they were fried. If you don't have an electric mixer, you can mix the dough by hand.

To make the dough: Cut the butter into ¼- to ½-inch cubes, put in a bowl, and refrigerate until ready to use. In a small bowl, stir together 4 tablespoons of the ice water with the vanilla and place in the refrigerator. In a separate small bowl, refrigerate the remaining 2 tablespoons ice water.

In the bowl of a stand mixer fitted with the paddle attachment, combine the flours, granulated sugar, and salt and beat on low speed until well blended. Turn the mixer off and add the chilled butter cubes to the bowl all at once; using your fingers, toss to separate the cubes and coat them nicely with the flour mixture. Again with the mixer on low speed, beat the butter into the dry ingredients, using a rubber spatula to scrape down the sides of the bowl as needed, until most of the mixture has been cut up into pea-size bits and the rest resembles coarse cornmeal, 3 to 5 minutes. Note: After about 3 minutes of beating, turn off the mixer periodically to check the large chunks—they may appear to be all butter, but are likely to be butter mixed with the dry ingredients and readily crumbled apart with your fingers. Once these chunks start appearing, immediately stop beating the mixture and do crumble the chunks by hand, or your crust will end up less flaky.

Add the chilled vanilla mixture to the bowl all at once and beat on low speed until the ingredients are moistened and beginning to stick together but not yet forming a ball, about 30 seconds. If the mixture still seems dry, add the reserved 2 tablespoons ice water and continue beating on low for just a few seconds longer.

With the dough still in the bowl, press it into a single mass; do not knead. Divide the dough mass in half and very gently press each half into a ball. Gently flatten each ball into a 7- to 8-inch disk. Wrap the disks snugly with plastic wrap and refrigerate for at least 2 hours or up to overnight. Or, wrap each disk in double layers of plastic wrap, put in a zippered plastic bag, and freeze, lying flat, for up to 1 month. Thaw in the refrigerator overnight before using.

To make the filling: Start the sweet potatoes at least a couple of hours ahead. Position a rack in the middle of the oven and preheat to 400°F. Arrange the sweet potatoes on the rack and bake until very tender when pierced with a fork, 45 minutes to 1 hour. Let cool, then peel the potatoes and process the pulp in a blender or food processor until smooth. Measure out 2½ cups of the purée. (Snack on any remaining purée or save for another use.)

In a large bowl, whisk together the sugars, salt, cinnamon, allspice, and nutmeg. Add the sweet potato purée, whole egg and egg yolk mixture, melted butter, cream, and vanilla and stir with a rubber spatula until the filling is well blended and smooth. Set aside if you are ready to roll out your dough, or cover and refrigerate until ready to assemble the turnovers.

Remove 1 disk of the chilled dough from the refrigerator and unwrap. If it is too stiff to roll out, let sit at room temperature for about 5 minutes. Dust a work surface very lightly with flour. Dust the top of the dough disc and a rolling pin with flour as well. Starting with the rolling pin in the center of the disk, roll the dough away from you, working in only one direction and using even pressure. Turn the disk a quarter turn and again roll out from the center using even pressure. Continue rolling out the dough in this manner just to a uniform ⅛-inch thickness; passing over it as few times as possible makes for the flakiest crust. Mend any large cracks as they form simply by pinching the cracks together. You should end up with a more or less round shape of even thickness.

(If you are a beginner at rolling out dough, it's a good idea at this point to cut out a round near the edge of the dough—see the next step for how—to assess if the dough is uniformly thick. If the little dough round you cut is lopsided, find the thicker areas on the big piece of dough and gently roll them out as needed.)

Using a floured 4 ¾-inch round pastry cutter or a large round jar lid, cut out dough rounds as close together as possible, working quickly so the dough doesn't get sticky. Arrange the rounds on a large baking sheet lined with parchment paper and refrigerate. Gather together the dough scraps and refrigerate separately. Repeat to roll out the second disk of dough and cut into rounds, arranging them on a second parchment-lined large baking sheet. Add the second round of scraps to those in the refrigerator and chill for at least 15 minutes, then press all the scraps together, roll out again, and cut out more rounds; discard the remaining scraps.

Position one rack in the upper third of the oven and one in the lower third and preheat to 375°F. Lightly flour a clean work surface. Have handy a fork and small bowl of flour.

Remove the first tray of dough rounds from the refrigerator. Transfer the rounds to the floured work surface in a single layer and set the pan alongside with the parchment still in place (or discard the paper and lightly grease the pan with butter). Using a pastry brush, brush a ½-inch border of the egg wash around the edge of each round. Spoon about 1½ tablespoons of the filling into the center of each round. Fold each round into a half-moon, gently pulling the top half snugly over and around the filling. Pinch the edges to seal. Dip the tines of the fork in flour and lightly press the edges of the turnovers together to make sure they are sealed. Turn the turnovers over and lightly press the edges again with the floured fork, being careful not to mash the tines completely through the dough. Transfer the turnovers to the prepared baking sheet; place any with tears in the dough hole-side up. Cut a slit in the tops to release steam during baking. Repeat to assemble the second tray of turnovers.

(At this point, the unbaked turnovers may be frozen for up to 1 month. Place them in the freezer on the baking sheet until the surface feels frozen, about 30 minutes. Carefully place the turnovers in resealable freezer bags and store in the freezer. When you're ready to serve the turnovers, thaw at room temperature for 20 minutes, brush with egg wash, sprinkle with sugar, and bake.)

Brush the tops (but NOT the edges) of the pastries lightly with the egg wash. Sprinkle with sugar, if desired. Bake for 15 minutes. Rotate the baking sheets top to bottom and back to front and continue baking until the turnovers are evenly browned on the bottoms and golden brown on the tops, 9 to 12 minutes more. Remove from the oven and let cool on the pans for 15 to 20 minutes before serving (they will still be warm), or serve at room temperature.

Bayona's Sweet Potato Brioche

1 large or 2 small (about 12 ounces) sweet potatoes

1 envelope (2¼ teaspoons) active dry yeast

1 teaspoon sugar, plus 2 tablespoons

2 tablespoons warm water

6 large eggs

¼ cup whole milk

3½ cups unbleached all-purpose flour

1 teaspoon salt

1 cup (2 sticks) cold unsalted butter, cut into small pieces

Makes 1 large brioche, one 9-by-5-inch loaf, or about 20 rolls

Susan Spicer has a whole other life making delicious, incredible artisan bread. She and Sandy Whann from G.H. Leidenheimer Bakery co-own the WildFlour Breads company. Whenever I eat dinner at Susan's restaurant, I make sure I grab the bread basket and get a sweet potato brioche before the last one is gone.

Start the sweet potato(es) a couple of hours ahead. Position a rack in the middle of the oven and preheat to 400°F. Arrange the sweet potato(es) on the rack and bake until very tender when pierced with a fork, 45 minutes to 1 hour. Let cool, then peel and mash in a bowl until smooth. Measure out 1 cup of the purée. (Snack on any remaining purée or save for another use.)

In a small bowl, dissolve the yeast and the 1 teaspoon sugar in the warm water.

Put the sweet potato purée in the bowl of a stand mixer fitted with the paddle attachment. Beat on medium speed for 1 minute, then add 5 of the eggs, the milk, and the yeast mixture and beat for 1 more minute. Add the flour, the 2 tablespoons sugar, and the salt and beat, still on medium speed, for about 5 minutes. Let the mixture rest for 10 minutes, then beat in the cold butter pieces, one-third at a time, allowing time for the butter to be fully incorporated into the batter. Increase the mixer to high speed and beat about 2 minutes until shiny, smooth, and elastic. Remove the bowl from the mixer, cover lightly with plastic wrap, and let the dough rise at room temperature until doubled in size, about 1 hour.

Uncover the bowl. Using your fist, gently punch down the dough to release the air pockets. Re-cover the bowl, put it in the refrigerator, and let the dough rise a second time for at least 6 hours, or preferably overnight.

Remove the dough from the refrigerator and scoop it into a greased 6-cup brioche mold or a 9-by-5-inch loaf pan. Or, divide it among the cups of a standard muffin tin or similar individual molds, for rolls; you should have enough dough for about 20 rolls. Let the dough rise at room temperature until doubled in size, about 2 hours.

At least 25 minutes before baking, preheat the oven to 400°F. Beat the remaining egg in a small bowl. Brush the surface of the dough with the beaten egg and prick in several places with a toothpick. Bake for 10 minutes, then reduce the oven temperature to 325°F and continue baking until golden brown, about 20 minutes longer for a large loaf or about 10 minutes for rolls. Let cool for 10 minutes in the pan(s), then invert onto a wire rack and let cool completely.

DOMENICA'S CRISPY KALE

CHEF ALON SHAYA

I met Alon Shaya when we both worked at Brulard. Even then his passion was Italian food. Not long after leaving the Brulard madness, he joined Chef John Besh's team. Together, they opened Domenica, a showplace for Alon's skills with pasta, pizza, *verdure*, *carni*, and *salumi*. Don't be misled by the vegetable headlines. Kale or no kale, this dish is joyfully decadent.

In a small skillet over medium-low heat, lightly toast the pine nuts until golden brown, about 3 minutes. Set aside to cool.

Pour the oil into a deep-fryer or saucepan with tall sides and clip a deep-frying thermometer to the side of the pan. (You can also use a candy thermometer.) If you are using a saucepan on the stovetop, make sure the pan is no more than halfway full, or the oil may bubble up and overflow or splatter excessively and burn you as you add the kale. Heat the oil over medium-high heat until it reaches 350°F.

While the oil is heating, tear the kale leaves into rough 2-inch squares and set aside. In a large bowl, whisk together the chickpea flour and cold water until thoroughly combined. The batter will be thick.

When the oil has reached 350°F, put all of the kale pieces into the bowl of batter and, using tongs, toss to coat well. Working in batches, add some of the kale to the hot oil, easing it in carefully so the oil doesn't splatter. Be sure not to crowd the pan. Watch the thermometer and adjust the heat to maintain the oil's temperature at as close to 350°F as possible during frying. Once the kale stops bubbling in the oil, about 1 minute, use the tongs or a slotted spoon to transfer the kale to paper towels to drain. Sprinkle evenly with the salt while still warm and transfer to a large bowl.

When all of the kale is fried and salted, add the tomato, green and red onions, pine nuts, lemon juice, and vinegar and toss until well combined. Immediately transfer to a serving dish and sprinkle with the cheese. Serve at once while the kale is hot.

2 tablespoons pine nuts

About 2 quarts vegetable oil

1 to 2 bunches Tuscan kale (also called black kale or lacinato kale) or regular green kale (about 20 ounces), tough stems and spines removed and rinsed well

1 cup chickpea flour

¾ cup cold water

Kosher salt for sprinkling

¼ cup very finely chopped heirloom tomato or any vine-ripened tomato

2 tablespoons sliced green onion, tender green part only

1 tablespoon minced red onion

1½ teaspoons fresh lemon juice

1½ teaspoons good-quality aged balsamic vinegar

¼ cup freshly grated Parmesan cheese, preferably Parmigiano-Reggiano

Makes 4 servings

KARMA KITCHEN'S HUSK-WRAPPED MUSHROOM BOUDIN TAMALES

Every month, a different chef cooks the lunch special at the farmers' market. One day I saw a sign for Blue Plate Lunch: Mushroom Boudin Tamales, and I had to try them. It seemed like such an oddly appropriate combination. I should have known long before I read Anne Churchill, Karma Kitchen on the sign that the chef was my old line-cook buddy from the Bayona days. Anne Churchill is not a vegan, or even a vegetarian. But in a city dedicated to meats and sea creatures, and in a profession where most folks scoff at non-meat eaters as if they are beings of a lower evolutionary status, she's carved a niche for herself as vegan/vegetarian caterer. But don't be fooled. Anne makes a pretty mean pot of seafood gumbo, too.

Green Garlic Coleslaw

½ cup chopped green garlic, white parts only (if not available, use young leeks and 2 cloves garlic to equal ½ cup)

1 tablespoon chopped fresh lemon basil, regular basil, or Thai purple basil

2 teaspoons honey or agave syrup

1 teaspoon Creole mustard

1 to 2 teaspoons raw sugar

2 to 3 tablespoons fresh lemon juice

2 to 4 tablespoons water

1 teaspoon Kosher salt, or more to taste

1 cup canola oil

4 cups finely sliced or shredded green cabbage

1 cup shredded purple cabbage

½ cup peeled and shredded carrot

1 cup wood chips such as hickory or mesquite

One 14-ounce block firm tofu

Kosher salt and freshly ground black pepper

1 or 2 pinches of cayenne pepper

1 pound ripe plum (Roma) tomatoes

1 teaspoon dried oregano

1 teaspoon dried thyme

¼ cup olive oil

1 large yellow onion, diced

3 tablespoons chopped garlic (about 1 head)

1 pound white button mushrooms, brushed clean and chopped in a food processor

1 pound shiitake mushrooms, stems discarded, caps brushed clean and sliced

4 cups cooked rice, brown or white, cooled

17 dried cornhusks (about one-third of a 12-ounce bag), soaked in cold water for 1 hour

To make the slaw: In a food processor, combine the green garlic, basil, honey, mustard, 1 teaspoon sugar, 2 tablespoons lemon juice, 2 tablespoons water, and 1 teaspoon salt and pulse to blend. With the machine running, slowly pour in the canola oil and process, just until a thick emulsion forms. Taste and add more sugar, lemon juice, and/or salt as needed. Process just until well blended. Add another tablespoon or 2 of water to loosen if needed, pulsing just to blend. Taste and adjust the seasoning again. In a large bowl, toss together the cabbages and carrot with the dressing until well coated. Cover and refrigerate until ready to serve.

Build a hot fire for indirect cooking in a charcoal grill or preheat a gas grill to high. While the coals are heating, soak the wood chips in a bowl with water to cover. Meanwhile, preheat the oven 350°F.

Season the tofu all over with salt, black pepper, and cayenne. Set the seasoned tofu on a wire rack. When the grill is ready, drain the wood chips and arrange them on top of the hot coals or in a smoker box or foil packet on the burner of a gas grill. Place the wire rack with the tofu on the grill rack over indirect heat. Cover the grill and open the vents. Smoke the tofu until it is lightly golden and no longer jiggly, about 20 minutes. Remove from the grill and set aside.

Cut the tomatoes in half crosswise. Arrange on a baking sheet, cut-side up. Season with salt and pepper, and sprinkle on the oregano and thyme. Roast until collapsed and starting to brown in spots, 20 to 30 minutes. Remove from the oven and let cool. Transfer to a food processor and process to a smooth purée. Set aside.

In large sauté pan or skillet, heat the olive oil over medium heat. Add the onion and sauté until translucent, about 5 minutes. Add the garlic and sauté for 1 minute. Add the mushrooms and cook, stirring occasionally, until they give up their liquid and the liquid cooks off, about 15 minutes. Season with salt and pepper and continue to cook, stirring constantly, until the mixture begins to stick and brown deeply. Stir in the roasted tomato purée. Cut the smoked tofu into bite-size cubes and add to the vegetables. Stir in the rice until well coated and all the ingredients are evenly distributed. Taste and adjust the seasoning.

Drain the cornhusks. Cut 2 of the husks into a total of 15 long, thin strips to use for ties for the tamales and set aside. Open the remaining cornhusks and stack them flat on a clean work surface. To assemble, scoop about ⅓ cup of the mushroom mixture into the center of a cornhusk, leaving about 3 inches of husk unfilled at the bottom. Fold the long sides of the cornhusk snugly over the mixture, then fold the bottom flap of husk up over the filling and tie the whole packet closed snugly around the middle with 1 of the reserved strips of husk. Repeat to assemble the rest of the tamales. (Note: cornhusks can vary in size. You can reduce the amount of filling to accommodate smaller husks or overlap 2 husks to make larger tamales.)

Pour water into a large saucepan to a depth of 1 inch and bring to a boil. Place a steamer basket over (but not touching) the boiling water and add the tamales, stacking them neatly. Cover tightly and steam for 15 minutes. Remove from the steamer, let cool slightly, and serve.

Note: The steamed tamales can be stored, tightly wrapped in plastic wrap in the refrigerator, for up to 5 days. To serve, unwrap and reheat gently in a steamer basket over steam or in a microwave.

*Makes 15 boudin tamales;
serves 6 to 8*

MOMOFUKU'S POACHED EGGS WITH CAVIAR

Onion Soubise

¾ pound yellow onions

4 tablespoons unsalted butter, at room temperature

½ cup water

1 teaspoon kosher salt

8 eggs

Fingerling Potato Chips

4 finger-size fingerling potatoes, very well scrubbed

Grapeseed or other neutral oil for deep-frying

Kosher salt

Fines Herbes Salad

6 tablespoons fresh chervil leaves

1 tablespoon fresh parsley leaves

1 tablespoon snipped fresh chives

2 ounces American hackleback caviar (about ¼ cup)

Smoked salt

4 teaspoons sweet potato vinegar (preferred) or top-quality sherry vinegar

Makes 8 servings

David Chang's inspiration for this dish comes from the fact that Alain Passard, Jean-Georges Vongerichten, and a lot of other great French chefs have created signature egg dishes. This is his contribution to that luminary list. Whether you do the dish itself is up to you. But keep this in mind: his 5-minutes-and-10-seconds technique is something to follow any time you need to poach eggs.

To make the soubise: Cut the onions in half through the root-stem axis and then, working in the same direction, cut the halves into ¼-inch-or-so-thick slices—they should be thin but not too thin—with a knife or on a mandoline. You should have 2½ to 3 loosely packed cups sliced onions.

In a saucepan large enough to accommodate the ingredients snugly, combine the onions, butter, water, and salt. Turn the heat to its lowest setting and cook, keeping the heat low and gentle, for 2 hours, stirring occasionally. Remember that you are trying not to color or brown the onions at all.

After 2 hours, the onions should be tender and sweet and the butter and water should have quietly reduced into a satiny sauce that cloaks the onions (if it's still loose and watery or the onions are not completely yielding, continue cooking). Set the soubise aside while you make the rest of the dish. (The soubise can be made up to 3 days in advance and refrigerated, then warmed gently before serving.)

While the onions are cooking, poach the eggs. Bring a saucepan halfway full of water to a boil. Gently lower the eggs, in their shells, into the boiling water with a slotted spoon or spider. (Some may crack, though they should still be usable even if they're not beautiful.) Set a kitchen timer for 5 minutes and 10 seconds from the moment the eggs go into the water, and fill a large bowl with water and ice cubes to make an ice water bath.

When the timer rings, use the spoon or spider to transfer the eggs to the ice water. Peel the eggs when they are cool enough to handle, cracking them open on a cutting board and then peeling them underwater, in the bowl. (We've found that the little bit of water that sneaks in between the shell and the white as you work helps with the peeling.) Reserve the eggs in the fridge until ready to use, or for up to 8 hours. Warm them for 1 minute under hot running tap water before serving.

To make the potato chips: Working over a small bowl nearly full of cold water, slice the potatoes into as-thin-as-possible disks using a mandoline or knife. (The slices should be see-through thin.) Rinse the potatoes in one or two changes of water, until the water is clear, to remove excess starch.

Pour oil into a deep fryer or heavy-bottomed saucepan with tall sides to a depth of 1½ inches and heat to 360°F, using a thermometer to monitor its temperature. (Oil that's too hot can impart a nasty flavor; oil that's too cool won't crisp the potatoes.) Have ready a plate lined with a double thickness of paper towels.

Place a couple of handfuls of potatoes in a clean kitchen towel and wring out the moisture in the potatoes, blotting them even drier with a paper or kitchen towel, and pile them in a spider or slotted spoon with a long handle. Plunge the potatoes into the hot oil and immediately stir them, agitating the contents of the pan until the bubbling subsides. Fry them for 3 to 3½ minutes, stirring regularly to prevent the potatoes from sticking to each other, until crisp and very lightly browned. Transfer the fried potatoes

continued

to the paper towels to drain and season immediately (and heavily) with salt. Wring out another handful of potatoes and repeat, replacing the paper towels you're draining the chips on as necessary and keeping an eye on the temperature of the oil. When all of the potatoes are cooked and cooled, transfer them from the paper towels to a plate or airtight container and reserve until ready to use.

To make the salad: Combine all of the herbs in a small bowl and toss gently to mix well.

We serve this dish in a very wide, very shallow bowl, almost like a concave plate. Putting together the dish, we imagine the middle of the plate as a circle: the right half of the circle should be onion soubise, two-thirds of the left half should be potato chips, and the remainder—the part of the circle that will face the diner—a little pile of herb salad.

Using the back of a spoon, make a small indentation in the onions on each plate, and nestle a warmed egg in each. Split each egg open a little more than halfway with a small knife, and then use a small spoon to sneak about ½ tablespoon of the caviar into each egg, letting it settle into the yellow river of yolk spilling out onto the plate. Add a few grains of smoked salt on top of each egg and a tiny splash of sweet potato vinegar over by the onions. Serve at once.

Soa's Garden Vegetable "Fettuccine" with Fresh Tomato Sauce

CHEF SOA DAVIES

Soa Davies is amazing. She's been Eric Ripert's right hand for years. She can talk endlessly about the joys of making cassoulet. She was one of the first people I met when I worked at Le Bernardin, and she really helped me get acclimated. When she invited me to her apartment for dinner, I didn't know what to expect; she can come at you from so many angles. It turns out that when she eats at home, she likes to eat simple food. Roast chicken and a salad, maybe. The night I came over, she knocked me out with this beautiful "fettuccine" made of tender ribbons of super-fresh vegetables. Who needs pasta?

In a heavy skillet over medium heat, heat the olive oil. Add the garlic and toast, stirring, until fragrant and light golden brown, 3 to 4 minutes.

Stir in the wine and tomatoes and bring to a simmer. Reduce the heat to medium-low and simmer gently until the sauce is slightly thickened, 8 to 10 minutes. Season with salt and pepper. Remove from the heat and cover to keep warm.

In a large sauté pan or skillet, melt the butter over medium heat. Add the onion and sauté until tender, about 3 minutes. Add the zucchini, yellow squash, and carrot ribbons and lightly sauté just until wilted, about 30 seconds. Season with salt and pepper.

Divide the vegetable "fettuccine" among four plates and spoon the fresh tomato sauce on top. Garnish with the basil leaves and pecorino. Serve at once.

Note: Substitute any sturdy vegetables you like that will hold up to shaving into these delicate ribbons; use the freshest vegetables available to you.

¼ cup extra-virgin olive oil

2 cloves garlic, minced

¼ cup dry white wine

2 large ripe tomatoes, peeled, seeded, and diced

Fine sea salt and freshly ground pepper

2 tablespoons unsalted butter

1 yellow onion, halved and thinly sliced lengthwise

1 zucchini, shaved with a vegetable peeler into long strips

1 yellow squash, shaved with a vegetable peeler into long strips

1 carrot, peeled and shaved with a vegetable peeler into long strips

¼ cup fresh basil leaves, torn

½ cup shaved pecorino cheese

Makes 4 servings

Herbsaint's Shrimp and Louisiana Brown Rice Risotto

4 tablespoons unsalted butter

2 yellow onions, cut into ¼-inch dice (about 3 cups)

2 jalapeño chiles, seeded and minced

2 cloves garlic, minced (about 1 tablespoon)

2 pounds whole shrimp, medium or large, peeled and deveined

1½ cups brown jasmine rice

2 acorn squash (about 2½ pounds total weight), peeled, seeded, and cut into ½-inch dice (about 3 cups)

3 teaspoons salt

1 teaspoon freshly ground black pepper

Generous pinch of cayenne pepper (optional)

7 cups Basic Chicken Stock (page 230) or store-bought chicken broth

¼ cup sliced green onions, white and tender green parts

¼ cup chopped fresh parsley

Hot sauce to taste

It seems like no one ever makes risotto with brown rice—probably because it would add time (and therefore trouble) to a dish that is already slow (and labor intensive). But Donald Link does it, at his restaurant Herbsaint. Part of his secret is that he uses organic "Cajun Grain" brown jasmine rice, produced by Kurt and Karen Unkel in Kinder, Louisiana. The brand is distinct from other brown rices because the Unkels include some of the stray grains of red wild rice that grows in the field with their main rice.

In another personal touch, instead of the usual cheese that most chefs put in risotto for the creaminess, Donald uses acorn squash, which melts into a dreamy sweetness. Ryan Prewitt, one of Donald's chefs, says depending on the size of your shrimp, they too might cook until they fall apart and become more a flavoring ingredient than a recognizable component. Don't worry if that happens. If you use larger shrimp and they don't cook apart, that's fine, too. People in Louisiana are perfectly happy if their shrimp are cooked a bit more than the fine-dining norm.

In a heavy 8-quart saucepan or Dutch oven over medium-high heat, melt the butter. Add the onions, jalapeños, and garlic and sauté until soft, about 5 minutes. Add the shrimp, rice, squash, salt, black pepper, and cayenne, if using, and stir until the rice grains are thoroughly coated with the fat and the ingredients are hot, about 5 minutes.

Reduce the heat to medium and stir in 1 cup of the stock. Bring the liquid in the pan to a slow simmer, then cook, stirring often, until the rice has absorbed most of the liquid but is still very moist, about 15 minutes. Add another 1 cup stock, stir until combined, and slowly simmer until the rice has again absorbed most of the liquid, still stirring often. Continue this process of adding 1 cup of stock at a time, cooking and stirring between additions, until the rice has absorbed the stock but is still quite moist. By the time the risotto is done, you will have used roughly 7 cups of stock total and the rice will have cooked for about 1½ hours from the time you started adding the stock. The finished rice should be creamy and tender.

Stir in the green onions, parsley, and hot sauce. Season the risotto with more salt and pepper, if desired. Remove from the heat, spoon onto warmed plates, and serve at once.

Makes 6 to 8 servings

CRAWFISH RAVIOLI
WITH SEA URCHIN BUTTER SAUCE AND MISSISSIPPI PADDLEFISH ROE

This may be the happiest moment of my professional life! Maybe by putting this recipe in this book, I won't have to make it anymore. It's a great dish. Crawfish tails are small and their flavor is delicate. Many of the usual preparations—crawfish bisque, crawfish étouffée—include so many other ingredients that much of the crawfish flavor is obscured beneath the seasoning in the sauce. The delicacy of ravioli is perfect for crawfish. Just don't commit yourself to making fifty orders of them a night. That's enough to take the love out of any dish.

To make the dough: Sift the flour and salt together into a large bowl. Make a well in the center of the flour mixture and add the egg yolks and whole eggs. Using a fork, slowly pull the eggs into the edges of the well, until all the eggs have been absorbed by the flour and a rough dough has formed. Turn the dough out onto a lightly floured work surface. Using the heel of your hand, knead the dough until smooth and elastic, about 4 minutes. The dough is done when you press your finger into it and the dough bounces back into shape. Wrap the dough in plastic and place in the refrigerator to rest for 30 minutes.

To make the filling: In a small saucepan over medium heat, bring the cream to a simmer and cook until reduced by half, about 5 minutes. Remove from the heat and let cool.

In a sauté pan over medium heat, melt the butter. When the butter starts to brown, add the shallots and garlic and sweat until tender, about 3 minutes. Remove the pan from heat and stir in the garlic chives. Set aside and let cool.

In a large bowl, stir together the crawfish, shrimp, sautéed shallots and garlic, cooled reduced cream, and lemon zest. Season with hot sauce, salt, and white pepper to taste. Cover the filling and refrigerate until you're ready to fill the ravioli.

Remove the pasta dough from the refrigerator. Cut into quarters. Work with one-fourth of the dough at a time, keeping the remainder covered with a clean dish towel so it doesn't dry out. Using a pasta machine, roll out 1 dough piece from the thickest setting to the thinnest setting. Dust the work surface and the dough sheet with additional flour if needed to prevent sticking. Repeat to roll out the remaining 3 dough pieces.

When you have rolled out all 4 sheets of dough, fill the ravioli. Lay a sheet of dough on a floured work surface and lightly spray or brush the surface with water. Place 1 teaspoon of the crawfish filling in 2 rows about 3 inches apart on 1 of the pasta sheets. Top with another pasta sheet. Seal the edges, being careful not to trap air inside the ravioli. Cut the ravioli into 3-inch squares using a ravioli cutter or the tip of a knife, or cut into rounds with a 3-inch cookie cutter. Press on the edges with your fingers or the tines of a fork to seal. Place the finished ravioli on a baking sheet dusted with flour. Repeat with the remaining 2 sheets of dough and filling. Cover the ravioli with another clean dish towel and refrigerate until ready to cook.

To make the sauce: Combine the butter and sea urchin roe in a food processor and pulse until smooth. Transfer to a small bowl, cover, and refrigerate. In a saucepan over medium-high heat, bring the shrimp stock to a boil and cook until reduced by half, about 15 minutes. Season with salt and pepper. Meanwhile, bring a large pot three-fourths full of salted water to a boil over high heat.

Whisking constantly, add the sea urchin butter to the boiling stock until all the butter has been incorporated. Add the ravioli to the salted water and cook until they float to the top and the thick edges are al dente, about 5 minutes. Drain thoroughly.

To serve, place 3 or 4 ravioli on each plate and scatter around the chive flowers, if you have them. Place 1 teaspoonful of the paddlefish roe on top of each serving and spoon the sauce around the ravioli. (Gently reheat the sauce if needed at serving time, but do not bring to a boil or the sauce will break.) Serve at once.

Pasta Dough

2 cups all-purpose flour, plus more for dusting

1 teaspoon fine sea salt

5 large egg yolks, plus 2 whole large eggs

Filling

½ cup heavy (whipping) cream

3 tablespoons unsalted butter

1½ tablespoons minced shallots

1 clove garlic, minced

¼ cup thinly sliced garlic chives, any flowers reserved for garnish

1 pound Louisiana crawfish tail meat

½ pound small (60 count) shrimp, peeled and deveined

1 teaspoon grated lemon zest

2 tablespoons Crystal hot sauce, or to taste

Fine sea salt

Freshly ground white pepper

Sauce

½ cup (1 stick) unsalted butter

3 ounces sea urchin roe, puréed, or tomato paste

1½ cups Rich Shrimp Stock (page 229) or store-bought shrimp or seafood stock

Fine sea salt and freshly ground black pepper to taste

Garlic chive flowers for garnish (reserved; optional)

4 ounces Mississippi paddlefish roe for garnish

Makes 4 to 6 servings

CLEMENCEAU'D SHRIMP

You see Shrimp Clemenceau on classic New Orleans menus at places like Dooky Chase and Galatoire's. Traditionally it's a composed dish, with all the ingredients ending up in the same skillet before plating. For a twist and a dare (forgive me, tradition!), I like to separate the components. I think this pretties the Clemenceau up, and, instead of all the flavors colliding in one pot as in the classic version, it allows the diner to the bring the flavors together at the table.

Believe it or not, so-called "Meyer" lemons are not lemons at all. They are thought to be a cross between a lemon and a mandarin orange. They are sweeter and rounder in flavor than a regular lemon, so they can be an exciting substitute for more common citrus. Microplanes used to be exclusively for carpenters and woodworkers. But now that chefs have discovered them, they are in every commercial kitchen in town. If your housewares department doesn't have them, check your hardware store (or use your grater, but really, the 'plane is amazing for zest!).

Line a baking sheet with parchment paper. Peel and devein the shrimp, making sure to keep the heads attached. Arrange the peeled shrimp in a single layer on the prepared baking sheet, cover with plastic wrap, and keep refrigerated until ready to serve.

Preheat the oven to 350°F. Scrub the potatoes (but do not peel), pat dry, and place them in a large mixing bowl. Add the mushrooms. Drizzle with the olive oil and season with salt and pepper. Toss gently to mix well and coat evenly with the oil. Spread them in a single layer on a large, rimmed baking sheet. Scatter the thyme sprigs and crushed garlic on top. Roast until tender, 25 to 30 minutes. (The potatoes can be made up to 1 day ahead.)

Bring a medium saucepan of salted water to a boil. While the water is heating, prepare an ice bath by filling a large bowl halfway with ice, then adding enough water just to cover the ice. Add the peas to the boiling water and blanch just until tender, about 2 minutes. Drain the peas and immediately plunge them into the ice bath to stop the cooking and preserve their color. Using a slotted spoon, remove them from the ice bath and set aside.

Using a microplane or the smallest holes on a box grater, finely grate the lemon zest. Set aside the zest. Using a sharp paring knife, remove the skins of the lemons and discard. Over a small bowl, supreme the lemons by gently cutting in between each segment to remove the flesh, letting the segments fall into the bowl as you work. Squeeze the rinds and pulp over the lemon supremes to extract any remaining juice, and discard the peels. Set aside.

Bring ¼ cup water to boil in a small saucepan set over medium-high heat. Reduce the heat to low and whisk in the cold butter, 1 tablespoon at a time, until all the butter is melted and a fully emulsified sauce forms. Season to taste with salt. Remove from the heat and cover to keep warm.

If the potatoes were cooked ahead of time, rewarm them in a 350°F oven. Place the cooked sugar snap peas in a medium saucepan with 2 tablespoons water and heat over medium-high heat until hot. Season with salt and pepper. Spoon 2 tablespoons of the butter sauce over the peas and toss to coat. Remove from the heat and cover to keep warm.

Remove the tray of shrimp from the refrigerator. Divide the canola oil between 2 large nonstick skillets and heat over medium-high heat. (Alternatively, you can cook the shrimp in 1 pan but in 2 batches; what's important is to avoid overcrowding the pan.) Season the shrimp on both sides with salt and pepper. Add the shrimp to the hot pans and sear until the shrimp start to turn opaque, 1 to 1½ minutes. Turn the shrimp and continue cooking just until cooked through, 1 to 1½ minutes longer.

Arrange the potatoes and a spoonful of sugar snap peas in the center of each of six large plates, along with 3 or 4 shrimp. Stir the lemon segments and juice into the butter sauce and spoon the sauce over and around the shrimp. Serve at once.

18 large or 24 medium Gulf shrimp, heads intact

1½ pounds baby new potatoes, preferably some combination of red, white, yellow, and purple

4 ounces enoki or cremini mushrooms, wiped clean

¼ cup extra-virgin olive oil

Sea salt and freshly ground pepper

2 fresh thyme sprigs

6 cloves garlic, unpeeled, lightly smashed

1 pound sugar snap peas, ends trimmed

2 Meyer lemons

¾ cup (1½ sticks) cold unsalted butter, cut into tablespoons

3 tablespoons canola oil

Makes 6 servings

Pickled Chanterelle Salad

½ cup rice wine vinegar

¼ cup water

1 tablespoon sugar

Fine sea salt

10 ounces fresh chanterelle mushrooms, brushed clean, tough stems discarded

1 fresh thyme sprig

2 ears corn, husks and silk removed

1 dried apricot, split in half and julienned

1 tablespoon pistachio oil or walnut, pecan, or hazelnut oil

½ cup mâche leaves

½ cup watercress leaves

Freshly ground white pepper

Roasted Corn Coulis

2 cups Basic Chicken Stock (page 230) or store-bought chicken broth

4 to 5 ears corn, husks and silks removed and kernels cut from cobs (about 2 cups) with cobs reserved

2 pieces star anise

2 shallots, thinly sliced

3 tablespoons heavy (whipping) cream

Fine sea salt

Freshly ground white pepper

Kosher salt

Two 2-pound live Maine lobsters

¼ cup water

1 cup (2 sticks) unsalted butter, cut into ½-inch cubes

Fine sea salt

Freshly ground white pepper

Makes 4 servings

Changing the nightly special in the middle of service may not be unheard of. But changing the special to a dish featuring an ingredient that you don't even have in the kitchen is, well, insane. Enrico Brulard did it, and the result was typical Brulard—fabulous, ethereal, "peppy" lobsters. Of course, this dish didn't just occur to him out of nowhere. Lobsters and corn are a typical New England combination. Looking over this recipe, you can get a good sense of how a great chef re-imagines something ordinary and makes it something extraordinary.

Note that you will need a total of 6 or 7 ears of corn—2 for the salad and 4 or 5 for the coulis.

To make the salad, first pickle the mushrooms: In a small saucepan over medium-high heat, stir together the vinegar, water, sugar, and a pinch of salt and bring to a boil. Put the chanterelles and thyme sprig in a heatproof container with a lid. Pour the boiling vinegar solution over the mushrooms and let stand at room temperature for 1 hour. (The pickled mushrooms can be made up to 1 week ahead. Cover tightly and refrigerate.)

Fill a large bowl with ice cubes and water to make an ice water bath. Put a pot half full of water on to boil that is big enough to accommodate the 2 ears of corn. When the water is boiling, blanch the ears for 4 minutes. Transfer the cobs to the bowl of ice water. Once they are chilled, cut the kernels from the corn. (If the kernels are cut off before the ears are blanched, you will lose some of the natural sweetness.) Set aside the blanched kernels with the pickled mushrooms; you will compose the salad with the remaining ingredients when you are ready to serve.

To make the coulis: In a 3-quart saucepan over medium-high heat, bring the chicken stock to a boil. Add the 4 to 5 reserved corn-cobs, the star anise, and the shallots and simmer for 15 minutes. Strain the corn stock and set aside.

Meanwhile, heat a dry large cast-iron skillet over high heat. Working in batches and stirring constantly, toast the corn kernels from the 4 to 5 ears until lightly browned on all sides, 5 to 7 minutes per batch. Transfer each batch to a blender as it's finished. When all of the corn has been toasted, process to a coarse purée. Strain the corn purée through a chinois or fine-mesh sieve into a medium heavy-bottomed saucepan and place over low heat. Add the cream and just enough of the corn stock to give the coulis a saucelike consistency that is thick enough to coat a spoon evenly. Continue simmering over low heat as you season with salt and white pepper. Thin the coulis with more corn stock, if needed. Remove from the heat and strain through the chinois into a bowl, then return to the saucepan and set aside.

Bring a large pot of water salted with kosher salt to a boil. Meanwhile, on a cutting board (wear gloves to protect your hands, if desired), kill each lobster by plunging a heavy knife through its head just above the eyes, making sure the knife goes all the way through the head; then pull the knife in a downward motion through the eyes toward the cutting board without splitting the head in half. Twist off the claws where they join the bodies and set aside. Twist the tails away from the bodies, use the knife to split each tail lengthwise, and pull out the vein that runs down the center of the tails along the top, if visible; refrigerate the tails until ready to use. (Discard the bodies or reserve for another use, such as stock.) Separate the claws from the knuckles. Set the knuckles aside and add the claws to the boiling water. Boil, uncovered, for 5 minutes. Add the knuckle shells to the pot and continue cooking for 3 minutes longer. Using a slotted spoon, transfer the claws and knuckles to a bowl and refrigerate until cool enough to handle. (Discard the salted water.)

When the claws and knuckles have cooled, using kitchen scissors, cut through the knuckles and remove the meat. Crack the claws with a cracker or the back end of a knife and twist to open. Extract the claw meat and set aside with the knuckle meat.

In a small saucepan, bring the water to a boil. Gradually whisk in the butter, 1 cube at a time, whisking each until fully emulsified before adding the next cube. Season the butter emulsion with salt and reduce the heat to low. Season the lobster tails with sea salt and white pepper and add them, still in the shell, to the emulsified butter. Poach the tails for 3 minutes, then add the claw and knuckle meat. Continue warming the lobster until the tail meat turns opaque throughout, about 5 minutes longer.

While the lobster is cooking, gently rewarm the corn coulis over low heat, stirring often to prevent scorching.

Using a slotted spoon, transfer the pickled chanterelles to a bowl and add 1½ teaspoons of the pickling liquid. Add the corn kernels, apricot, pistachio oil, and mâche and watercress leaves. Season with salt and white pepper and toss gently to coat.

Remove the lobster from the emulsified butter and remove the tail meat from the shells. (Discard the shells.) Place 1 half-tail, 1 knuckle, and 1 claw in the center of each of four individual plates. Artfully arrange the salad on top of and to the side of the lobster and spoon the coulis around all. Serve at once.

LISTEN-TO-YOUR-FISH FISH

Whenever I tell people about working at Brulard's, they tell me they would have quit the first day. But there are two things you have to understand about a chef like Enrico Brulard. First, he's a genius. You can learn more working for him in six weeks than you can working at a lot of good restaurants for six years. Second, he was insane. It was a relief to go to Le Bernardin.

To begin the fricassee: In a medium, heavy skillet over high heat, heat the oil until hot, about 1 minute. Add the morels and sauté until tender, 3 to 5 minutes. Remove from the heat and season with salt and white pepper. Set aside.

Bring a 2-quart saucepan halfway filled with lightly salted water to boil over high heat. While the water is heating, prepare an ice bath by filling a large bowl halfway with ice, then adding enough water just to cover the ice. Add the peas to the boiling water and cook until tender, 5 to 7 minutes. Using a slotted spoon, immediately transfer the peas to the ice water to stop the cooking and preserve their color. Cook the fava beans the same way and transfer to the ice bath. Drain the peas and beans well in a colander set in the sink. Slip off the tender inner skins from the fava beans. Set the peas and beans aside while you make the sauce.

To make the sauce: In a heavy nonreactive saucepan, combine the wine and shallot and cook over high heat without stirring until the liquid reduces to about 1 tablespoon, 8 to 10 minutes. Reduce the heat to low and whisk in the cold butter 1 tablespoon at a time, whisking until each addition of butter is fully incorporated before adding the next. Whisk in the mustard and lemon juice, then season with salt and white pepper. Strain the sauce through a fine-mesh strainer into a bowl, then return to the saucepan and cover to keep warm. You can also hold the sauce in the top of a double boiler with hot water in the bottom.

Season the salmon fillets on both sides with salt and white pepper. Divide the 1 tablespoon oil between 2 nonstick 10-inch skillets and heat over medium-low heat for about 2 minutes. Place 2 fillets in each skillet and cook slowly until the top of each fillet is just warm to the touch, 8 to 10 minutes; while the fillets cook, do not turn them or try to loosen them from the bottoms of the skillets. Remove from the heat. Using a sturdy spatula, transfer the fillets onto paper towels to drain, cooked side down, for a few seconds.

Meanwhile, finish the fricassee. Heat a small, dry skillet for about 1 minute over medium-high heat. Add the butter, garlic, and shallot, cooking them until they are soft and their liquids have released, about 2 minutes, stirring occasionally. Add the reserved morels, peas, and fava beans and season with salt and white pepper. Sauté just until all the vegetables are heated through, about 1 minute, then add the 2 tablespoons water to emulsify the butter in the skillet (this will add a nice glaze to the vegetables). Stir. Remove from the heat.

Spoon a portion of the fricassee in the center of each of four individual plates and arrange a salmon fillet on top. Spoon some of the sauce over and around the salmon and garnish each plate with a few pieces of mustard cress or sprouts. Serve at once.

Fricassee of Peas, Fava Beans, and Morel Mushrooms

1 tablespoon canola oil

4 ounces fresh morel mushrooms, stem ends trimmed, washed quickly under cool running water and drained

Fine sea salt

Freshly ground white pepper

¼ cup shelled fresh English peas

¼ cup shelled fresh fava beans

1 tablespoon unsalted butter

2 cloves garlic, finely minced

1 large shallot, finely minced

2 tablespoons water

Mustard-Butter Sauce

½ cup dry white wine

1 large shallot, finely minced

6 tablespoons cold unsalted butter, cut into tablespoons

1 tablespoon Dijon mustard

1½ teaspoons fresh lemon juice

Fine sea salt

Freshly ground white pepper

4 skinless fillets wild Alaskan salmon (about 6 ounces each)

Fine sea salt

Freshly ground white pepper

1 tablespoon canola oil

Micro mustard cress or mustard sprouts for garnish

Makes 4 servings

LE BERNARDIN'S POUNDED TUNA WITH FOIE GRAS

CHEF ERIC RIPERT

Foie Gras Terrine

One 1½-pound whole grade-A foie gras, cleaned and deveined (see page 24) or a prepared foie gras terrine or torchon (preferably from D'Artagnan)

1 tablespoon fine sea salt

½ teaspoon freshly ground white pepper

¼ teaspoon sel rose or other pink salt

1½ quarts Basic Chicken Stock (page 230) or store-bought chicken broth

12 ounces sushi-grade yellowfin tuna fillet, in one chunk

One 4½-by-9-inch marquise-shaped template (see recipe introduction)

One 6-inch mini-baguette

Fine sea salt

Freshly ground white pepper

4 tablespoons extra-virgin olive oil

2 small shallots, minced

2 tablespoons minced fresh chives

1 lemon, cut in half

Makes 4 servings

The pounded tuna appetizer is probably the most popular dish at Le Bernardin. If you're not charged with wielding the mallet, I agree, it's exquisite. Perhaps I lost sight of the rewards for the palate, and the stomach, because I pounded enough of these in my time to depopulate a large sushi-grade school.

But now that I am no longer spending my days that way, I have realized that this is not only a delicious dish, it's an ingenious dish. The tuna and foie gras are both subtle and rich in flavor, so they don't overpower each other.

At Le Bernardin, this dish is marquise-shaped, like an oval with pointy ends. You can make it round if you want. To make the marquise template, take one side of a cardboard box, measuring at least 6 by 12 inches. Place the pointy end of a clothes iron (unplugged, unheated) at the end of one long side of the cardboard, with the point of the iron centered on the short side. Using a pencil, trace the shape of the iron. Now you have the shape of one side of the template. Turn the iron around so the pointy end is in the opposite direction. Position the point of the iron so it is 9 inches from the point at the other end of the cardboard, also lining up the points where the body meets in the middle. Using the pencil, trace the shape of the iron. Using a sharp knife or razor blade, cut out the oval shape so that you have a template roughly 4½ by 9 inches. Wrap the template in aluminum foil.

A fervent note: If you're going to go through all the trouble of making this dish, please use the best extra-virgin olive oil you can get your hands on. You'll really taste it here. Oh, and make sure you plan well in advance, because you have to start preparing the foie gras a full 3 days ahead.

To make the terrine: Clean and devein the foie gras as directed. In a small bowl, stir together the salt, white pepper, and sel rose. Season both lobes of the foie gras on all sides with the salt mixture. Lightly press the lobes together and wrap the foie gras in plastic wrap. Refrigerate overnight.

The next day, in a 6-quart saucepan or large Dutch oven over high heat, bring the chicken stock to a boil. Meanwhile, remove the foie gras from the plastic wrap and place it centered crosswise on one end of a 13-by-18-inch piece of parchment paper. Wrap the foie gras in the parchment paper snugly and roll it back and forth, pressing gently, to form a tight log about 6 inches long and 2½ inches in diameter. Twist the ends of the parchment tightly closed while compressing the log gently at the same time, to remove any air pockets from the foie gras. Unwrap the foie gras from the parchment paper and discard the paper. Make a double layer of cheesecloth about 12 by 24 inches and place

the log of foie gras centered crosswise at one end. Rolling away from you, shape the foie gras into a tight log again, wrapped in cheesecloth this time, making sure to remove any remaining air pockets and again twisting the ends to compact the shape. Tie off each end snugly with a piece of kitchen twine.

Reduce the heat under the boiling chicken stock to bring it to a steady simmer. Using tongs, ease the foie gras log into the simmering stock and cook until an instant-read thermometer inserted in the middle registers 90°F, about 2 minutes. Carefully remove the foie gras from the stock and immediately refrigerate until well chilled, at least 2 hours and up to 2 days. (Save the stock for another use.)

When the foie gras is chilled, remove the cheesecloth and discard. Gently reshape the foie gras log once more by rolling it in plastic wrap and smoothing with your hands. Refrigerate overnight.

On the day you are serving and at least 2 hours ahead, prepare the tuna: Cut the tuna chunk horizontally through the thickness into 4 slices about ¼ inch thick. Set up a sheet of plastic wrap (you may need to use two sheets overlapping) at least 2 by 3 feet on a work surface. Arrange the tuna slices on the plastic wrap about 1 inch apart. Cover with another same-size sheet of plastic wrap. Using a kitchen mallet, gently pound the tuna pieces to a uniform ⅛-inch thickness. Using the marquise template and the tip of a sharp knife, cut through the tuna and both layers of plastic to form 4 marquise-shaped portions of tuna. (Save the tuna trimmings for another use.) Leaving the plastic wrap in place on both sides of the tuna ovals, refrigerate until serving time.

Preheat the oven to 350°F. Trim the ends of the baguette and trim off the crust. Cut the loaf lengthwise into 4 very thin slices. Arrange the slices on a baking sheet lined with parchment paper. Cover the slices with another sheet of parchment paper, and then position a second baking sheet on top to keep the slices as flat as possible while they toast. Toast the slices in the hot oven until lightly browned and crisp, 5 to 7 minutes. Remove from the oven and let cool on the pan to room temperature.

Unwrap the foie gras log and cut lengthwise into 4 slices about ⅛ inch thick; make sure each slice is as long as the baguette slices. (You will have foie gras left over for other uses.) Arrange each foie gras slice on top of a baguette toast and spread into a smooth, even layer. Place a foie gras toast in the center of each of four oval-shaped individual plates. Peel off the top piece of plastic wrap from 1 tuna portion and take up the tuna in your hand, with the plastic-wrap side on your palm. Invert the tuna carefully over a foie gras toast like a blanket, pulling it smooth and centering the edges on the plate. Remove the remaining piece of plastic. Repeat to assemble the remaining plates. Sprinkle the tuna with salt and white pepper and brush each portion with 1 tablespoon of the olive oil. Sprinkle the shallots and chives over each. Wipe off any excess garnish from the plates. Squeeze lemon juice over each portion and serve at once.

GENGHIS KHAN'S WHOLE FRIED FISH

Americans don't like to see their dinner staring back at them. But growing up in Louisiana, folks are used to shrimp, crawfish, crabs, and even fish gazing up from the plate. The best whole fried fish I have ever eaten came from Genghis Khan, a Korean restaurant that used to be on a shady stretch of Tulane Avenue. Henry Lee, a classical violin player, originally opened the restaurant with his three brothers and their wives. Eventually, only one sister-in-law, Myung Yun, and Henry's wife, Myung Hee, remained on the team. But the Lees' two gorgeous daughters, Patricia and Erica, played piano, and they hired waiters who were classical singers. So between courses they would serenade you. It was magical and surreal and wonderful.

You may need to remove the tails of the fish (ask your fishmonger, if you prefer, or just sever with a large, sharp knife) to fit your fryer. "This sauce is great on anything fried," Patricia told me. "We served it with the Chicken Imperial, which was also battered in the tempura. I love to pour it all over rice and just eat it like that. YUM."

Marinated Fish

2 quarts room-temperature water

2 cups dry white wine

½ cup salt

1¾ tablespoons ground pepper

1¾ tablespoons garlic powder

3 whole black drum or other flaky white fish such as trout, striped bass, snapper, or flounder, (12 to 24 ounces each, depending on the size your fryer can accommodate), cleaned and scaled, skin and head intact

Tempura Batter

7 large eggs, separated

3 cups cornstarch

2½ cups self-rising flour

4 tablespoons unsalted butter, melted

1 teaspoon salt

2½ cups water, or as needed

3 to 4 quarts peanut or vegetable oil for frying

All-purpose flour for dredging

Ginger Sauce

2 tablespoons vegetable oil

6 small dried red chiles

2 tablespoons peeled and minced fresh ginger

3 cloves garlic, minced

1 cup Basic Chicken Stock (page 230) or store-bought chicken broth

2 tablespoons dark soy sauce

2 teaspoons sesame oil

1 tablespoon sugar

1½ teaspoons cornstarch, dissolved in water

1 to 2 onions, peeled and cut into thick slices

1 sweet potato, peeled and cut into thin wedges

1 head broccoli, trimmed into florets

Hot cooked rice for serving

2 green onions, thinly sliced on the diagonal, for garnish

Makes 6 to 8 servings

To marinate the fish: In a large bowl or pot, combine the 2 quarts water, wine, salt, pepper, and garlic powder and stir until dissolved. Add the fish. Cover and refrigerate overnight.

To make the batter: In a bowl, using an electric mixer set on high, beat the egg whites until stiff peaks form. Add the cornstarch and self-rising flour, using your fingers to break up any large lumps, and beat until the dry ingredients are well incorporated, stopping to scrape down the sides of the bowl as needed. In a bowl, whisk the egg yolks until well combined. Add to the egg white mixture along with the melted butter, salt, and 2½ cups water and beat on low speed until well combined. If the batter seems too thick, add more water, a little at a time. The batter should be about the consistency of heavy cream.

Pour the peanut oil into a deep fryer or heavy-bottomed saucepan with tall sides to a depth of 3 inches and heat to 360°F on a deep-frying thermometer. Meanwhile, pour all-purpose flour onto a large plate or into a shallow bowl. Remove the fish from the brine and pat dry. Dredge each fish in the flour to coat on all sides. Tap off any excess. When the oil is hot, dip a flour-coated fish into the tempura batter to coat thoroughly and then transfer immediately to the hot oil. Fry for 10 minutes, just to parcook. Transfer to a platter. Repeat to parcook the remaining fish. Remove the oil from the heat and reserve for second frying.

To make the sauce: Place a wok or large skillet over high heat and add the vegetable oil, swirling to coat sides. Add the chiles, ginger, and garlic and stir-fry for 30 seconds. Add the stock, soy sauce, sesame oil, and sugar and bring to a boil. Pour the cornstarch mixture slowly into the pan and cook until the sauce bubbles and thickens, about 30 seconds. Set aside and cover to keep warm.

When ready to serve, return the reserved oil to 360°F. Re-fry each fish until perfectly brown, 5 to 7 minutes. Quickly dredge the onion, sweet potato, and broccoli in the flour and dip in the remaining tempura batter. Fry until golden brown. Transfer to a paper towel–lined plate to drain while you debone the fish.

To debone the fish, fan the belly side of a fish slightly to support it upright on a platter or work surface. Using a fork to hold the fish between the body and head, run a fish knife or other very sharp, thin-bladed knife from head to tail, pressing the knife edge close to the bone to release the fillets. Lay the fish down and open it on the plate like a book, flesh-sides up. Gently lift away the head, tail and spine. Repeat to debone the remaining fish.

Make a mound of hot rice on each of four individual plates. Place half a fish on top of the rice. Add some of the vegetable tempura. Spoon the ginger sauce over and garnish with the green onions. Serve at once.

CHEF JOHN BESH

GRANDMOTHER BESH'S BRAISED RABBIT WITH CAVATELLI

3 whole rabbits, quartered (about 6 pounds total weight)

Kosher salt and freshly ground black pepper

¼ cup olive oil, plus more as needed

1 yellow onion, cut into ¼-inch dice

1 large carrot, peeled and cut into ¼-inch dice

1 tablespoon tomato paste

2 tablespoons water

½ pound wild mushrooms such as cremini, chanterelle, shiitake, or oyster or a combination, brushed clean, stemmed, and sliced

1 celery stalk, cut into ¼-inch dice

4 cloves garlic, chopped

Leaves from 1 fresh thyme sprig

Leaves from 1 fresh sage sprig, minced

1 teaspoon red pepper flakes

¼ teaspoon fennel seed

1 bay leaf

5 large ripe tomatoes, peeled, seeded, and cut into ¼-inch dice

1 cup dry white wine

2 quarts Basic Chicken Stock (page 230) or store-bought chicken broth

1 quart Veal Stock (page 230) or good-quality store-bought veal or beef broth

3 tablespoons unsalted butter

Ricotta Cavatelli

2¼ cups "00" flour or all-purpose flour

2 large eggs

8 ounces fresh ricotta cheese

½ cup freshly grated Parmesan cheese, preferably Parmigiano-Reggiano

Salt

For all his European training, John Besh brings a Southern grandmother's sensibility to his kitchen. One taste of this rabbit and you'll recognize the slow-simmered goodness of an authentic Louisiana stew. Grandmother made her version with traditional stew dumplings, but John's touch is to instead use *cavatelli*, ricotta-based pasta hand-rolled into tender-chewy mini dumplings, each with a little dimple in the middle to capture the sauce.

Don't be afraid of making fresh pasta from scratch. It's really not that hard, and making individually shaped pasta like cavatelli can be satisfying, creative, relaxing. It's also a great way to spend time in the kitchen with friends, if they are willing to help. And this pasta is very forgiving. Even if yours don't come out as the best cavatelli you've ever had, they'll still be delicious in a dumpling kind of way.

Season the rabbit pieces evenly on both sides with a generous 1 tablespoon salt and 2 teaspoons black pepper.

In a heavy-bottomed 8-quart saucepan or a large Dutch oven over medium-high heat, heat the ¼ cup olive oil until hot, about 3 minutes. Working in batches to avoid crowding the pan, sear the rabbit pieces in the hot oil until golden brown on both sides, about 5 minutes on the first side and 3 to 4 minutes on the second side. If the pan needs more oil after browning half of the rabbit, add 2 tablespoons or so to the pan and let it heat a few seconds before browning the remaining pieces. Transfer the browned rabbit pieces to a baking sheet as they are finished.

When all of the rabbit is browned, add another tablespoon olive oil to the same saucepan and heat for a few seconds over medium-high heat. Add the onion and carrot and cook, stirring often, until the vegetables are browned, 8 to 10 minutes.

Reduce the heat to medium and stir in the tomato paste and water. Cook, stirring often, until the liquid is absorbed, about 5 minutes. Add the mushrooms, celery, garlic, thyme, sage, red pepper flakes, fennel seed, and bay leaf and stir to mix well. Cook, stirring occasionally, to release the aromas, about 5 minutes. Next, stir in the tomatoes, wine, and chicken and veal stocks. Raise the heat to high and bring the mixture to a boil. Reduce the heat to low and return the rabbit pieces

to the pan. Cover the pan and simmer gently, stirring occasionally, until the rabbit is fork-tender and nearly falling off the bone, 1 to 1½ hours.

While the rabbit is braising, make the cavatelli: Mound the flour on a work surface and use your fist to make a well in the center of the mound. Add the eggs, ricotta, Parmesan, and a pinch of salt to the well. Using your hands, begin mixing the wet ingredients together with the flour, pulling the flour in from the edges of the well a little at a time, until the mixture forms a cohesive dough. Add a little additional flour if the dough still seems too wet to knead without sticking to your hands. When a soft but not sticky dough has formed, knead the dough, dusting the work surface with more flour as needed to prevent sticking, until firm and elastic, about 10 minutes. Cover with a clean kitchen towel and let rest at least 30 minutes, or wrap in plastic wrap and refrigerate for up to 1 day.

When the rabbit is done, using tongs or a slotted spoon, transfer the meat to a baking pan and set aside. Place the saucepan over high heat and simmer the sauce briskly until reduced by half, about 30 minutes. Stir in the butter and remove from the heat. Taste and adjust the seasoning, then return the rabbit pieces to the pan. Set aside.

Bring a large pot three-fourths full of generously salted water to a boil over high heat. While the water is heating, finish shaping the cavatelli: Pinch off a piece of dough slightly larger than a golf ball. Rubbing it between your palms or with one palm against a lightly floured work surface, roll the piece of pasta into a rope about ½ inch in diameter and 7 to 8 inches long. Cut the rope crosswise into ½-inch pieces to form small squares of dough. Repeat to roll and cut the remaining dough. To create a dimple in each little dumpling of dough, dust the work surface in front of you with more flour and scatter a handful of dough squares on top. Using a butter knife or your finger, roll each dough piece toward you, using just enough pressure to make it curl over on itself and create the little hollow pocket that defines the cavatelli shape. (You may need a little practice to get the touch, and you probably won't produce the indentations that you'd get if you had an actual cavatelli machine; but no need to worry—even a very rough version of the shape cooks just fine.)

When all the pasta is rolled, working in small batches, add the cavatelli to the boiling water and stir once. After the pasta floats, which only takes a few seconds, cook just until tender, about 2 minutes. Using a slotted spoon, transfer to the pan with the rabbit and stir to coat with the sauce. After all the pasta is cooked and the stew is completely assembled, place the saucepan over medium-high heat and simmer for 2 minutes to allow the flavors to blend. Remove from the heat. Taste and adjust the seasoning. Spoon onto large rimmed dinner plates or into large pasta plates or shallow bowls. Serve at once.

Makes 6 to 8 servings

MiLa's Chicory Coffee–Glazed Quail with Swiss Chard and Creamy Grits

7 tablespoons olive oil

2 bunches Swiss chard (about 1½ pounds total weight), tough stems and spines removed

8 shallots, 3 diced, 5 thinly sliced

6 cloves garlic, 2 crushed, 4 thinly sliced

Fine sea salt and freshly ground pepper

10 quail (about 4 ounces each), deboned by the butcher

4 fresh thyme sprigs

1 fresh or dried bay leaf

1 cup dry white wine

1 quart Veal Stock (page 230) or good-quality store-bought veal or beef broth

½ cup sugar

2 tablespoons ground chicory coffee

1 quart whole milk

1 cup quick-cooking grits

½ cup heavy (whipping) cream

2 tablespoons unsalted butter

Makes 4 servings

Allison Vines-Rushing won a James Beard Award in 2004, when she was cooking in New York at Jack's Luxury Oyster Bar, where her then-boyfriend-now-husband Slade Rushing joined her in 2005. At the time, it appeared they were on the fast track to chef stardom in New York City; but the thing was, they wanted to come home, or at least close to it—he's from Tyler Town, Mississippi, and she's from West Monroe, Louisiana. So now they're cooking at their own place, the elegant eatery MiLa.

Their signature dish, Oysters Rockefeller Deconstructed, is a masterpiece that finely turns the usual oysters-and-green-gunk preparation on its head. This dish features a similar combination of the familiar and the unexpected: quail—a Louisiana staple because there are always so many hunters around—is cloaked in a glaze made from another local signature, chicory coffee.

In a 12-inch sauté pan or skillet, heat 3 tablespoons of the olive oil until smoking. Add the chard, diced shallots, and crushed garlic cloves to the pan, season with salt and pepper, and cook, stirring often, until the chard is wilted completely, about 5 minutes. Scrape the contents of the pan onto a baking sheet and let cool. Discard the garlic cloves.

Stuff about 2 tablespoons of the cooled chard mixture into the body cavity of each of eight of the quail. Arrange the legs of each quail in a crisscross fashion over the breast, close with a toothpick, and place, breast-side up, on a baking sheet. Season the stuffed quail generously on all sides with salt and pepper. Refrigerate while you make the sauce.

Note: if your quail has already had the backbone removed, spread the quail skin-side down on a work surface, add the 2 tablespoons of chard stuffing, then enclose the chard by securing the wing portions of the quail around the filling with toothpicks.

Chop the remaining two quail into ½-inch pieces and season with salt and pepper. Place a large skillet over high heat and add 2 tablespoons olive oil. When the oil is smoking, reduce the heat to medium and add the seasoned quail pieces to the pan. Sear, turning as needed, until thoroughly browned on all sides, about 3 minutes per side. Add the sliced shallots and garlic, the thyme sprigs, and the bay leaf to the pan. Sauté until the

shallots and garlic are soft, about 3 minutes, then pour in the wine, scraping up any bits stuck to the pan bottom. Bring to a simmer and cook until the liquid is reduced by half, about 15 minutes. Add the stock, adjust the heat to maintain a gentle simmer, and cook until falling apart, about 45 minutes. Strain the sauce through a fine-mesh sieve or chinois into a small saucepan and set aside.

Meanwhile, preheat the oven to 450°F.

Heat a saucepan over high heat. Add the sugar to the pan and cook, swirling the pan periodically (but not stirring), until the sugar melts and forms a deep-amber caramel, about 5 minutes. Remove the caramel from the heat and add the coffee grounds and the strained quail sauce. Return the sauce to high heat and bring to a simmer, then reduce the heat to medium-low and cook until the sauce has reduced to a syrupy consistency, about 40 minutes. Strain the glaze through a fine-mesh sieve into a small saucepan again and cover to keep warm, or place near (but not directly over) very low heat until needed.

While the sauce is cooking, in a medium saucepan over medium heat, whisk together the milk and 1 teaspoon salt and bring to a simmer. Carefully whisk in the grits, reduce the heat to low, and cook, whisking occasionally, until the grits are tender, 10 to 12 minutes. Finish the grits with the heavy cream and butter, stirring gently until well mixed. Season with salt and pepper. Set aside and cover to keep warm.

In a large sauté pan or skillet, heat the remaining 2 tablespoons olive oil over high heat. When the oil is smoking, add the stuffed quail to the pan, breast side down. Sear the quail, turning as needed, until nicely browned on all sides, about 2 minutes total. Return the quail to the baking sheet as they are finished browning. Using a pastry brush, brush the quail generously all over with the glaze. Place the quail in the oven and bake until they develop a lacquered surface, about 8 minutes. Remove from the oven and let rest for about 5 minutes to allow the juices to redistribute throughout the meat, keeping it moist.

Spoon a mound of the creamy grits on each of four individual plates. Arrange the quail on the grits and serve at once.

Gabrielle's Slow-Roasted Duck with Cracklin' Skin

Two ducks (about 5 pounds each), rinsed and patted dry

Salt and freshly ground pepper

2 pounds yellow onions, coarsely chopped

½ cup (1 stick) unsalted butter, melted, plus 2 tablespoons at room temperature

4 large fresh rosemary sprigs

2 cups fresh orange juice

1 cup dry sherry

½ cup soy sauce

2 carrots, peeled and julienned

4 ounces cremini or button mushrooms, brushed clean and thinly sliced

One 7-ounce jar roasted red peppers, rinsed, drained, and cut into strips

½ cup vegetable oil

1 pound dried linguini

4 fresh chives, cut into 1-inch lengths

Makes 4 to 6 servings

Greg and Mary Sonnier's restaurant, Gabrielle, was a casualty of the levee failures. It was a small building near City Park, and it served some of the best updates on the Creole tradition you ever tasted. At first, I'd order different dishes on the menu every time I went. Finally I decided that the duck was my favorite and there was nothing wrong with getting it every time. Later I found out he modeled it on Duck Pasta K, a dish Paul Prudhomme served for a staff meal back when Greg and Mary worked at K-Paul's. At first, Greg served the duck on a bed of linguini, my favorite approach. Eventually, he started substituting unsalted potato chips or shoestring potatoes for the pasta. The chips get soggy in the duck sauce, but that's okay. It's supposed to happen. Sweet potato fries or sweet potato chips would also work well.

If you braise a duck, much as when you stew a hen, you'll get tender meat with seasoning throughout, but you'll miss getting the crisp, cracklin' skin that is half the reason for cooking duck in the first place. On the other hand, if you sear duck breast, you get the crispness, but not all the deeply simmered flavors you get with braising. Greg has a solution to this conundrum: he removes the skin and crisps it separately. *Voilà*: the best of both worlds.

Preheat the oven to 500°F. Season the ducks inside and out with salt and pepper.

In a large bowl, toss the onions with the melted butter. Place 2 of the rosemary sprigs inside each duck's body cavity, then tightly pack the cavities with the buttered onion mixture, dividing it evenly. Place the ducks in a large roasting pan so they are not touching. Roast for 10 minutes. Reduce the oven temperature to 300°F and loosely cover the pan with aluminum foil. Continue roasting, draining the fat from the roasting pan every hour, until the ducks are falling-apart tender, about 4½ hours.

Remove the ducks from the oven and discard the fat from the roasting pan one more time. Add the orange juice, sherry, and soy sauce to the pan and stir into the drippings, scraping up any bits stuck to the pan bottom. Return to the oven and roast the ducks, uncovered, for 30 minutes longer. Transfer the ducks to a platter and let cool slightly.

Meanwhile, pour the pan juices into a saucepan, discarding any pieces of duck skin. Skim the fat off the juices and bring to a boil over medium-high heat. Add the carrots, return to a boil, and cook until the liquid is reduced to about 1½ cups, about 10 minutes. Strain the sauce through a fine-mesh sieve and return to the saucepan. Set aside.

Cut the ducks in half lengthwise and discard the onions and rosemary sprigs. (They will be falling off the bone and very easy to section.) Remove all the bones except the leg bone, keeping the breast attached to the leg bone. Remove the skin from the ducks and set aside. Transfer the ducks to a clean roasting pan or a baking sheet and keep warm in a low oven.

Bring a pot three-fourths full of salted water to a boil over high heat.

In a skillet, melt the remaining 2 tablespoons butter. Add the mushrooms and sauté until nicely browned, about 10 minutes. Add the red peppers and sauté briefly, then add the reduced sauce. Taste and adjust the seasoning. Remove from the heat and cover to keep warm.

Meanwhile, for the cracklings garnish, in a skillet over medium-high heat, heat the oil. Add the reserved duck breast skin and fry, turning as needed, until golden and crispy all over, about 4 minutes total.

Add the pasta to the boiling water, return to a boil, and cook, stirring once or twice, until al dente, about 8 minutes or according to the package directions. Drain but don't rinse; you want to leave a little of the cooking water clinging.

Make a bed of pasta on each plate. Place a duck half on top of each. Spoon the vegetables and sauce on top, top that with a piece of cracklin skin and garnish with the chives, and serve at once.

Paper-Skin Chicken and Rice-Flour Waffles with Asian-Cajun Red Pepper Syrup

I love the fried chicken I grew up on, but this version, which I came up with when I was at Lucky Peach, takes the beauty of the comfort-food classic to another level, and adds a spicy sauce with a twist, for excitement. The technique here uses basically the same principle as twice-fried French fries: you fry the chicken pieces once at medium heat to just cook them through, and then fry them a second time at a higher heat to brown and crisp the skin. The key to achieving this chicken's extra-crispy skin on the outside and juiciness on the inside is to pat the raw chicken pieces dry and refrigerate uncovered for several hours, or preferably overnight, to let the skin dry out. Moisture is the enemy of crispness.

With the rice flour and tapioca starch, these waffles have a chewier texture than wheat flour waffles. If you don't have a waffle iron, the same batter can be used for cooking up 4 large pancakes or 8 smaller ones in a lightly buttered skillet; top them with melted butter and cane syrup as directed for the waffles.

Preferably 1 to 2 days ahead, or at least 2 hours in advance, make the glaze: In a small bowl, combine the red pepper paste, soy sauce, cane syrup, and garlic and stir to blend well. Set the glaze aside at cool room temperature if you make it on the same day you are using it. Otherwise, cover and refrigerate until ready to use.

To make the chicken: The day before frying the chicken, rinse the chicken pieces and pat dry thoroughly with paper towels. On a baking sheet lined with several thicknesses of paper towels, arrange the pieces in a single layer without touching. Refrigerate, uncovered, for at least a few hours or preferably overnight.

When ready to fry the chicken, pour oil into a deep fryer or pot with tall sides to a depth of 2 to 4 inches. Place over medium-high heat and heat to 350°F on a deep-frying thermometer. Line a large baking sheet with parchment paper.

Put about 1 cup of the rice flour in a large pan or shallow bowl and dredge each chicken piece in the flour, turning over to coat all the surfaces well, then shaking off the excess flour and brushing off as much of the flour as possible still holding the chicken with your fingertips, so there remains only an extremely light, transparent dusting of flour on each piece. As you work, place the finished pieces in a single layer on the prepared baking sheet.

In a medium bowl, combine the ½ cup cornstarch and ½ cup cool water and whisk until completely blended and smooth. When the oil reaches 350°F, whisk the cornstarch mixture again (it separates readily). One at a time, dip the chicken pieces in the cornstarch mixture, let excess drip off, then ease into the hot oil. Make another batch of the cornstarch mixture if needed. Fry for 10 minutes, working in small batches to avoid crowding the pan. Adjust the heat to maintain a constant 350°F temperature as much as possible. Using tongs, transfer the pieces to paper towels to drain.

When all of the chicken has been fried at 350°F and drained for at least 2 minutes, raise the oil's temperature to between 360°F and 375°F. Again working in small batches as needed to avoid crowding, return the chicken to the hot oil and fry until golden brown all over, about 12 minutes, maintaining the hotter temperature range as closely as possible. Drain the chicken on a wire rack placed over a baking sheet to catch the drippings. While the chicken is still hot, use a pastry brush to brush the pieces all over with a thin layer of the red pepper glaze, then

continued

Asian-Cajun Red Pepper Glaze

½ cup Korean red pepper paste (also labeled "Korean fermented hot pepper paste"; available in Asian markets)

1½ tablespoons soy sauce

1½ tablespoons pure cane syrup, preferably Steen's, or honey

5 cloves garlic, minced (about 1½ tablespoons)

Fried Chicken

8 bone-in chicken wings, legs, or thighs, or any combination (2½ to 3 pounds total weight)

Vegetable oil for frying

White rice flour for dredging (available in Asian markets)

½ cup cornstarch, plus more if needed

½ cup cool water, plus more if needed

1 tablespoon minced fresh cilantro

Rice-Flour Waffles

2 cups white rice flour (available in Asian markets, or in supermarkets that carry Bob's Red Mill products)

½ cup cornstarch or tapioca starch (available in Asian markets)

2 tablespoons sugar

2 teaspoons baking powder

1 teaspoon kosher salt

¾ cup whole milk

¼ cup well-shaken buttermilk

2 large eggs, lightly beaten

4 tablespoons unsalted butter, melted, or bacon fat

4 teaspoons sesame seeds

Melted butter for serving

Pure cane syrup, preferably Steen's, or honey for serving

4 teaspoons sesame seeds for garnish

Makes 4 servings

sprinkle with the minced cilantro. Set the chicken aside or keep warm in a 200°F oven while you make the waffles.

To make the waffles: Preheat a waffle iron according to the manufacturer's instructions. Meanwhile, in a large bowl, whisk together the rice flour, cornstarch, sugar, baking powder, and salt until well blended. In a small bowl, combine the milk, buttermilk, and eggs and mix well. Add the milk mixture to the flour mixture and whisk or stir to mix well. Whisk in the melted butter. Pour some of the batter into the hot waffle iron, sprinkle 1 teaspoon of sesame seeds over the batter and cook until golden according to the manufacturer's instructions, stirring the batter again just before measuring out each portion.

When all the waffles are done, divide them among four individual plates and top each portion with a tablespoon of melted butter and 1 teaspoon or 2 of cane syrup. Arrange 2 pieces of the chicken on each plate, garnish with the sesame seeds, and serve at once.

Bacon-Wrapped Pork Loin
with Smothered Greens, Butternut Squash,
and Cane Syrup Jus

The quality of pork these days is getting better and better—and what better way to highlight that than some pork-on-pork action. The loin is not the richest part of the pig, but it is one of the most tender. Bacon, now that's another story. I know vegetarians who make a bacon exception. This was one of the dishes I couldn't wait to put on the menu at Desautel's on the Avenue.

Season the pork loin all over with salt and pepper. On a clean work surface, lay out the bacon slices vertically, side by side and slightly overlapping, until you have a "sheet" of bacon wide enough to cover the length of the pork loin. Center the seasoned pork loin crosswise along the end of the bacon "sheet" closest to you and wrap the loin completely in the bacon by rolling it away from you, lifting the ends of the bacon and pressing to help it adhere to the meat as you roll. Cover the bacon-wrapped pork loin in a large piece of plastic wrap and refrigerate until well chilled, at least 1 hour and up to 1 day.

About an hour before you are ready to serve, preheat the oven to 350°F and bring a large pot of salted water to a boil over high heat. Meanwhile, prepare an ice bath by filling a large bowl halfway with ice, then adding enough water just to cover the ice.

Add the kale leaves to the boiling water and blanch until tender, about 4 minutes. Using tongs, remove the leaves from the boiling water and immediately plunge into the ice water to stop the cooking. Drain the kale, gently squeezing to remove the excess water, and set aside.

Peel and trim the butternut squash, scraping out any seeds. Cut crosswise into 6 rounds about ½ inch thick and cut the rounds into half-moons. Arrange the squash pieces in a single layer on a baking sheet. Drizzle the 2 teaspoons cane syrup, 1 tablespoon of the oil, and the melted butter over the squash and season with salt and pepper. Toss to coat. Roast in the preheated oven until tender and deep golden brown in spots, 25 to 30 minutes.

Remove the pork loin from the refrigerator and remove the plastic wrap. Secure the ends of the bacon with toothpicks. In an ovenproof skillet over medium-high heat, heat the remaining 1 tablespoon oil. Sear the pork loin, seam-side down, turning as needed, until golden brown on all sides, about 8 minutes total. Transfer the skillet to the oven and roast until an instant-read thermometer inserted in the middle registers 135°F, 10 to 15 minutes.

While the pork is roasting, in a saucepan over medium heat, melt the 2 tablespoons butter. Add the shallot and garlic and cook until tender, 2 to 3 minutes. Add the blanched kale and ¼ cup of the stock and simmer until the kale is heated through, about 3 minutes longer. Remove from the heat and cover to keep warm.

When the pork loin is ready, remove the skillet from the oven and transfer the pork loin to a cutting board. Tent loosely with a piece of aluminum foil to let rest for about 5 minutes. (The pork loin will continue to cook as it rests.)

Put the skillet back on the stove over medium heat and add the 3 tablespoons cane syrup and the remaining ¾ cup stock to the skillet, scraping up any bits stuck to the pan bottom. Simmer until the sauce is slightly reduced, about 5 minutes. Season with salt and pepper.

Rewarm the butternut squash in the oven for 2 minutes.

Carve the pork loin into 8 slices. Arrange 2 slices of pork on each of four individual plates, along with 3 pieces of butternut squash and a mound of the greens. Spoon the jus over and around the pork and serve at once.

Makes 4 servings

---

1 center-cut boneless pork loin (2½ to 3 pounds)

Salt and freshly ground pepper

10 to 12 slices bacon, depending on the length of the pork loin

1 bunch dinosaur (lacinato) kale (about 12 ounces), tough stems and spines removed

1 small butternut squash

2 teaspoons pure cane syrup, preferably Steen's, plus 3 tablespoons

2 tablespoons canola oil

1 tablespoon melted butter, plus 2 tablespoons at room temperature

1 small shallot, minced

1 clove garlic, minced

1 cup Basic Chicken Stock (page 230) or store-bought chicken broth

PEPPERED HANGER STEAK
WITH CRISPY RICE CAKES

Rice Cakes

1 cup sushi rice

1½ cups water

Fine sea salt

3 tablespoons canola oil

Peppered Hanger Steak

4 hanger steaks (about 6 ounces each)

3 to 4 tablespoons cracked black pepper

Kosher salt

2 tablespoons canola oil

2 tablespoons extra-virgin olive oil

4 cups packed pea shoot leaves or spinach leaves

1 teaspoon Vietnamese chili-garlic sauce, preferably Huy Fong

3 tablespoons Chile–Sweet Soy Glaze (see Note)

Fine sea salt

Freshly ground black pepper

Makes 4 servings

I knew I had to have a steak item on the menu. Even at Stella!, Chef Scott Boswell's innovative restaurant, they sell more of the filet mignon than any other dish. As much as I would like to think my customers want to travel with me to flavor regions unknown, a lot of them want the protein on their plate to be familiar. You can't write a menu with Guinea hen or wild boar or Patagonian toothfish if you want it to sell. But, if you start off with steak or chicken, the customers will often follow you all over the map. So instead of filet mignon, I went with hanger steak. Instead of potatoes, I went with sushi rice. Instead of spinach, I went with pea shoots. Instead of steak sauce, I created this Asian variation inspired by the garlic sauce David Chang makes at Lucky Peach.

If your hanger steak hasn't already been trimmed, be sure to ask your butcher to remove the silver skin that runs down the middle. The rice can be made a couple of days in advance and cut and toasted just before serving.

Make the rice cakes: In a sieve, thoroughly rinse the sushi rice under cold running water until the water runs clear. Place the rinsed rice in a small saucepan with the water and a generous pinch of salt. Bring the rice to a boil, uncovered, over medium-high heat. Reduce the heat to medium and simmer until most of the water has been absorbed by the rice, about 5 minutes. Cover the pan tightly, reduce the heat to low, and continue cooking for about 7 minutes longer. Remove from the heat and let stand, covered, for 15 minutes. The rice should be tender and all of the water absorbed. (Even very slightly overcooked rice is not a problem in this recipe, as that may help the rice cakes keep their shape.) Scoop the rice onto a small baking sheet lined with plastic wrap. Form the rice into a rough square ¼ to 1 inch thick. Cover tightly and refrigerate overnight until cold and set. When the rice has set, cut 8 equal-size tri-angles of rice cake and set aside until ready to fry and serve.

Preheat the oven to 400°F.

To make the steak: Generously season the hanger steaks with the cracked black pepper and kosher salt. In a cast-iron skillet over very high heat, heat the 2 tablespoons oil until almost smoking. Add the steaks to the pan and sear until nicely browned on both sides, about 3 minutes per side. Transfer the pan to the oven and bake until steaks are medium-rare, 7 to 10 minutes. Transfer the steaks to a cutting board and let rest for 5 minutes.

While the steaks are cooking and resting, finish the rice cakes. Heat the 3 tablespoons canola oil in a large nonstick sauté pan over medium-high heat. Carefully add the rice cakes to the hot oil. Cook until golden brown and toasty on one side, 3 to 4 minutes. Flip the rice cakes and continue cooking until golden brown on the other side, another 1 to 2 minutes. Transfer the rice cakes to a plate and cover to keep warm. Set aside, reserving the pan.

Wipe out the pan you used to fry the rice cakes, if necessary, and add the olive oil and pea shoots. Stir in the chili-garlic sauce, the sweet soy glaze, and season with sea salt and ground pepper. Sauté the pea shoots until just barely wilted.

Carve each of the steaks into 5 slices. Place 2 toasted rice cakes in the center of each plate, spoon the sautéed pea shoots over one side of the toasted rice cakes, and arrange the sliced beef around. Spoon the sweet soy glaze over and around the steak and serve at once.

Note: To make a versatile Chile–Sweet Soy Glaze, in a bowl, stir together 1 tablespoon Vietnamese chili-garlic sauce, preferably Huy Fong; 1 red Thai chile, minced, or a pinch of red pepper flakes; 2 tablespoons soy sauce; ½ cup ketchup manis (Indonesian sweet soy sauce, available in Asian markets); and 1 teaspoon toasted sesame oil. Store in a tightly sealed jar in the refrigerator for up to 2 weeks.

Gautreau's Citrus–Olive Oil Cake with Kumquat Marmalade and Almonds

Kumquat Marmalade

3 pints kumquats

3 cups sugar

5 to 5 ½ cups water

Citrus–Olive Oil Cake

1½ cups all-purpose flour, plus more for dusting

3 large eggs

¾ cup sugar

1 cup extra-virgin olive oil

1 cup whole milk

½ cup fresh satsuma or orange juice

1 tablespoon very finely chopped satsuma or orange zest

2 tablespoons Grand Marnier liqueur

½ cup yellow cornmeal

¾ teaspoon baking powder

½ teaspoon baking soda

½ teaspoon fine kosher salt

About ½ cup dry-roasted sliced or slivered almonds for garnish

Makes 8 to 12 servings

Gautreau's has been the launching pad for a lot of great chefs, but Sue Zemanick is special even among such distinguished company. She wasn't even thirty years old when Patrick Singley appointed her to the top spot in his restaurant. It's been a joy to welcome her into the small sorority of New Orleans women chefs.

I've always imagined kumquats in marmalade. Their sour pulp and sweet skins seem natural for it. Sue beat me to the punch, but don't be surprised if you see some kumquat marmalade on a Desautel's menu soon. If you don't have kumquats, or don't have time to make your own marmalade, buy a good-quality commercial one. Even orange marmalade will do.

To make the marmalade: Using a sharp knife, cut the kumquats in half lengthwise. Squeeze out the inside of each kumquat half, pulp and seeds and all, into a medium nonreactive bowl. Set aside. Finely julienne the kumquat rind, place in a large nonreactive bowl, and pour the sugar over to cover the rind evenly. Cover the bowl with plastic wrap and set aside. Fold a large piece of cheesecloth into a square of four layers. Pour the kumquat pulp and seeds into the middle of the square; lift up the 4 corners and tie the cheesecloth into a bundle. Secure the cloth knot by tying another knot underneath with kitchen twine to seal the bundle tightly. Place the bundle in a bowl. Refrigerate both bowls, one with the rind and one with the pulp, overnight.

The next day, put the bundle of kumquat pulp and seeds in a nonreactive 4-quart saucepan. Add 3 cups of the water and bring to a simmer over medium heat. Simmer for 20 minutes, pushing the bundle down with a large spoon as needed to keep it covered with liquid. Remove from the heat and let stand until the bundle is cool enough to handle, about 40 minutes.

When the contents of the bundle are cool, gently squeeze into the saucepan to extract as much of the pectin from the pulp as possible; discard the bundle. Pour the liquid in the pan, which is now a mixture of the infused cooking liquid and the pectin, into a large measuring jar; you should have about 1½ cups. Add enough water to bring the total liquid back to 3 cups. Return the pectin mixture to the same saucepan. Add the rind-sugar mixture and stir to mix. Place over medium-high heat and cook, stirring to dissolve the sugar, until the mixture reaches 220°F on a candy thermometer, about

10 minutes. Remove from the heat and let the marmalade cool (it will thicken as it cools, but note, the level of pectin in the kumquats varies from season to season, so the marmalade may be thinner than a standard marmalade).

Set aside 1½ cups of the marmalade for the cake; cover tightly and refrigerate. (You will have 3 to 4 cups marmalade remaining for another use. Transfer to sterilized glass jars, cover tightly, and keep in the refrigerator for up to 1 month; or transfer to zippered plastic freezer bags and freeze for up to 3 months.)

To make the cake: Preheat the oven to 325°F. Grease and flour a 10-inch round cake pan with 1½-inch sides. Tap to shake out the excess flour.

In a large bowl, briskly whisk together the eggs and sugar until the mixture thickens slightly and lightens in color, about 4 minutes. Add the olive oil, milk, satsuma juice and zest, and Grand Marnier and whisk until well blended.

In another large bowl, whisk together the 1½ cups flour, cornmeal, baking powder, baking soda, and salt. Add the liquid ingredients to the dry ingredients and whisk just until the batter is smooth; do not overmix.

Pour the batter into the prepared pan and bake until the top is golden brown and a toothpick inserted into the center comes out clean—that is, without crumbs; the toothpick will be moist from the oil—35 to 40 minutes. Let cool in the pan on a wire rack at least 10 minutes. Remove the cake from the pan. Cut into wedges and serve, garnishing the top of each serving with about 2 tablespoons kumquat marmalade and about 2 teaspoons toasted almonds.

BAYONA'S CAFÉ AU LAIT POTS DE CRÈME WITH MUDSLIDE COOKIES

CHEF SUSAN SPICER

When I was trying to butter up my parents for another small business loan, this is one of the desserts I presented to them. I didn't tell them it was Susan's recipe. Susan wasn't the one who needed the loan.

Note you can tailor the number of servings to suit your party (although remember, pot de crème is a very rich dessert; not many sweet teeth I know will want to go beyond a 4-ouncer; even just a bite or two of this luscious elevated pudding is transporting). Choose a baking pan not much larger than the space you need to fit your ramekins.

To make the cookies: Combine the chopped chocolate and butter in the top of a double boiler set over (but not touching) hot, barely simmering water and slowly melt together, stirring occasionally and lifting the top of the double boiler occasionally to keep the water below a simmer. Remove from the heat, whisk in the vanilla, and set aside to cool.

Sift the flour, baking powder, and salt together into a large bowl or onto a sheet of parchment paper.

In the bowl of an electric mixer fitted with the whip attachment, beat the eggs and sugar at medium-high speed until they form smooth, glossy ribbons that rest on the batter for a moment after the whip is pulled out of the batter. Using a rubber spatula, fold in the cooled chocolate mixture and then the sifted ingredients, folding in just until mixed. Fold in the chocolate chips, walnuts, and cocoa nibs.

Divide the dough into 4 equal portions. Place each portion on a piece of wax paper on a work surface and roll into a log (or pat into a long rectangular slab) about 1½ inches in diameter. Put the logs in the freezer until firm, at least 1 hour or up to several days.

When ready to bake, preheat the oven to 325°F. Cut the frozen logs into ¼-inch-thick slices and place at least 2 inches apart on parchment-lined baking sheets. Bake until the cookies are slightly crusty on the outside but still gooey in the middle, 13 to 15 minutes. Let cool completely on the baking sheets. (Store mudslides in an airtight container for up to 1 week.)

Preheat the oven to 275°F (or if you just baked off your cookies, reduce the temperature).

To make the crème: In a heavy-bottomed 2-quart saucepan, combine the cream, half-and-half, and sugar. Using the tip of a paring knife, split open the vanilla bean half lengthwise and scrape out the seeds in each side of the pod into the cream mixture. Drop the pod halves into the cream mixture as well. Heat slowly over low heat until the mixture reaches 180°F, about 40 minutes.

Meanwhile, place the egg yolks in a large bowl and whisk until smooth. Set aside at room temperature.

When the cream mixture reaches 180°F, immediately remove the pan from the heat and add the espresso powder, stirring until dissolved. Very gradually pour the hot cream mixture into the bowl of egg yolks, whisking constantly. Stir in the vanilla. Taste and add more vanilla or espresso powder, if desired. Strain the custard into a bowl through a very fine-mesh strainer.

Pour warm (not hot) water into a baking pan just large enough to hold your ramekins or pudding cups (with a little room to spare) to a depth of ½ inch. Ladle the custard into the ramekins and gently place in the baking pan, being careful not to splash any water on top of the custard. If needed, carefully add more water around the containers; the water should come up the sides of the containers slightly less than halfway.

continued

Mudslide Cookies

1½ pounds semisweet (63% cacao) chocolate, coarsely chopped

6 tablespoons unsalted butter

1 tablespoon vanilla extract

1½ cups all-purpose flour

¾ teaspoon baking powder

¼ teaspoon salt

6 large eggs

3 cups sugar

12 ounces semisweet chocolate chips

2 cups finely chopped toasted walnuts

1 cup cocoa nibs

Pots de Crème

2 cups heavy (whipping) cream

2 cups half-and-half

½ cup plus 3 tablespoons sugar

½ vanilla bean

6 large egg yolks

2 tablespoons instant espresso powder

1 teaspoon vanilla extract

Whipped cream for serving

Chocolate-covered espresso beans for garnish

Makes twenty 2-ounce servings, ten 4-ounce servings, or eight 6-ounce servings of pots de crème. Makes about 8 dozen cookies total, or 2 dozen cookies per log.

Cover the pan and the ramekins with aluminum foil and very carefully transfer to the oven. Bake until the custard is set around the edges but still jiggles in the center, 45 minutes to 1½ hours; the time will vary according to size of ramekins used. If you are using 2-ounce ramekins, after about 30 minutes, carefully lift a corner of the foil to uncover one pot de crème and peek to see if it seems to be cooking too fast; if so, reduce the oven temperature to 250°F and continue cooking until the edges are set.

Carefully remove the pan from the oven and remove the foil. Let the custards cool in the hot water, about 45 minutes. Serve at once, or cover and refrigerate until serving time. Serve each pot de crème topped with whipped cream and 1 or 2 chocolate-covered espresso beans with the cookies on the side.

THYME-SATSUMA–BLACK PEPPER ICE

Satsumas may have originated in Japan, but when the Spanish Jesuits got them to Plaquemines Parish, Louisiana, the fruits were made to feel right at home. So much so that people in Louisiana seem to think that these sweet, easy-to-peel citrus fruit are natives, and indeed a bevy of varieties grow plentifully on farms in the coastal and other southern parishes.

This isn't the lemon ice I served right after the storm. Not only had the local citrus crop been devastated by Katrina, but the few satsumas left weren't in season yet. This is a recipe I came up with in better times, when the satsumas were so sweet and good that they could handle a little savory spice. Be careful not to grind the black pepper too finely or it will discolor the sorbet.

2 tablespoons satsuma zest

2 cups water

1 cup sugar

6 fresh thyme sprigs

Freshly ground pepper

4 cups fresh satsuma juice (from about 20 satsumas)

In a small saucepan, combine the satsuma zest, water, sugar, thyme, and 4 grinds of a pepper mill. Bring to a boil over medium-high heat, stirring to dissolve the sugar. Remove from the heat and set aside to steep for 20 minutes.

In another small saucepan, bring the satsuma juice to a simmer over medium heat. Cook until reduced by half, about 30 minutes, then stir it into the sugar mixture.

Strain the sorbet base through a fine-mesh sieve into a metal bowl nested in a bowl of ice water. Discard the solids. Refrigerate the base until well chilled, at least 2 hours. Alternatively, you can strain the mixture into a heatproof container, set aside until cool, then cover and refrigerate overnight.

When the base is thoroughly chilled, freeze in an ice-cream machine according to the manufacturer's directions. Transfer the sorbet to a container, cover, and freeze until firm, at least 2 hours or up to overnight.

Makes 1 quart

THE FOOD *of the* STREETS

It's amazing how many people didn't die in the days before health inspectors and restaurant regulations. Vendors could just walk the streets at will, selling food of all descriptions, and eke out a living doing so. Not just in New Orleans; this was happening all over. Think of the strawberry vendor's cries in the opening of the song "Who Will Buy?" from the musical *Oliver!* Think of the Strawberry Woman in *Porgy and Bess*. But those are old shows about times long ago. In most cities in America, vendors like that are as rare as hen's teeth.

Street vending was especially important around New Orleans. During slavery, it provided a way for African-American women, free and enslaved, to earn money. For many Italian immigrants, selling produce door to door was the stepping stone to opening a corner grocery store. And in the case of the Uddo-Taormina family, what started as a small street-vending business ultimately evolved to become the Progresso food brand.

There are still a few vestiges from those times. The most famous, Arthur "Mr. Okra" Robinson, became something of a cause célèbre. For years, he drove a brightly painted but otherwise beat-up old pickup truck all around the city, selling fresh produce—including, but not limited to,

his signature vegetable. He drives slowly through the street, calling over an attached loudspeaker, "I have okra; I have tomatoes; I have peaches; I have plums." You might hear him from the back of your house and, because he drives so slowly, you can run to the street and catch him before he makes it to the corner.

One day, in a shocking development, the Okramobile broke down, and it looked like the days of the fruit-and-vegetable vendor in New Orleans had finally come to an end. But a mini movement rose up: bands played benefits; Mr. Okra fans donated online. And they collected enough money to save the day. Now Mr. Okra is driving around in a new truck, albeit one painted to look like the old one. There was even a documentary made about Mr. Okra, which made it to the Sundance Film Festival. And there are plenty of amateur YouTube videos about him online.

But the dean of New Orleans' street vending is Ron Kotteman, the Roman Candy Man. He doesn't have all the modern equipment Mr. Okra does. He gets around in a wagon drawn by a mule. Kotteman's grandfather, Sam Cortese, started the business almost a century ago. Cortese had lost both his legs in a streetcar accident when he was a child.

He had a wagon built that would allow him to sell the candy that his Sicilian immigrant mother made. As the business grew, Sam started to make the taffy, or "Roman chewing candy," as it says on the wagon, himself. He was still at it in 1969. After his grandfather died that year, Ron, who had just come back from Vietnam, took over the business. Probably the biggest change since the old days is that Ron's wagon has a butane stove instead of the old coal-burning one his grandfather used.

The candy comes in three flavors—chocolate, vanilla, and strawberry. The chocolate has been described as "artisanal Tootsie Roll," and I agree that about sums it up. All three of the candies come in strips about a foot long and wrapped in wax paper. In a nod to the modern era, it seems, Kotteman has started selling his candy online at http://romancandy .gourmetfoodmall.com.

There are certain streets you can drive down—South Carrollton Avenue, South Claiborne Avenue, Napoleon Avenue—where you see the descendants of the truck farmers selling fresh produce from the back of pickup trucks on the side of the road. These men aren't literally the descendants of truck farmers. They aren't farmers at all. But it's good to have easy, drive-by access to fruits and vegetables.

As workers from Latin America and Texas started coming here after the flood, taco trucks started popping up in the neighborhoods where they worked. It wasn't quite the gourmet food truck movement that's happening on the West Coast. But it has reintroduced the New Orleans food scene to some of the Latin influences it had back in the days when the city was a popular entry point for immigrants from various Gulf of Mexico countries. Restaurant owners, especially in Jefferson Parish, groused at the competition. But, for the most part, the taco trucks endure.

There are other street vendors around the city. But it seems to me that for most of them, selling on the street is a temporary way to make some occasional money rather than a real job. Sometimes in the afternoon, I'll be walking in the French Quarter and I'll see a woman selling pies out of a basket like in the old days. But come to think of it, I've only seen her like twice. You still see praline vendors at bus stops and walking along Canal Street. Mostly I've seen men doing this. But with fast food driveups on every corner, there's not much need for the food vendors to come to you. It's easy and convenient to find something to eat. Jacques tells me that the one place you still see peddlers selling everything from gumbo, jambalaya and Sock-It-To-Me-Cake to knock-off designer bags and perfumes is at black beauty parlors and barber shops. There the vendors have a captive audience and will probably have one as long as people grow hair.

ANTOINE BATISTE AND DESIREE

Antoine

Now that it's all over, everybody knows what they would've took with them. So when you tell them you walked out of your house with pretty much the clothes on your back, they tell you they would have grabbed the baby pictures, or the insurance policy, or the letter from when their daddy got discharged from the army. They don't know. And Desiree was rushing me so, I didn't know which way was up. So, instead of taking it, I put my Kid Ory's Creole Jazz Band 1954 album up high.

Not high enough. You know how that all ended.

It wasn't Kid Ory made me want to play the trombone. I wanted to play because of hearing the St. Augustine Marching 100 during Carnival parades and hearing my teacher, Danny Nelson, play the second line parades that passed through the 6th Ward. But when Freddie Lonzo gave me that Kid Ory album, it was special to me. First of all, it came from Freddie, and I got to admit it, he was Danny Nelson's star student. Freddie had a huge, loud tone. He could tailgate or he could play progressive. I remember hearing him one time at a club playing with Ellis Marsalis when I was just in high school. They played Ellis's tune "Nostalgic Impressions." Freddie could walk off of Ellis's bandstand and right into Preservation Hall and not miss a beat. Now how many cats you know can do that?

So that Kid Ory album was special because Freddie gave it to me. But it was special too because of those recipes on the back. You listen to music and you get to know a person. You can hear that Kid Ory was a proud man from the way he plays. You can tell he was smart. He knew how to listen and complement what else was going on. But you also know that he wasn't taking no shit from nobody just cause they played in the upper register like the trumpet or the clarinet. He stood his ground, and then some. But those recipes made me feel something about Kid Ory that even the music couldn't.

See, music and food have always gone together in New Orleans. Sunday meant two things to me: the music during church and the Sunday dinner after. I know I was supposed to be worrying about my soul and what the preacher was saying, but I was listening to the music in his voice. After a while, he would get to the sweet part of the sermon and he couldn't hardly get out real words, but he would be kind of humming, cause it was too powerful to say. Then the organ would get behind him and punctuate and my grandmother would get the spirit and start doing the holiness dance and the drum would come in. Then the preacher would get to the point where he couldn't say nothing more and he would just have to break into some kind of song like "Soon I Will Be Done (With the Troubles of the World)" or "Something's Got a Hold of Me." That was music to me. It was trombone music, the way he talked. Then we would go to Gramma's house and she would have baked hen with sweet potatoes and mustard greens and smothered okra and coconut cake. And for me, you couldn't have the preaching without the music and the eating any more than you could have fried catfish without potato salad.

When I heard Kid Ory's music, I felt like I was in the audience, across from him, listening to him play. When I read those recipes, I felt like I was in the kitchen, listening to him talk.

I knew John McCusker because he's a photographer at the *Times-Picayune*. He would shoot a lot of the parades I was playing in, plus I would always see him taking pictures at Indian practice. So one day, we was kicking it and he told me he was writing a book called *Creole Trombone*, on Kid Ory. So I told him there was nothing that his book could tell me about Ory I didn't already know, and he immediately commenced to proving me wrong. He asked me if I knew that when Ory first went to Los Angeles he was a chef cook. He got there in 1919 and the whole time he was there, he cooked and played. I got to admit, I didn't know all that.

Lots of musicians cook. Kermit Ruffins spends as much time in front of the barbecue pit as he does on the bandstand. This here goes way back. Fats Domino used to bring hot plates to Europe and cook in the hotel room when he was on the road. Narvin Kimball, the banjo player at Preservation Hall, used to brag about his red beans, and they were good, too, full of sausage and ham. But it's very seldom you see anybody really talk about musicians and food.

Louis Armstrong talks about food in all his books. Like in *Satchmo: My Life in New Orleans*, he writes, "Mayann taught us both how to cook her best dishes. Her jambalaya was delicious. It is a concoction of diced bologna sausage, shrimp, oysters, hard-shelled crabs, mixed with rice and flavored with tomato sauce. If you ever tasted Mayann's jambalaya and did not lick your fingers, my name is not Louis Satchmo Daniel Armstrong.

"With fifteen cents, Mayann could make the finest dishes you would ever want to eat. When she sent me to the Poydras Market to get fifteen cents worth of fish heads, she made a big pot of 'cubie yon's' [court bouillion], which she served with tomato sauce and fluffy white rice with every grain separate. We almost made ourselves sick eating this dish."

That's the thing about this. You can't really separate the music and the food. Whether it's good times or bad, they are locked in together. Sometimes, I'll hear a certain song and it will remind me of something I ate or something my mother used to make. Danny Barker used to talk about how when he was a kid, they would have what you call "spasm bands," kids just parading through the neighborhood playing kazoos, beating on old pots and a few instruments maybe. In a way, everything we play down here is the sound of the pots and pans.

Desiree

Antoine would never admit it, but it was my cooking that got him.

We started seeing each other sort of now and then, hitting and missing. Nothing too serious. You know how Antoine is, never wanting to commit to anything. I would invite him to come by for dinner and he would always have an excuse. Some gig came up or something. But I knew he was interested because we kept going out. When I invited him for Sunday dinner, he took me to eat at his mama's house. So you know what that means: I was good enough to meet his people, but not good enough to cook for him. That was all right. My mama always taught me, if it's worth having, it's worth waiting for. (Incidentally, I didn't think his mama's macaroni and cheese was all that.)

I got my chance for his birthday. He told me he had a gig and couldn't come by for dinner, but I was there when he got the call canceling the gig. I made Creole succotash and rice. It was over then. Suddenly he was all "Baby" this and "Honey" that. I fixed him breakfast the next morning. It was a Sunday. I put on Mahalia Jackson while I was cooking. That might have been the same day he moved in.

You be around a person and you learn their ways. Antoine don't like nothing too fancy. If I'm watching Eric Paulsen and Sally-Ann Roberts on the morning news, they might have a chef on there making a dish I want to try. One time they had Greg Reggio from Zea's making alligator with some peanuts and sweet potato. I thought Antoine was asleep. But he saw I was watching and writing down how you could get the recipe. He looked up just long enough and said, "Any alligator comes into this house better be a size 9½ and go with my good suit." Don't even talk about the time Trombone Shorty tried to get him to eat some sushi. He still talk about that. For Antoine, if it ain't fried, it better be smothered. And if it ain't fried or smothered, it better have some gravy on it. And if it ain't fried, smothered, or covered in gravy, it better be baked and sweet and covered in ice cream.

Come to think of it, a lot of the best times we ever had were over food. I had made some white beans and shrimp and he was talking about how good it was and how we should give the baby some. But you don't give no little baby nothing with spice and stuff in it. You wait till they're at least a little older. I stepped outside for one minute, and all of a sudden the blender is cranked. When I walked back in, there he was feeding the baby liquified white beans and shrimp. But I couldn't say nothing—she was laughing and smiling like she was happy eating her mother's cooking.

That was the same thing that happened when we went to Hansen's Sno-Bliz uptown. I grew up in the 9th Ward, so I didn't know a thing about snowball stands uptown. But back when he had his band, they were playing a gig at this club on Tchoupitoulas Street. We were driving my mama's car and he wanted to show me where the gig was and we passed Hansen's. He liked to gave me and the baby whiplash slamming on the brakes. They had a line going all the way out the place, but he made us stand there and wait. He ordered a combination of two flavors: nectar cream and cream ice cream. It was like a snowball for grown people, not all sweet and syrupy like a lot of them be. I don't think Antoine even tasted it. He spent the whole time feeding Honorée, who was just smiling and giggling like she was tasting sunshine.

When Danny Nelson died, it hit him hard. Danny was his teacher, but he was also like his father, too. In New Orleans, music is one thing that can help keep boys out of trouble. But you have to get good enough to play and get gigs—and, yes, have some of them little girls looking at you. You have to get all of that together before you start hanging out with the wrong crowd. If you just play a little bit, you think you can make more money or get more props selling dope on the corner or something. Whenever Danny couldn't make a gig, he told them to hire Antoine. Sometimes he told them to hire Antoine even if he could make the gig, and Danny didn't have it like that financially. He just wanted to see a young man have a chance. Antoine was young, he couldn't really play. Half the time Danny would show up at the gig late or leave early or do something so Danny was the one who was playing most of the time. That way, the bandleader couldn't complain and Antoine would still make a little money to give his mama or have in his pocket. I know this because Antoine told it to me after Danny died. We were lying in bed, but he couldn't sleep. So we talked about Danny till I had to get up and go to work.

At the repast, when Danny's family and friends were all there and they had all those pots of jambalaya and red beans and fried chicken, Antoine was all jokes. Everything he said was something funny about how he kept doing stupid things or making mistakes with the music and Danny would straighten him out. Pretty soon, everybody was having a good time and remembering Danny like they were supposed to do.

Antoine can be like that. Sometimes he knows just the right time to crack a joke or feed a baby table food. And he can't get enough Creole succotash.

DUTCH MORIAL'S OYSTER DRESSING

2 quarts (about 100 small) shucked fresh oysters, with their liquor

1 to 1½ loaves French bread

2 tablespoons vegetable oil

1 pound ground beef

1 large yellow onion, finely chopped

1 green bell pepper, seeded and finely chopped

4 celery stalks, finely chopped

Leaves from 3 fresh parsley sprigs, finely chopped

¼ to ½ cup dry unseasoned bread crumbs (optional)

Salt and freshly ground black pepper

Desiree: Dutch Morial was the first black mayor of New Orleans. He was tough, didn't take no mess off of nobody. Had to be, being the first. When he got elected, all of us were proud. I always loved Mayor Morial. When I saw his recipe reprinted in the *Times-Picayune*, I had to try it. Now this is the only oyster dressing I ever make.

Place a colander or mesh strainer over a nonreactive bowl. Drain the oysters into the colander and reserve the juices. Remove any shell or bits of grit from the oysters and discard. Cut any large oysters in half. Refrigerate the oysters.

Tear the French bread into bite-size chunks. You should have roughly 14 cups. Spread the pieces in a large, shallow, nonreactive bowl. Sprinkle in the reserved oyster liquor; the bread should be moist but not too soggy. Set aside.

In a 12-inch sauté pan over medium heat, heat the oil. Add the ground beef and cook, breaking up the meat with a spoon, just until slightly browned, about 5 minutes. Add the onion, bell pepper, celery, and parsley. Reduce the heat to medium-low and cook slowly, stirring often, until the beef is well done and the vegetables are soft, about 20 minutes.

Add the oysters to the beef mixture and cook until the additional liquid the oysters give off has been absorbed, about 5 to 10 minutes. Add the moistened bread chunks to the meat mixture, cooking and stirring until the dressing is well mixed and warmed through, about 10 minutes longer. If the dressing is too loose to hang together, add bread crumbs 2 tablespoons at a time until it comes together, and cook 2 to 3 minutes longer. Season with salt and pepper and serve at once.

Makes 6 to 8 servings

Tee's Smothered Okra

Antoine: It didn't occur to me until my mama started to write down this recipe for me that smothered okra is basically gumbo without the liquid. It usually doesn't have crabs or oysters in it, but a lot of people don't put that in their gumbo, anyway. You can add those things, or even some chopped ham, if you want to. If I had to choose a last meal, this would be it. My mother learned this recipe from her sister, my auntie, Althea Pierce. That's why we call it Tee's Smothered Okra.

You can make this whole dish up to 1 day ahead. Reheat gently to serve.

½ cup canola oil or olive oil

2 pounds fresh or thawed frozen okra, trimmed and cut crosswise into ½-inch pieces

1 yellow onion, chopped

1 green bell pepper, seeded and chopped

1 celery stalk, chopped

1 clove garlic, chopped

One 15-ounce can diced tomatoes, with their juices

1 pound smoked pork sausage, cut into ½-inch slices (optional)

1 pound medium shrimp, peeled and deveined

Salt and freshly ground pepper

Hot cooked rice for serving

In a large heavy-bottomed, nonreactive saucepan or Dutch oven over medium heat, heat the oil until hot, 1 to 2 minutes. Add the okra, onion, bell pepper, celery, and garlic and stir to coat with the oil. Cover and cook, stirring occasionally to prevent sticking or burning, until the okra is so tender it's breaking apart and is an army-green color, about 45 minutes.

Add the tomatoes and their juices and the sausage, if using, and stir to mix well. Re-cover the pan and cook, stirring occasionally, until the juices thicken slightly, about 15 minutes. Stir in the shrimp and cook, stirring often, until the shrimp are cooked through and the flavors have blended, 10 to 15 minutes longer. Remove from the heat and season with salt and pepper. Serve at once over the rice.

Makes 8 servings as a main course or 16 servings as a side dish

CREOLE STUFFED BELL PEPPERS

5 large bell peppers, halved, seeded, and membranes thoroughly removed

¼ cup plus 2 tablespoons canola oil or olive oil

1 pound smoked ham, cut into 1-inch cubes

2 pounds large shrimp, peeled and deveined

1 onion, chopped

2 ribs celery, chopped

Basic Creole Seasoning Blend to taste (page 228)

3 cups very fine, dry, unseasoned bread crumbs (preferably from day-old French bread), broken into crumbs by rubbing between your hands

8 tablespoons very fine, dry, Italian-seasoned bread crumbs, for sprinkling

Water for baking

Olive oil for drizzling

Desiree: My mama used to grow bell peppers in the yard. When I was growing up, everybody in the 9th Ward had a little garden with tomatoes or okra or peppers in it. Those days are probably gone forever now. You don't know what you might catch eating stuff planted in all that pollution and oil that came up with the storm. But back in the day, when the summer peppers first came out and got big, it would just be a few. Then before you knew it, we would have so many peppers we couldn't give them away. We stuffed most of them; I never got tired of eating them this way.

Preheat the oven to 350°F. Coat a 9-by-13-inch glass baking dish with cooking spray.

Chop 2 green bell pepper halves and set aside the remaining 8 halves. In a large skillet over medium heat, heat the canola oil. Add the ham, shrimp, onion, celery, and chopped bell peppers. Cook, stirring often, until the shrimp are cooked through and the ham is tender, about 5 minutes. Add the Creole seasoning and unseasoned bread crumbs to the pan and sauté, stirring constantly, until the bread crumbs have absorbed all the moisture, about 3 minutes. Remove from the heat.

Arrange the bell pepper halves, cavity-side up, in a large baking pan. The peppers should just be touching each other. Spoon the cooked stuffing into each pepper half, dividing it evenly and packing it into each pepper half. Sprinkle the Italian-seasoned bread crumbs on top.

Pour the water carefully into the baking dish around the peppers so that the water reaches ¼ inch up the outside of the peppers. Bake the peppers for 35 minutes and, if the stuffing appears dry, drizzle oil over the top. If the water has baked away, carefully add more water and bake for 10 more minutes, or until the peppers are tender when pierced with a fork and the stuffing is heated through. Serve at once.

Makes 8 servings

Smothered Cabbage
with Onion and Bacon

Desiree: My neighbor Neecy used to always try to get me to go to the St. Patrick's Day Parade. I told her I didn't want be around a bunch of drunk Irish people. She told me I was missing out. Then one time she came home in the evening with a bag full of cabbages and potatoes she had caught at the parade. She say they was just throwing vegetables off the float like it was Carnival. Now it look like every year one of us goes out there to make groceries.

A lot of people boil their cabbage and it tastes kind of weak to me. But when you smother it with bacon and you don't have all that water, you can really taste your cabbage. It gets a little sweetness to it, too, which is good. It's just a richer dish when you fix it like this. If you do go to the parade and come back with a few potatoes or even some carrots in your bag, just peel them and put them in the pot when you put the cabbage in. It'll be good like that, too.

6 to 8 slices bacon, cut into 2-inch pieces

2 tablespoons unsalted butter

1 large yellow onion, coarsely chopped

1 large head green cabbage, cored and cut into 8 to 10 chunks

1 green bell pepper, seeded and cut into ¼-inch strips the length of the pepper

Salt and freshly ground pepper

Hot cooked rice for serving

Place the bacon (a little more or a little less, however you like) in a large pot and place over medium heat. Cook until the fat is rendered and the bacon is crisp, about 10 minutes.

Put the butter, onion, and cabbage in the pot, place over medium-high heat, and cook, stirring the pot every minute or so, until the vegetables are soft and starting to brown, about 15 minutes. Reduce the heat to medium-low, add the bell pepper and cover the pot. Cook, covered, until the cabbage is tender, 45 minutes to 1 hour.

Season with salt and pepper and serve hot over the rice.

Makes 4 servings

CREOLE SUCCOTASH

Desiree: My mama always used to talk about how succotash was summer food. When she was growing up, my grandma used to make this when the corn and the okra and the tomatoes were in season. But by the time I was coming up, you could buy all of that frozen, so we used to have succotash all year round.

Why do we call it Creole? We from New Orleans. Pretty much all the main dishes we cook, we call Creole. We don't have Creole hamburgers and hot dogs, but we do have Creole tomatoes, Creole okra, Creole gumbo, and Creole succotash, Creole cream cheese, just to name a few. The succotash is even better if you make it a day ahead and let all the flavors coagulate for a while. Refrigerate and reheat gently just before serving.

In a large heavy-bottomed saucepan or Dutch oven over medium heat, melt the butter. Add the tomatoes, onion, bell pepper, and celery and stir to coat well in the fat. Cook, uncovered, stirring occasionally, until the vegetables are tender, 10 to 15 minutes.

Stir in the okra, lima beans, corn, sausage, ham, bay leaves, and thyme. Cook, still uncovered, until vegetables are soft, about 1 hour, stirring occasionally. If the mixture seems dry toward the end of the cooking time, stir in water to moisten, a little at a time, then cover the pan and continue cooking.

Reduce the heat to low and stir in the shrimp. Cook, stirring often, until the shrimp are cooked through and the flavors have blended, about 15 minutes longer. Remove from the heat. Mound the rice on large plates, spoon the succotash over the rice, and serve at once.

Makes 8 main-course servings

2 tablespoons unsalted butter

One 28-ounce can crushed tomatoes

1 yellow onion, chopped

1 green bell pepper, seeded and chopped

2 celery stalks, chopped

1 pound fresh or frozen okra, trimmed and cut crosswise into 1-inch pieces

1 pound fresh or frozen lima beans

1 pound fresh or frozen corn kernels

1 pound smoked pork sausage, cut crosswise into ¾-inch slices

1 pound boneless smoked ham, cut into 1-inch cubes

2 bay leaves

Pinch of dried thyme

½ to 1 cup water, if needed

1 pound medium shrimp, peeled and deveined

Hot cooked rice for serving

KERMIT RUFFINS'S BUTTER BEANS

8 ounces pickled pork rib tips

8 ounces pickled pigtails

2 pounds dried large white lima beans

2 yellow onions, chopped

½ cup (1 stick) butter

4 bay leaves

1 teaspoon granulated garlic

½ teaspoon dried thyme

12 cups water

8 ounces andouille or smoked sausage

8 ounces smoked pork neck bones

1 tablespoon Basic Creole Seasoning Blend (page 228)

Hot cooked rice for serving

Antoine: Bethany Bultman from the New Orleans Musicians' Clinic once explained it to me this way: In the South—and, yes, that includes New Orleans sometimes—when people say they are having beans or greens, a lot of times what they really mean is they are having pork stew seasoned with beans or greens. The pork is just assumed.

It used to be a little pickle' meat or smoked neck bone was just for seasoning. Nowadays, people put as much meat in the pot as beans. That's how Kermit does it. When I was coming up, all this meat here would have made 5 or 10 pounds of beans. I miss the old days, but I love this recipe.

Don't let it scare you, though. You can use this recipe as your guide and make it the old way. Use whatever combination of sausage or smoked or pickle' meat you can get. And even if it doesn't add up to the exact amount of pounds the recipe calls for, improvise. You can even use this recipe with black-eyed peas or pinto beans. As Kermit himself would say, "Do Watcha Wanna."

Put the rib tips and pigtails in a large pot. Add water to cover by 2 inches and bring to a boil over high heat. Reduce the heat to medium-low and cook until the tips and tails are fork-tender, 60 to 90 minutes.

Meanwhile, in another large pot, combine the white beans, onions, butter, bay leaves, garlic, thyme, and water. Bring to a boil over high heat, then reduce the heat to very low, cover the pot, and cook the beans slowly, stirring occasionally, for 4 hours.

When the rib tips and pigtails are tender, drain the liquid and set the pot of meat aside.

Add the sausage and pork neck bones to the beans and cook until the beans are totally tender and the juices in the pot have formed a thick liquid with a saucelike consistency, another hour or so. Add the rib tips and pigtails. These meats will add salt to the dish, so taste the beans, add half of the Creole seasoning, and taste again. Add more Creole seasoning, if desired. When everything is heated through, serve the beans in big bowls, ladled over the cooked rice.

Makes 8 to 10 servings

White Beans and Shrimp

Desiree: The first time I had this dish was on the buffet at Dooky Chase. I know in a lot of places people put beans and seafood together, but we don't really do that here. If you have red beans and rice, you have it with some smoked sausage or a fried pork chop or fried chicken. So the first time I had it, it kind of took me aback. When Miss Chase makes hers, she uses green limas. I use different kinds of white beans when I make mine. It doesn't matter which ones—navy beans, baby limas, butter beans, Great Northern beans. Most of the time, I use a combination. If you put in just a handful of the really big beans in the mix, it almost tastes like you're biting into a piece of meat when you run across one of them from time to time.

Peel and devein the shrimp, reserving the heads and shells to make a quick shrimp stock. Cut each shrimp in half lengthwise, and put in a clean bowl. Add the wine, the 1 teaspoon garlic, ½ teaspoon salt, and ¼ teaspoon pepper and stir to mix well and evenly coat the shrimp with the seasonings. Cover the bowl tightly and refrigerate.

In a large heavy-bottomed saucepan or Dutch oven over medium heat, heat 2 tablespoons of the olive oil until hot, 1 to 2 minutes. Add the reserved shrimp heads and shells and cook, stirring occasionally, until the shrimp shells turn pink and then start to turn lightly golden, about 5 minutes. Add the water to the pan, raise the heat to high, and bring to a vigorous boil. Return the heat to medium and simmer briskly, uncovered, for 10 minutes.

Remove the stock from the heat and strain into a bowl through a fine-mesh strainer. Discard the solids. Return the strained stock to the pan.

Pick over the beans for stones or grit. Rinse and drain well. Stir the beans into the stock with the remaining 4 tablespoons olive oil, the 2 tablespoons garlic, the onion, celery, bell pepper, and bay leaves. Bring to a boil over high heat. Reduce the heat to maintain a slow simmer and cook until the beans are tender, 2 to 2½ hours, stirring about every 20 minutes.

When the beans are tender, add 1 tablespoon salt, ½ teaspoon pepper, and the butter to the pot, stirring over low heat until the butter melts into the beans. Remove the pot from the heat, stir in the seasoned shrimp, and let the mixture stand until the shrimp turn pink in the residual heat, about 3 minutes, stirring once or twice. Season with more salt and pepper, if needed.

Serve at once on large plates alongside the rice.

Note: You can make the shrimp and beans up to 1 day ahead. Be sure to reheat only briefly when ready to serve, to prevent overcooking the shrimp.

1 pound medium shrimp, heads and tails intact

1 tablespoon dry white wine

2 tablespoons minced garlic, plus 1 teaspoon

Salt and freshly ground pepper

6 tablespoons olive oil

2½ quarts water

1 pound dried navy beans, Great Northern beans, or baby white lima beans, or a combination

1 yellow onion, chopped

2 celery stalks, chopped

½ green bell pepper, seeded and chopped

4 bay leaves

6 tablespoons unsalted butter, at room temperature

6 cups of hot cooked rice for serving

Makes 6 to 8 servings

Kermit Ruffins:
Life Is a Picnic Every Day

I asked Kermit Ruffins for one of his recipes, but something became immediately clear: Kermit's a musician, a cook, and a talker, not a writer. So I decided to pull out my tape recorder and let him tell all about his life and love of food. As you'll hear, Kermit and cooking go way back:

I came up in the Lower 9th Ward. I have two brothers and one sister. I was the oldest out of all the cousins and siblings. Whatever I woke up with in the morning, that's what we were going to do. Be a baseball team. Go fishing. Whatever.

Almost every Saturday, about thirty family members would wake up at about 4 o'clock in the morning and go down to Hopedale, Louisiana, and go fishing or crabbing. We'd come back in the backyard by about 11:00 in the morning. Start cleaning fish, frying fish, boiling crabs. That's where it kind of started.

My daddy and them would be cleaning rabbits, turtles, raccoons, in the backyard. And I do the same thing. Clean 'em. Musk 'em. Take a turtle; knock his head off; put him in some red gravy with some angel hair pasta. I don't hunt. That's the only part I miss. I'd like to. I used to catch them bullfrogs though. I'd catch them and my daddy would be frying them like in the next thirty minutes.

My grandmother was the head chef at Lawless Senior High School. I was in junior high then. So I was still a little kid. I used to get out of school early, so I had a chance to go work with her with all those ladies in the kitchen, cooking for all those teenagers. They were cooking for real back then. I would always be in the kitchen. I was a sous chef and didn't even know it: peeling shrimp, cutting onions, cutting bell pepper, skinning carrots.

Every Saints game, all the uncles, they had to have a pot of gumbo on. Right after church, you know, something about that okra gumbo they used to make. Between my grandmother and my mama, my daddy, my grandfather, they all were just excellent cooks. Just down home, you know. I was just around them and paying attention. And before you know it, when I was like twelve, thirteen years old, that roast that my mama had for Sunday morning to cook? She would wake up and I would already have it in the oven. And that's the way it kind of started. I just wanted to get in that kitchen so bad, I don't know what it was, it was just some kind of itch I had to scratch. And I'm like that today. I don't know; it's a fine line between trumpet and cooking.

I'm always the first one up, 6:30 easily. I'm in the kitchen, putting on grits. I might lay down and go to sleep with that low fire on and let 'em cook a good while. I want it to cook good. Something about grits, you want them to cook long. At least an hour. Something about being a kid and you get up every morning and smell that trinity cooking (onions, bell pepper, celery), you know. Now I make sure my kids smell that every morning.

In terms of restaurants, I love that top of the line. Ruth's Chris Steak House, Maximo's, Crescent City Steak House. I love Emeril's. I love to call them early and request that table in the kitchen. I be watching them more than I be eating. I got lucky by Maximo's letting me hang out with the chefs over there. They taught me about that Italian high-heat cooking. Searing it with olive oil and popping it in the oven. Pasta, crawfish diablo, and all that stuff. I do that a lot when I got a lot of company to show off with, the pasta and that crawfish and that shrimp and that heavy whipping cream.

I love them hole-in-the-walls, too. I love my girl over there at Willie Mae's. I like Sammy's Deli. I was lucky enough to hang out with Lula Belle when she had her restaurant and when I thought I could cook. She taught me a few things; I realized I really *couldn't* cook. But after I hung out with Lula Belle for about five years, because I used to date her daughter, she started showing me some things. Her and her daughter. Badass cooks. Lula Belle's is gone now, though.

Lula Belle's was right on St. Ann's, they just tore it down after the storm. And she took over Steve's kitchen for a while. Steve's was on Claiborne. She's an elderly lady now. And she only cooks on Thursday and she brings it to all the ladies at the beauty shop, her daughter's beauty shop, right there in Gentilly.

I like to barbecue my quail. Put them in an ice chest or plastic bag, about twelve of them, with some olive oil, seasonings. I like my Tony Chachere's, my granulated garlic, paprika, slap a little rosemary in there, a half of a bottle of beer, shake it up good, let it marinate in the ice box for about 5 hours. Take it out. Let it get to about room temperature. Grill them for about 2 minutes on each side. I just cooked that for the Food Network.

When I starting doing it, nobody was cooking on the street. I take total responsibility for every food truck you see out there with the second lines today. When my babies were three and four years old, we used to like to go to second lines and sell beer. Just for the fun of it. My little girl, four years old, calling out "Ice cold beer!" The funniest thing in the world, you know?

Nothing like cooking outside. I always say, life is a picnic every day. I always have that picnic frame of mind, from the time I wake up to the time I got to sleep. I program myself to think like that. Before a gig? Standing at my stove cooking, or standing at my grill cooking? Those are always my best shows. Leaving the pots to the stage, I mean literally—when they say, "Okay Kermit, we got show time in five minutes," I flip a couple of more burgers, holler at one of my boys, "Watch that for me, Chippie," and go out on stage. You talking about the best feeling in the world! That's how the name of the band, the Barbecue Swingers, came about. Tailgating at Vaughn's. I started tailgating with a little hibachi. Take a break go out there, eat a little hot sausage, come back. You know you get the munchies in my band.

TONI AND CREIGHTON BERNETTE

Toni

My daughter still can't figure out why anybody asked me to contribute to a cookbook. And she's right. There is an irony here. If I were a great cook, I wouldn't eat out all the time. I probably wouldn't have gotten to know Janette and she probably wouldn't have asked me to contribute to this book. But Janette's been on a mission ever since she came back from New York. She has no patience for excuses. And we shouldn't have patience. Before you know it, the whistle sounds and it's over, time to get out of the pool whether you had a good swim or not.

I have three things to contribute here. I have a few recipes. They're simple but they're good. If you're busy, or if you just don't want to spend your life facing the stove, you'll appreciate these. I'm not a great cook, but I hate bad food and wouldn't knowingly give you a recipe for it.

The second thing I offered Janette was some recipes from some of our favorite restaurants. Some of the places didn't survive the levee failures. (I started to write "didn't survive Hurricane Katrina." Creigh would have killed me!) Who knows if the recipes will taste the same prepared in your kitchen. But they'll be good. And if you ever ate at these places, they'll be seasoned with delicious nostalgia.

Looking back, each of these restaurants has special meaning. JoAnn Clevenger and her chef, Ken Smith, combine an atmosphere and a menu at Upperline that's both comfortable and sophisticated. Frank Brigtsen has fought hard for Louisiana fishermen in the months and years since August 29, 2005. His Shell Beach Diet is really a tribute to the men and women of the water. It's also my favorite dish on his menu, after the banana bread pudding, of course. I think of Ken whenever I eat oysters. I think of Frank and his wife, Marna, whenever I eat bread pudding.

After my husband died, I went through all the things he was writing when he was supposed to be writing his novel about the great flood of 1927. I was hard on him for not getting the book finished. But he wrote some journal entries and little reflections that I think are just beautiful. I hope you can see that. Even when he was writing about eating dinner one night at the Upperline, he was thinking like a novelist, with little leitmotifs and epiphanies and structure.

I hope you like it. It's what I have.

Creighton

Tonight, JoAnn was smiling and warm, with Lafcadio pinned to her chest just like nothing had happened. If you're Lafcadio, a bejeweled lizard of long standing in this place, I suppose nothing had. And if you were JoAnn's laugh, you couldn't be defeated by any circumstance either. You would still erupt, unbidden and unbowed, and ring through the Upperline like the Nile flooding its banks. Or the Mississippi. Or Mr. Go. There's a good metaphor in there somewhere.

Roy Blount was there. Talk about timing. His book on New Orleans came out last April. But nobody wants to read anything about the city now unless it was written by Dame Katrina.

Mary Howell says Tom Piazza's writing a book-length essay about why New Orleans will survive or why it must survive. He's a good writer. He's going to need to be a great writer to get a hearing in these naysaying times. We still have the jeremiads, but old Jerusalem's a distant memory.

He recognized me, Roy did. He was there with JoAnn and this writing couple from Ole Miss, Beth Ann Fennelly and Tom Franklin. I barely know the guy, but he remembered me and he was talking shit about the YouTube stuff. Toni thinks he really likes it. But I never know with Roy. He's funny. While you're laughing at his jokes and his Georgia-ness, he's throwing out books you never read and allusions to stuff you never heard of. He's the master of control. You can't imagine him on a rant. How could he like that YouTube shit?

I saw something tonight I had never seen before. The way JoAnn has all that art on the wall . . . it's mostly portraits of people. It feels like you're at some big cocktail party. It's like there're a few tables in the middle where people are sitting down and eating. But the musicians and the French Quarter denizens are standing around, and Tom Dent is staring out alive from his funeral program and Willie White and his giant watermelons are just sitting on the porch watching wisely.

It could have been January 2005.

Then Jessica Harris, the cookbook writer, walked in with some lady. The lady hugged JoAnn and she kept hugging her. It was like she couldn't let go or everyone would see she was crying. She did let go, and then Jessica was crying. And Willie White and Tom and that crowd in the painting behind the hostess stand all looked like they had seen it before and understood.

There's a lot of that now, but sometimes it hits you differently.

When JoAnn came to the table, she was JoAnn again. She was talking about how Chef Ken has created this oyster dish as a tribute to the old Maylie's Restaurant on St. Claude, and how they had to rip out the carpet and clean out the walk-in, but she felt it was important that they be open again because that's her job and we need her. And her husband's tending bar because no one's back. It's loud in there without the carpet. It feels alive and that's important now.

She was saying that the word "restaurant" comes from French and Latin words meaning "to restore." Places served restorative soup by name back then. That's what this is all about for her, restoring people even when you can't restore houses and heirlooms and so much.

Outside people pilgrimage here every year like it's the black Madonna at Czestochowa. They take their communal food and communal music at the altar bar and they can survive another year in the Babylon of back home, saved by the blood of this place.

Now we're the pilgrims, coming here and looking for whatever bowl of soup or lucky lizard might restore us.

The oysters were good. Lots of garlic.

PECAN PANCAKES

½ cup pecan halves

1 cup all-purpose flour

1 tablespoon baking powder

1 tablespoon sugar

¼ teaspoon salt

1 ¼ cups whole milk

2 large eggs

½ teaspoon vanilla extract

1 tablespoon vegetable oil, plus more for frying

½ cup (1 stick) unsalted butter, melted

Maple syrup for serving

Toni: This is Creighton's recipe. He wasn't especially handy around the kitchen. For him, fixing dinner usually meant warming up leftovers or ordering takeout. But after I had Sofia, he was just so happy, he wanted to be the perfect father and husband. So he took to making me breakfast in bed on Sundays. That lasted about two weeks. When I reminded him of it years later, he insisted that he would make family breakfast every Sunday from then on. He worked hard at it. No frozen waffles or instant grits for him. It got to the point where all Sofia wanted was pecan pancakes, pecan pancakes. When it comes to fathers and daughters, who cares about Mom and her expanding waistline or rising cholesterol level? We had pecan pancakes every Sunday.

Preheat the oven to 350°F.

Spread the pecans on a small baking sheet or in an ovenproof skillet and toast in the oven until fragrant and lightly toasted, about 10 minutes. Transfer the pecans to a food processor and add the flour, baking powder, sugar, and salt. Process the mixture until some of the pecans are chopped into fine crumbs but not all of them are completely uniform in size, about 30 seconds. Transfer the pecan mixture to a medium bowl. Reduce the oven to warm, about 175°F.

In a medium bowl, whisk together the milk, eggs, vanilla, and 1 tablespoon vegetable oil until well blended, then whisk in the melted butter. Whisk the milk mixture into the flour mixture until just combined.

Heat 1 teaspoon oil in a large nonstick skillet over medium-low heat. Brush or swirl the oil to coat the pan bottom. Working in batches, drop pancake batter by generous tablespoonfuls onto the skillet and cook the pancakes until bubbles have formed on the top, 1½ to 2 minutes. Flip the pancakes and cook on the other side until nicely browned, 1½ to 2 minutes longer. Transfer the pancakes to a plate and keep warm in the oven. Repeat with the remaining batter. Serve hot with the maple syrup.

Note: The batter will thicken as it sits. You may thin the batter to your liking with up to ¼ cup more milk, if desired.

Makes 4 servings

Crawfish Calas with Green Garlic Mayonnaise

Green Garlic Mayonnaise

3 cloves garlic

5 green onions, white and tender green parts

1 large egg

Juice of 1 lemon

1 cup olive oil

½ cup flat-leaf parsley leaves

2 tablespoons ketchup

Crawfish Calas

Vegetable oil for deep-frying

2 cups cooked rice (not instant or parboiled)

6 tablespoons all-purpose flour

2 teaspoons baking powder

¼ teaspoon salt

2 large eggs, lightly beaten

3 green onions, white and tender green parts, very thinly sliced

¼ cup chopped cooked crawfish tails or boiled shrimp (see page 164)

Toni: Poppy Tooker is on a mission to save the *calas*, the emblematic New Orleans rice fritter that gets second billing to the beignet among Creole fried foods. Usually, calas are served dusted in powdered sugar, like beignets. But Poppy's recipe for crawfish calas are savory and delicious; no sugar needed on top. If you can't get crawfish, substitute shrimp.

To make the mayonnaise: Put the garlic and green onions in a food processor and pulse to chop thoroughly. Add the egg and lemon juice and pulse to blend. With the machine running, slowly drizzle in the olive oil until a thick emulsion forms. Add the parsley and ketchup and process just until well mixed, about 1 minute. Transfer the finished mayonnaise to a bowl. Cover and refrigerate to allow the flavors to marry, preferably at least 2 hours, and up to 5 days.

To make the calas: Pour oil into a deep fryer or heavy-bottomed saucepan with tall sides to a depth of 3 inches and heat to 360°F on a deep-frying thermometer.

While the oil is heating, in a large bowl, whisk together the rice, flour, baking powder, and salt. Add the eggs, green onions, and crawfish and stir gently to mix well. Using a tablespoon, scoop up a heaping spoonful of the crawfish mixture and gently scrape it into the hot oil. Working quickly, repeat to add 6 to 8 calas; do not overcrowd the pan. Fry until golden brown, 2 to 3 minutes. (Usually the calas will turn themselves over after they have browned on one side. But if not, gently turn them.) Transfer to paper towels to drain. Repeat to fry the remaining calas. Serve hot, with the garlic mayonnaise for dipping.

Makes 12 calas; serves 4 to 6

UPPERLINE'S OYSTERS ST. CLAUDE

St. Claude Sauce

½ cup (1 stick) unsalted butter

3 tablespoons paprika

1 lemon, zested and juiced

½ bunch flat-leaf parsley, disciplined a few times with a knife

1 cup whole garlic cloves, peeled

1½ tablespoons **Crystal** hot sauce

1½ tablespoons **Tabasco**

3 tablespoons **Worcestershire** sauce

Salt

Sugar

Canola oil for frying

2 cups corn flour (not cornmeal)

1 teaspoon salt

1 pint (12 large to 15 medium) shucked fresh oysters, drained and picked over for shell bits or grit

1 loaf French bread

Toni: On the menu at Upperline Restaurant, JoAnn Clevenger offers a list of her favorite dishes at her favorite restaurants. Who but JoAnn would offer free advertising to her competition? It's in that spirit that her chef, Ken Smith, created Oysters St. Claude, a tribute to the now-shuttered Mandich's Restaurant on St. Claude Avenue. Incidentally, *USA Today* voted this one of the best new dishes in the United States in 2007. Since then, Chef Ken has left the kitchen to become a priest. David Bridges, the new executive chef, wrote this, based on Chef Ken's recipe. He says "it serves 6 close friends or 8 out-of-towners." It calls for 2 cups of corn flour, but that's a minimum. Four cups would be better. Corn flour is pretty cheap and having another cup or two minimizes the chance that your last oysters will be dredged in soggy flour.

To make the sauce: In the bowl of that cumbersome food processor you own, place the butter, paprika, and zest and juice of that lemon you liberated from your neighbor's tree. (The depth of flavor that emancipation lends to Creole cooking should not be overlooked.) Add the parsley, garlic, hot sauces, Worcestershire, 2 pinches of salt, and 1 pinch of sugar. Process the mixture into a paste.

Transfer the paste to a small saucepan and set over low heat. Gently heat the mixture to poaching temperature, never letting the bubbles rise from the bottom of the pan and get angry. Constantly stir to prevent any sticking and scorching. Over time, the mixture will become dark red. This will take any responsible citizen about the same amount of time as drinking two glasses of decent Alsatian wine. About an hour. Set the sauce aside and let it cool to room temperature. Skim off any of the vibrant red fat that may accumulate at the top of the sauce.

Pour enough oil into a heavy-bottomed pot to deep-fry some bivalves. Heat the oil to 350°F on a deep-frying thermometer. Put the corn flour in a bowl and whisk in the salt. Discard any remaining liquor off the oysters and lightly toss them in the seasoned flour to coat well. Working in batches so as not to overcrowd the fryer like the French Quarter during Mardi Gras, carefully lower the oysters into the hot oil. When each batch is lightly golden and the sound of them singing in the fat starts to weaken, transfer them to a few sheets of the *Times-Picayune* to drain.

Using one of your best serving platters, bedazzle the vessel with tablespoons of the sauce. Place an oyster on top of each one of the saucy jewels. Serve to your friends and pass the fresh loaf of French bread to be torn in celebration of French wine, Louisiana seafood, and, of course, Creole emancipation.

Makes 6 appetizer servings

TROUT FARCI

CHEF POPPY TOOKER

Toni: This is another dish I learned in one of Poppy Tooker's cooking classes. She learned it while working as a chef at Christian's, another restaurant that didn't survive Hurricane Katrina's floodwaters. *Farci* just means "stuffed." In New Orleans, you'll often find stuffed shrimp or stuffed crabs on the menu, both likely using a mixture something like the crabmeat-based stuffing here.

Poppy's trout dish is wonderful for dinner parties. It's elegant enough to make guests think I'm a real chef. Since you have the oil hot already, consider dredging eggplant sticks in flour, then egg wash and then some seasoned bread crumbs and frying them to serve alongside the fish.

To make the stuffing: In a medium skillet, melt 3 tablespoons of the butter over medium heat. Add the flour and stir into the butter until smooth, to make a roux. Cook until the roux is a very lightly browned color, about 5 minutes. Meanwhile, in a small saucepan, heat the milk over medium-high heat until hot. Pour the hot milk into the roux and whisk until smooth. Reduce the heat to low and cook, stirring, until a thick béchamel sauce forms, about 10 minutes. Pour into a bowl and stir in the remaining 1 tablespoon butter. Set aside and let cool. Stir in the shrimp, crab, green onions, and parsley. Season well with salt and black pepper and stir in enough bread crumbs to hold the stuffing together nicely.

Pour oil into a deep fryer or heavy-bottomed saucepan with tall sides to a depth of 3 inches and heat to 375°F on a deep-frying thermometer. While the oil is heating, in a pie plate or shallow bowl, whisk together the flour, salt, and cayenne. In a second pie plate or shallow bowl, whisk together the milk, egg, and hot sauce. Put the bread crumbs in a third shallow bowl. Place the stuffing, the seasoned flour, the egg wash, and the bread crumbs on a work surface near the stove top.

Cut a pocket in the fat side of the trout fillets, being careful not to cut all the way through the fish or along the entire length of the fillet. Fill each fillet with a couple of tablespoons of the stuffing. Dredge in the seasoned flour, dip in the egg wash, and roll in bread crumbs. One or two at a time, lower the stuffed trout carefully into the hot oil and fry until golden brown, 8 to 10 minutes. Transfer the fish to paper towels to drain as they are finished.

Serve at once, with the garlic mayonnaise.

Makes 6 servings

Stuffing

4 tablespoons unsalted butter

3 tablespoons all-purpose flour

1 cup whole milk

½ pound boiled shrimp (see page 164), peeled

1 pound fresh claw or other lump crabmeat, picked over for cartilage and shell fragments

5 to 10 small green onions, white and tender green parts, thinly sliced

¼ cup chopped fresh parsley

Salt and freshly ground black pepper

¼ cup plain dried bread crumbs, or as needed

Canola oil for deep-frying

2 cups all-purpose flour

2 teaspoons salt

1 teaspoon cayenne pepper

1 cup whole milk

1 large egg

2 tablespoons hot sauce

2 cups plain dried bread crumbs

6 trout fillets (about 4 ounces each)

Green Garlic Mayonnaise (page 96) for serving

Pasta with Shrimp, Garlic, and Parsley

½ pound dried angel hair pasta or linguine

2 tablespoons olive oil

6 cloves garlic, finely chopped (about 2 tablespoons)

1 pound medium shrimp, peeled and deveined

Salt

½ teaspoon red pepper flakes

3 tablespoons chopped fresh parsley

2 tablespoons dry white wine

Toni: Fresh shrimp are cheap and plentiful in New Orleans, so you can make this dish any time of year. All this garlic, olive oil, and parsley smell up the kitchen so much that mouths are watering before the dish hits the plate.

Bring a pot three-fourths full of water to a boil over high heat. Add the pasta, stir once or twice, and cook until al dente, about 7 minutes for angel hair or according to package directions. Drain the pasta and set aside.

In a skillet over medium heat, heat the olive oil. Add the garlic and sauté for 2 minutes.

Add the shrimp, ½ teaspoon salt, and the red pepper flakes and sauté until the shrimp are cooked through, 3 to 4 minutes. Add the pasta, parsley, and wine and sauté for 1 more minute to allow the flavors to blend. Taste and adjust the seasoning. Serve at once.

Makes 2 servings

COMMANDER'S PALACE THANKSGIVING DINNER

Toni: Thanksgiving dinner at Commander's Palace was difficult the year after Creighton died. Now I get hungry just looking at these recipes for what we ate that day. If only I had had the same appetite when the food was actually in front of me. Commander's chef, Tory McPhail, is amazing. Even though Commander's is known as an "old line" restaurant, he's always inventing new takes on the New Orleans tradition.

Creole Roasted Turkey

One 11- to 13-pound dressed turkey, very fresh or just thawed, not injected with any flavorings

About 1 gallon cool water

½ cup crab-boil powder (preferably Zatarain's), or more or less to taste

1 tablespoon vegetable oil

2 tablespoons Commander's Creole Seasoning (facing page), Basic Creole Seasoning Blend (page 228), or store-bought Creole or poultry seasoning such as Chef Paul Prudhomme's Poultry Magic Seasoning Blend

Makes 6 to 8 servings

Injecting a crab-boil brine into the turkey (as well as letting the turkey soak overnight in the brine) helps give the meat a well-seasoned flavor and extra succulence.

Early on the day before baking the turkey, remove the metal or plastic prong holding the cavity closed, if present. Remove the neck and giblets from inside the bird and save for another use or discard. Trim the excess skin from the neck area and near the cavity. Rinse the turkey inside and out under cool running water. Drain the cavity well and pat dry with paper towels.

Pour the 1 gallon cool water and crab-boil powder into a large stainless-steel, ceramic, or glass mixing bowl and stir to dissolve the crab boil. Taste just a drop of the brine to assess the salt level. Some brands of crab boil, whether wet or dry, are saltier than others; let your personal taste and common sense guide you on how salty to make the brine and how much of it to inject. A happy medium is to have the brine taste salty but not as salty as the sea; inject less brine if it seems very salty. If the brine seems to need more flavor, add a little more crab boil.

Place the turkey, breast up, in a large shallow pan. Using a marinade injector, inject each breast and each leg-thigh area evenly to taste (my taste is 5 times in each breast half and 5 times in each leg-thigh) with a 1-ounce-full injector; set aside the remaining brine.

Put the injected turkey in a nonreactive pot large enough to fit the turkey but small enough to fit in your refrigerator. Fill the pot with enough of the leftover brine to submerge the turkey; you may need to mix up a little more brine solution to cover the bird. Refrigerate, uncovered, overnight.

As early as possible on the day you will roast the turkey, remove it from the brine and place breast-side up on a rack positioned on a jelly-roll pan to catch the drippings; discard the brine. Dry the outside and cavity of the bird thoroughly with paper towels and refrigerate the turkey to allow it to dry further before cooking.

About 1 hour before you are ready to put it in the oven, remove the turkey and let stand at room temperature to take the chill off. Meanwhile, position a rack on the next-to-lowest shelf of the oven and preheat to 475°F.

Put the turkey, breast up, on a clean rack in a roasting pan. Fold the wing tips back under the body and tie the legs together at the ankles with kitchen twine. Rub the oil all over the top and sides of the turkey and season evenly with the Creole seasoning, including in crevices, such as where the thighs join the body. Roast, uncovered, until light golden brown, about 30 minutes. Reduce the oven temperature to 325°F and continue roasting (the skin will brown further as it bakes) until an instant-read thermometer inserted into the thickest part of the innermost thighs (near but not touching the bone) and the thickest part of the breast on each side registers 165°F to 170°F, 3 to 4 hours. Remove from the oven and let rest for about 30 minutes before carving.

Shrimp and Mirliton Bread Pudding

Mirliton (see page 200) is the Creole name for the squash known as chayote in Latin America, as well as in many parts of the United States. It's what people in Jamaica call "cho-cho," and what people in the French Caribbean, other than Haiti, call "christophine." Creighton and I had it once on a trip to Jamaica; they boiled it and served it kind of plain, almost like you would serve boiled, buttered potatoes. A Haitian friend told me they spice it up and cook it with goat down there. As you can tell by the decadent savory and spicy bread pudding recipe here, New Orleans is closer in spirit to Port-au-Prince than to Kingston.

Make the seasoning mix: Combine all the ingredients in a blender or food processor and process until thoroughly mixed. You will have about 1 cup seasoning mix. Store in an airtight container for up to 4 weeks.

Preheat the oven to 350°F.

In a large heavy-bottomed saucepan or Dutch oven over high heat, melt the ½ cup butter. Brush or swirl the butter to coat the pan bottom. Add the garlic and ham and cook, stirring constantly, until the garlic is golden brown, about 5 minutes. Stir in the mirlitons, onion, celery, and bell peppers.

Cook until the onions are soft and just starting to brown, about 15 minutes, stirring occasionally. Add the shrimp and Creole seasoning and stir well. Continue cooking, stirring often, until the shrimp are just cooked through, about 5 minutes more. Remove from the heat and season with salt and pepper, if needed. Transfer the mixture to a large bowl and set aside.

In a medium bowl, whisk the eggs for a few seconds to blend. Whisk in the thyme and green onions and then the cream until well blended. Fold the bread into the shrimp mixture, then add the egg mixture, folding to blend thoroughly.

Grease a 4-quart casserole and pile the shrimp mixture into it. Spread evenly and press down all over with your fingertips to remove any air pockets. Cover loosely with aluminum foil and bake until heated through and the juices are bubbling rapidly around the edges, about 40 minutes. Serve at once.

Makes 6 to 8 servings

Commander's Creole Seasoning

2½ tablespoons plus ½ teaspoon salt

2½ tablespoons plus ½ teaspoon sweet paprika

2 tablespoons granulated or powdered garlic

2 tablespoons freshly ground black pepper

1½ tablespoons granulated onion

1 tablespoon ground cayenne pepper

1 tablespoon dried basil

1 tablespoon dried oregano

1 tablespoon dried thyme

½ cup (1 stick) unsalted butter

6 cloves garlic, finely chopped (about 2 tablespoons)

½ pound tasso or other smoked ham, finely chopped

3 medium mirlitons (about 2 pounds total weight), peeled, seeded, and finely chopped

1 large yellow onion, finely chopped

3 celery stalks, finely chopped

2 green bell peppers, seeded and finely chopped

2 pounds medium shrimp, peeled and deveined

3 tablespoons Commander's Creole Seasoning or store-bought such as Chef Paul Prudhomme's Poultry Magic Seasoning Blend

Salt and freshly ground black pepper (optional)

4 large eggs

2 teaspoons finely chopped fresh thyme

¾ cup thinly sliced green onions, tender green parts only

3 cups heavy (whipping) cream

1 to 1½ large loaves day-old French bread with crust on, chopped (about 8 cups)

Roasted Satsuma–Sweet Potatoes in Satsuma Cups

5 medium sweet potatoes (about 3 pounds total weight)

6 satsumas (select the largest ones available)

¾ cup firmly packed light brown sugar, or more to taste

½ cup (1 stick) salted butter, at room temperature

Salt

Freshly ground white pepper

The local satsumas are in full effect around Thanksgiving, so using them in this recipe is both timely and beautiful. If you can't find satsumas, substitute small oranges.

Sweet potatoes would probably have been important to Louisiana Agriculture, even if the LSU Ag Center hadn't spent so much time working on developing new varieties of the tuber. Sweet potatoes are the emblematic root vegetable of the South. The Ag Center has a whole Sweet Potato Research Station near Chase, Louisiana, that is dedicated solely and specifically to this tuber.

And while we are on the subject, one thing that always bothers me: sweet potatoes are not yams! Most Americans have probably never seen a real yam, let alone eaten one. Yams come from Africa and Asia. They are drier and more starchy than sweet potatoes and, well, not as sweet. The largest varieties of yams are far larger than the biggest sweet potatoes. So the next time someone offers you some candied yams, bear in mind, they are probably sweet potatoes.

Preheat the oven to 400°F. Place the sweet potatoes on a baking pan, pierce the skins in several spots with a fork, and bake until tender when pierced with a knife, about 1 hour 15 minutes.

Meanwhile, finely chop the zest of 1 satsuma and set the zest aside. Cut the zested satsuma in half and squeeze its juice into a measuring cup; discard the pulp. Cut off ⅛ inch from the tops and bottoms of the 5 remaining satsumas, and cut each in half horizontally. Create 10 satsuma cups by removing the pulp and its membrane from each half as follows (it's easier than it may sound): Use the tip of 1 teaspoon to separate a bit of the pulp and membrane from the skin and lift the pulp and membrane away from the skin in one piece. Set the cups aside at room temperature. Juice the pulp from the 5 satsumas into the same measuring cup with the satsuma juice until you have 1 cup juice. Reserve, covered, in the refrigerator. (Juice any remaining satsuma pulp and drink the juice or save it for another use.)

When the sweet potatoes are tender, remove them from the oven and reduce the oven temperature to 350°F. Let the potatoes cool for 20 minutes, then peel them and place the pulp in a food processor. Add the brown sugar, butter, 1 teaspoon salt, 1 teaspoon pepper, the reserved satsuma zest, and the reserved 1 cup satsuma juice. Process to a smooth purée. Taste and mix in more brown sugar, salt, or pepper, if you like.

Scoop the sweet potato purée into a pastry bag fitted with a star tip. Pipe the purée into the reserved satsuma cups in a circular motion, mounding it into an attractive pattern. Alternately, simply spoon the purée into the cups. You may have some of the purée left over; snack on it or save for another use. (You can make the cups up to four hours ahead up to this point; cover loosely with plastic wrap and refrigerate until time to heat for serving.)

Place the filled satsuma cups on a baking sheet and bake until the purée is heated through, 15 to 20 minutes. Serve at once, allowing 1 or 2 cups per serving depending on the size of the cups.

Makes 6 to 8 servings

CHUNKY PEANUT BUTTER AND CHOCOLATY BANANA CAKE

CHEF PAULETTE RITTENBERG

Toni: I got to know Paulette Rittenberg through her husband, Bill. He fights the good fight as a civil rights lawyer, while she tends to important matters like recipe testing for the late Jean-Louis Palladin, Paul Prudhomme, and Ralph Brennan. Paulette taught me this recipe. Without the icing, it's a perfect coffee cake. With the chocolate ganache on top, it's dessert.

Position a rack in the middle of the oven and preheat to 350°F. Grease a 9-by-13-by-2-inch glass baking dish and set aside.

In a medium bowl, whisk together the flour, baking powder, baking soda, and salt. Set aside.

In a large bowl, using an electric mixer (fitted with a paddle attachment if you have one), beat the ½ cup softened butter with ¾ cup of the sugar on medium speed until the mixture turns noticeably paler and fluffy, 3 to 4 minutes. Beat in the eggs, one at a time, mixing until well blended after each addition. When all the eggs are in, continue beating until the mixture is light and fluffy again, 2 to 3 minutes, scraping down the sides of the bowl and cleaning off the paddle or beaters with a rubber spatula as needed. Add the peanut butter and vanilla, beating on medium until thoroughly blended.

Still on medium speed, mix in one-third of the flour mixture just until incorporated into the batter, just a few seconds. Beat in one-third of the yogurt, then one-third of the bananas. Repeat twice until all the flour, yogurt, and bananas are blended in. Set the batter aside.

In a small bowl, using a large spoon, mix together the chocolate, the 2 tablespoons melted and cooled butter, and the remaining ¼ cup sugar.

Using a rubber spatula, scrape half of the batter into the prepared baking dish and spread evenly. Scatter half of the chocolate mixture evenly over the batter, then spread the remaining batter on top. End with the remaining chocolate mixture. Bake until the cake is dark golden and a toothpick inserted into the center comes out clean, about 30 minutes.

While the cake is baking, make the glaze: In a small bowl, combine the water, sugar, and orange liqueur and stir until the sugar dissolves.

When the cake is done, transfer the baking dish to a wire rack. Use a pastry brush to brush the cake all over with the glaze, using all of the glaze. Let the cake cool on the rack for at least 30 minutes before serving. If using as an un-iced coffee cake, just before serving, dust the top lightly with powdered sugar. If using the ganache, let the cake cool completely before icing.

To make the ganache, if using: Combine the chocolate chips and butter in the top of a double boiler set over (but not touching) hot, barely simmering water and slowly melt together until smooth, stirring occasionally and lifting the top of the double boiler occasionally to keep the water below a simmer.

Meanwhile, in a small saucepan, combine the cream and sugar and bring to a simmer over medium heat, stirring until the sugar is completely dissolved.

When the chocolate and cream mixtures are ready, remove both from the heat and very gradually add the cream mixture to the chocolate mixture, stirring constantly with a rubber spatula or metal whisk until the ganache is smooth.

Immediately spread the ganache evenly over the cooled cake with an icing spatula or rubber spatula. Freeze the cake until the ganache hardens, about 30 minutes. Remove from the freezer and let stand for a few minutes to allow the cake to return to room temperature. Cut into squares and serve.

2¼ cups all-purpose flour

2 teaspoons baking powder

1 teaspoon baking soda

¾ teaspoon salt

½ cup (1 stick) unsalted butter, at room temperature, plus 2 tablespoons melted and cooled

1 cup granulated sugar

3 large eggs

¾ cup crunchy or extra-crunchy peanut butter, at room temperature

1½ teaspoons vanilla extract

1 cup drained plain Greek yogurt

1 cup mashed very ripe bananas (from 2 medium bananas)

4 ounces top-quality 72% cacao dark chocolate, finely chopped (or substitute semisweet chocolate chips)

Glaze

¼ cup water

2 tablespoons granulated sugar

2 teaspoons orange-flavored liqueur

Powdered sugar for dusting (if not using ganache)

Ganache
(optional; see recipe introduction)

8 ounces semisweet chocolate chips

2 tablespoons unsalted butter

½ cup plus 2 tablespoons heavy (whipping) cream

1½ tablespoons granulated sugar

Makes 15 servings

CHEF FRANK BRIGTSEN

6 whole large eggs, plus 3 large egg yolks

2 very ripe, black-spotted bananas, mashed, plus 2 ripe still-yellow bananas, very thinly sliced

1½ teaspoons vanilla extract

2 teaspoons ground cinnamon

¼ teaspoon freshly grated nutmeg

1 cup granulated sugar, plus 1 teaspoon

¼ cup firmly packed light brown sugar

3 cups whole milk

1½ large loaves day-old French bread with crusts on, cut into ½-inch cubes (about 12 cups)

¾ cup raisins

1 cup heavy (whipping) cream

BRIGTSEN'S BANANA BREAD PUDDING

Toni: Brigtsen's Restaurant is really a side parlor house in the Riverbend neighborhood. That's as it should be. It feels like you're walking into someone's home. In fact, it's not a long walk from the Uptown house Creighton and I lived in. For more than twenty years, Frank and Marna Brigtsen have been putting their spin on Creole classics and food of their own invention.

Frank's is one of the best bread puddings in town. He included this note with the recipe: "Bread pudding is the most traditional of New Orleans desserts. As French bread is served at most New Orleans meals, there is almost always leftover bread that turns stale. This is the perfect way to utilize that stale bread. I like bananas in mine, but you may use the recipe as a base for many interesting variations by adding other ingredients such as pecans, chocolate chips, or coconut."

I've taken to adding a tablespoon or two of bourbon to my bread pudding, but the additions are up to you.

Preheat the oven to 350°F.

In a large bowl, whisk together the whole eggs and egg yolks until frothy. Add the mashed bananas, the vanilla, the cinnamon, and the nutmeg and whisk until well mixed. Add the 1 cup granulated sugar and the brown sugar and whisk until dissolved. Add the milk and whisk until well blended.

Add the bread cubes to the bowl and stir until the bread has absorbed most of the custard. Add the raisins and sliced bananas and stir to mix well.

Pour the bread pudding batter into a shallow baking pan and let stand at room temperature for 30 minutes. Place the baking pan in a slightly larger pan and pour in hot water to come 1 inch up the sides of the pudding pan, to form a water bath.

Bake, uncovered, until a toothpick inserted into the center comes out clean, about 1 hour.

In a bowl, using an electric mixer or by hand, beat the cream until soft peaks begin to form, about 3 minutes. Add the 1 teaspoon sugar and continue beating to soft peaks, 1 minute or 2 longer (or a little longer if mixing by hand). Spoon the bread pudding onto serving plates, top with a dollop of whipped cream, and serve at once.

Makes 12 servings

A Brief History of Bread Pudding

Bread pudding is the gumbo of New Orleans desserts. It's the go-to dessert for the home cook. It's on almost every menu in town, from the most exclusive to the least formal. Sometimes chefs try to fancy it up with different glazes or different kinds of fruit. But most of the time, they just stick to the basics and no one complains. If you told a New Orleanian that bread pudding didn't originate here, they might punch you in the nose. Or they might concede reluctantly that we got it from France, but that might not be totally true either. Bread pudding, or bread-and-butter pudding, as it's called sometimes, apparently originated in England. That makes sense; the English use the word "pudding" in so many more ways than anyone else, you'd have to assume that they had been perfecting and varying it the longest.

The ingredients for "Poor Man's Pudding," which dates to thirteenth-century England, looks a lot like the bread puddings of today. Water was used instead of milk to moisten the stale bread. Spices and sweetener were added. In 1723, when John Nott published *The Cooks and Confectioners Dictionary*, the recipe looked even closer to our own. It was called "white-pot," and the basic ingredients—bread, butter, eggs, raisins, nutmeg, and cream—are all there. The bits of marrow Nott includes as a possible alternative to butter might seem a little strange. Even though roasted marrow bones are coming back in style, you still don't see them on dessert menus too much.

As for French origins, Auguste Escoffier, the "emperor of chefs" and the man who everybody credits as the father of modern French cuisine, did have a recipe for *Pouding au Pain à la Française* in his 1903 book *Le Guide Culinaire*. But in another edition, he also had a recipe for *Pouding au Pain à l'Anglaise*. Among French Canadians, relatives of Louisiana Cajuns, you find recipes for *pouding chomeur*, or "pudding of the unemployed." You could also translate it as "poor man's pudding," which would bring this history full circle.

It's not a surprise that bread pudding recipes seem to have come out of at least two different culinary traditions. In cuisines where bread is as important as it is in England and France, the leftover-bread problem would be one to get a lot of people thinking about solutions. In New Orleans, we have our own leftover-bread problems, as one of the few cities in America with a local bread tradition. (Don't pay any attention to the adjective "French" in front of the name of our bread; it's not the bread you find in the boulangeries of Paris.) So New Orleanians are naturally inclined to believe that the "Bread Pudding Solution" belongs to us.

The Picayune's Creole Cook Book, a kind of Escoffier guide for New Orleans food, gives the English all the credit for creating puddings. "We have no real French word for pudding. Puddings are essentially English in origin," the authors wrote in the introduction to the pudding section. "The Creoles adapted the dish to many of the delightful fruits of Louisiana." The Picayune book was actually published in 1900, a couple years before Escoffier. But amid a chapter full of recipes for plum pudding, banana pudding, cocoanut (sic) pudding, cream pudding, cake or bread pudding, molasses pudding, and a couple of dozen others, the recipe for bread pudding doesn't really stand out as particularly special. Yet, bread pudding does have a special place in the cuisine of New Orleans, and New Orleans bread pudding has a special place in the cuisine of America. Some editions of *The Joy of Cooking* have specific recipes for "New Orleans Bread Pudding," which I like to think of as proof that the New Orleans pudding is the gold standard.

You can find bread puddings all around the country. We had them in Alabama, where I'm from, and nobody said we'd learned it from New Orleans. I guess with so many people coming down here to eat in New Orleans restaurants, and with bread pudding being so ubiquitous on the menus, the gospel of New Orleans bread pudding got spread farther and wider than any others.

Susan Tucker, the curator of the Newcomb Archives at Tulane University, wrote an essay on bread pudding in which she tried to figure out how this city and this dish came to be so intertwined. "This association of bread pudding with New Orleans may be best understood by looking to the retention of French culinary traditions—thrifty in the home and grand in the public spaces," she wrote in *New Orleans Cuisine: Fourteen Signature Dishes and Their Histories*. "Bread pudding can be both a taste of luxury and a taste of necessity or homeliness."

That is New Orleans cuisine in a nutshell. The home traditions and the restaurant traditions are always in dialog with one another, and there isn't really a sense that the gumbo or red beans or bread pudding that your mother made at home isn't good enough to serve to company, whether that company be Auguste Escoffier or Junior from down the block.

JACQUES JHONI

When I was twenty years old, I was in Operation Crossroads Africa. It was a program where American college students came to Africa and worked with African students. The Africans and the Americans were to get to know each other's cultures while we worked together in small villages on an irrigation project. The American women were always talking about how in Africa the women did all the work, while the African men had it easy. But something funny came to light when it was time to cook meals for the group: all of the African men in the group could cook. It's true we didn't cook at home, but we had learned how to cook—camping out in Boy Scouts. They teased us about all the work African women did, but none of the American women could cook. I really had fun cooking that summer, because we could tease the American girls. But I never thought I would be a chef.

My cousin Gabou had moved to New Orleans, and one by one, a lot of us followed him. When I got here, the first job I could find was washing dishes at Gabrielle Restaurant on Esplanade Avenue. I got to be a cook because I was reliable. Sometimes, when a cook didn't show up or was late, they let me cook. It was fun just trying to keep cool when all the orders were coming in. When Greg and Mary Sonnier opened Gamay on Decatur Street,

I moved there. That's where I met Janette. I was so excited to get the job, I called my mother to tell her and she told me (in Wolof), "Don't worry, my son. You will get a good job soon." I wanted to tell her about men like Lazone Randolph and Milton Prudence, men who'd earned respect working for years at Brennan's and Galatoire's. She didn't believe that I wanted to be a cook. The idea of traveling all the way to America just to cook didn't make sense to her, especially since I had one cousin here who was a doctor.

It was fun for me cooking in New Orleans because a lot of the ingredients, like okra, fish, and rice, are the food we eat every day in Senegal. And in New Orleans, the food is not hot. We just season it. Back home, we might take habanero pepper, boil it for just 1 minute, and then put on the table. If you want your food hotter, you must just touch your fork to the pepper. But for most dishes, the whole pot is not hot. And we use a lot of onions and tomatoes like here, as well.

"Family meal" is when one of the cooks in the kitchen prepares breakfast or lunch for the rest of the staff to eat between prep time and service time. Sometimes, I would make African dishes at family meal, the ones I thought people might like. They loved them. Especially peanut butter stew.

OATMEAL AND FRESH BERRY PARFAITS
WITH CHANTILLY CREAM

A common thing on menus these days is mixing up expectations—reversing sweet and savory recipes, or taking a breakfast classic and making it into a dinner dish. While everyone else was doing foie gras French toast or truffled bread pudding, I wanted to come up with a different way to use plain old oatmeal. Then I tasted a version of this dish that used to be on the brunch menu at the Palace Café. Before I could get back, they'd changed the menu. So I developed my own version. It's a perfect brunch dish.

You'll notice a lot of hints about timing in this recipe; read them carefully, as you want the berries macerated enough to be supremely juicy and flavorful, but not broken down too much or soggy, and a beautiful peak of soft whipped cream.

About 2 hours before assembling the parfaits for serving, if using strawberries, stem them and cut into pieces about the same size as the other berries. Put all the berries in a medium glass, ceramic, or stainless-steel bowl. In a small bowl, combine the granulated sugar and liqueur and stir until the sugar is completely dissolved. Add the sweetened liqueur to the berries and stir gently with a rubber spatula until the berries are well coated with the syrup, being careful not to break up the berries. Cover with plastic wrap and refrigerate until ready to serve, stirring very gently about every 45 minutes with the spatula.

Meanwhile, cook the oatmeal according to the package directions. Then cover and set aside at room temperature until ready to serve.

Just before assembling the parfaits, gently rewarm the oatmeal over low heat; thin with a little water, if needed. (It shouldn't be too hot, or it will melt the Chantilly cream.) Add the butter and brown sugar and stir to mix well. Cover to keep warm and set aside.

Also just before assembling, make the cream: In a large bowl, combine the heavy cream, sour cream, liqueur, and vanilla. Whisking by hand or using an electric mixer set on medium speed, beat the mixture just until soft peaks form, 5 to 10 minutes if beating by hand or about 3 minutes if using an electric mixer.

To assemble the parfaits, layer in each glass 2 tablespoons oatmeal, then 2 tablespoons drained berries, then 2 tablespoons Chantilly cream, then another 2 tablespoons oatmeal. Top with more berries, dividing them evenly, and end with 1 tablespoon Chantilly cream on top of parfait with a few more berries for garnish. Serve at once, with long-handled spoons.

6 cups fresh blueberries, black-berries, or strawberries, or a combination

2 tablespoons granulated sugar

6 tablespoons fruit liqueur such as Mandarine Napoleon, pear brandy, St-Germain, Grand Marnier or other orange-flavored liqueur

1 cup uncooked oatmeal, preferably steel-cut

5 tablespoons unsalted butter

¼ cup loosely packed light or dark brown sugar

Chantilly Cream

1 quart heavy (whipping) cream

2 tablespoons sour cream

2 tablespoons Grand Marnier or other orange-flavored liqueur

1 teaspoon vanilla extract

Makes 6 servings

4 tablespoons unsalted butter, at room temperature

Salt and freshly ground pepper

1 cup fresh lump or claw crab-meat, picked over for cartilage and shell fragments

8 large eggs

½ cup freshly cooked or leftover cooked rice (jasmine preferred, but any white is okay as long as it's not parboiled, instant, or converted; use real rice)

2 green onions, white and tender green parts, thinly sliced

My neighbors in Treme are always sharing food with me. Sometimes it's just a simple little dish. One morning, they invited me by for some egg and rice. We eat plenty of eggs and plenty of rice in Senegal, but somehow we never eat them together. In Cajun country, they scramble eggs into the leftover jambalaya. It's kind of like what the Chinese do with fried rice, only there's a lot more egg. That's what made me create this dish—as an uptown, upscale version of everyday New Orleans food.

In a small, heavy skillet or saucepan over medium heat, melt 1 tablespoon of the butter with a pinch of salt and ⅛ teaspoon pepper. When the butter is melted, reduce the heat to low, add the crabmeat, and cook just until the crabmeat is warmed through, using a rubber spatula or large spoon to fold gently and coat the crabmeat lumps with butter without breaking them up, 1 to 2 minutes. Remove from the heat and cover to keep warm.

Meanwhile, in the bottom of a double boiler, bring 1 to 2 inches of water to a boil over high heat. In a small bowl, lightly beat together the eggs and 2 tablespoons water; set aside.

Reduce the heat under the bottom pan of the double boiler to medium and add the remaining 3 tablespoons butter and ¼ teaspoon pepper to the top pan. Add the beaten eggs and the rice. Using a wooden spoon, slowly stir the egg mixture almost constantly as you cook it just until thickened to a very loose and creamy scrambled-egg consistency, 12 to 14 minutes. Toward the end of the cooking time, season with ½ teaspoon salt, or more, and more pepper, if desired.

Turn off the heat under the double boiler but leave the egg mixture in the top pan over the hot water while you continue stirring until the eggs are slightly thicker and cooked through but still very soft and moist, like a custard, about 1 minute longer. Remove the top of the double boiler from over the hot water and serve at once. To serve, spoon one-fourth of the warm crabmeat into each of four rimmed dinner plates, pasta plates, or shallow serving bowls. Spoon a portion of the egg and rice over the crab, garnish with the green onions, and serve.

Makes 4 servings

Black Beans and Rum à la Austin Leslie

The first second line parade after the levees failed was for Chef Austin Leslie. He survived the hurricane and seemed fine. But he died not long after. That's the way it was with a lot of people. It all hit them harder than they knew.

Chef Austin was famous for his fried chicken with pickle and minced garlic garnish. It really was some of the best fried chicken you'll ever taste. But the dish I remember him for is this one. I got to try it at an event the Southern Foodways Alliance had a month before Hurricane Katrina. A lot of the best chefs in the city were invited to cook a dish featuring some sugar product—molasses, sugar, cane syrup, rum, whatever. Chef Austin made this dish, and I fell in love with it. He told me that some Cuban or Brazilian guy gave him the idea, but he created the recipe himself. I never got the recipe from him, so I had to create my own. It doesn't taste quite like his, but it's entirely a tribute to him.

1 pound dried black beans

1 yellow onion, chopped

2 celery stalks, chopped

½ green bell pepper, seeded and chopped

¼ cup minced garlic (about 1 head)

One 4-ounce jar sliced pimientos in their juices

3 bay leaves

1 tablespoon dried Italian seasoning or herbes de Provence

¾ cup olive oil

2 quarts plus 3 cups water

Salt

1½ teaspoons habanero pepper sauce or other hot sauce

½ cup dark rum

Hot cooked rice for serving

Pick over the beans for stones or grit. Rinse and drain well. In a large heavy-bottomed saucepan or Dutch oven over high heat, combine the beans, onion, celery, bell pepper, garlic, pimientos and their juice, bay leaves, Italian seasoning, olive oil, and water and bring to a boil. Reduce the heat to medium-low, cover, and cook until the beans are tender, about 3 hours, stirring about every 15 minutes to prevent the beans from sticking to the pan bottom. The finished beans should be tender and most but not all of them still whole, all sitting in a thick bean jus.

Add 2 teaspoons salt, or more if desired, then the hot sauce, then the rum. Cook for 10 minutes longer to allow the flavors to blend. The beans should be soft and the liquid should have formed an almost creamy consistency. Spoon some rice onto large plates or into bowls, scoop the beans on top or alongside, and serve at once.

Note: You can make the beans up to 3 days ahead. Reheat gently over medium-low heat before serving.

Makes 4 to 6 servings

Bayona's Roasted Duck with Bourbon-Molasses Sauce and Sweet Potato Fries

2 ducklings (about 5 pounds each)

2 yellow onions, quartered

2 teaspoons chopped fresh sage leaves, plus a few of the plucked stems

2 teaspoons fresh thyme leaves, plus a few of the plucked stems

Salt and freshly ground pepper

Bourbon-Molasses Sauce

2 cups apple cider

1 cup cane vinegar or apple cider vinegar

4 large shallots, minced (about ⅔ cup)

½ cup molasses

1 quart Basic Chicken Stock (page 230) or store-bought chicken broth

6 tablespoons good-quality bourbon

4 tablespoons unsalted butter, at room temperature, cut into 8 pieces

Salt

Sweet Potato Fries

2 medium to large sweet potatoes (about 1¾ pounds total)

Salt

Vegetable oil for frying

When I worked for Susan Spicer at Bayona, this dish was my favorite. Duck naturally goes with sweet sauces, but the trick is not to make it too sweet. The technique here is to make a mixture that starts as a basting liquid and finishes as a sauce. The ample vinegar helps balance the dish, and the bourbon is that ingredient that has you asking yourself, "Now what's that other flavor I'm tasting?"

For slightly more exotic sweet potato fries, sprinkle with sugar, pepper, and a little bit of cinnamon along with the salt.

Remove the necks and giblets from the ducks and save for another use or discard. Trim the excess skin from the neck area and near the cavity of each. Rinse the ducks inside and out under cool running water. Drain the cavities well and pat dry with paper towels. Stuff the cavities with the onion quarters and sage and thyme stems (but not chopped leaves) and tie the duck legs closed at the ankles with kitchen twine. In a small bowl, mix together the chopped sage and thyme leaves, 2 teaspoons salt, and 1 teaspoon pepper. Place the ducks on a baking sheet and prick their skin lightly all over with the tines of a fork, then rub them evenly with the herb mixture, using it all. Set aside at room temperature for 1 hour, or refrigerate overnight.

About 1 hour before roasting the ducks, position a rack in the middle of the oven and preheat to 425°F. When the oven reaches temperature, fit a large roasting pan with a large rack (you don't want the ducks to touch) and preheat the pan on the middle shelf of the hot oven for at least 20 minutes.

Meanwhile, start the bourbon-molasses sauce: In a medium heavy-bottomed saucepan, combine the cider, vinegar, and shallots and bring to a boil over high heat. Reduce the heat to maintain a simmer and cook, stirring occasionally, until reduced by about half, about 15 minutes. Remove from the heat, pour half of the reduced mixture into a small bowl, and stir in ¼ cup of the molasses, blending well, for the basting liquid. Set aside the remaining vinegar reduction separately at room temperature until you are ready to finish the sauce.

To roast the ducks, place them, breast-side up, on the rack in the preheated roasting pan and roast, uncovered, for 30 minutes. Reduce the oven temperature to 400°F. Remove the ducks from oven, turn them breast-side down, and baste with about half of the basting liquid, then return to

the oven and roast for 45 minutes. Finally, turn the ducks breast-up again, baste again with the remaining liquid, and continue roasting until the skins are crisp and the juices run clear when you prick the thighs, about 30 minutes longer. Remove from the oven and let rest for 10 to 15 minutes before carving.

While the ducks roast, finish the sauce: In a heavy 3- or 4-quart saucepan, combine the stock and the reserved half of the vinegar reduction. Bring to a boil over high heat. Reduce the heat and simmer until the liquid reduces to 1 cup, about 30 minutes. Whisk in the remaining ¼ cup molasses and the bourbon and continue simmering, whisking occasionally, until the mixture is slightly syrupy, about 5 minutes more. Add the butter, 1 piece at a time, whisking constantly until all the butter is blended in and the sauce takes on a light and creamy consistency. Season with salt, then taste to consider if the sauce is nicely balanced between sweet and tart. If it's too tart, add a little more molasses; if it's too sweet, sprinkle in a little more vinegar. Set the sauce aside while the ducks finish baking.

Just before the ducks come out of the oven, start preparing the sweet potato fries: You want to finish the fries at the last moment possible so they will be piping hot when you serve. Peel the sweet potatoes and cut into sticks about 3 inches long and ¼ inch thick. Place the potato sticks in a bowl and add

lightly salted water to cover. Pour oil into a deep fryer or heavy-bottomed saucepan with tall sides to a depth of 2 inches and heat to 325°F on a deep-frying thermometer. Meanwhile, drain the sweet potatoes and dry them thoroughly with dish towels or paper towels. Working in small batches, gradually ease the potatoes into the hot oil, being careful not to add too many potatoes at once, as the oil may bubble up. Fry until tender but not yet brown, 3 to 5 minutes. Transfer the fries as they are finished to paper towels to drain.

When all of the potatoes have been fried once, raise the heat to boost the temperature of the oil to about 360°F, then fry the potatoes in batches again until browned and crisp, about 2 minutes. Drain on paper towels and salt lightly.

When the ducks have rested for at least 10 minutes, you can carve them at the table; or remove the breasts and leg-thigh pieces from the carcasses, slice the breasts, and arrange on a serving platter with the whole leg-thigh pieces alongside. Warm the sauce over low heat briefly, whisking constantly, and spoon it over the duck, or pass the sauce at the table. Serve with the sweet potato fries on the side.

Makes 4 to 6 servings

HABANERO-LACED LAMB SHANKS WITH SPICED COUSCOUS

4 lamb shanks (about 1 pound each)

4 teaspoons kosher salt

½ teaspoon freshly ground pepper

1 tablespoon olive oil

2 large yellow onions, cut into 1-inch cubes (about 3 cups)

4 carrots, peeled and cut into 2-inch chunks (about 2 cups)

1 head garlic, split horizontally

3 bay leaves

1 or 2 habanero chiles, poked with a fork to help flavor the dish

Zest of 2 oranges

1 cup fresh orange juice

1 cup Basic Chicken Stock (page 230) or store-bought chicken broth

1 tablespoon Jamaican picka-peppa sauce or other hot sauce

1 tablespoon white vinegar

1 teaspoon Angostura bitters

Spiced Couscous

3 tablespoons olive oil

2 cups Israeli couscous

1 teaspoon salt

¼ teaspoon ground allspice

1 cinnamon stick

2½ cups Basic Chicken Stock (page 230) or store-bought chicken broth

4 teaspoons fresh lime juice

1 tablespoon unsalted butter

¾ cup chopped fresh parsley

Before Hurricane Katrina, there was a great restaurant at the corner of Esplanade and Decatur called Marisol. Before they opened Marisol, every restaurant at that location had failed. Chef Pete Vazquez and Janis, his wife at the time, did some incredible things, including a Jamaican-inspired jerk lamb sandwich. It was my favorite dish at the restaurant, even more so than their Thai crab and coconut soup, which might have been the consensus favorite. Here's my twist, served on a plate with spiced couscous instead of on a sandwich.

Preheat the oven to 325°F.

Season the lamb shanks all over with the salt and pepper. In a Dutch oven over high heat, heat the olive oil. Add the shanks and sear, turning as needed, until nicely browned on all sides or until an instant-read thermometer registers 145°F when inserted into the thickest part of the shank, about 20 minutes total. Transfer the shanks to a plate and set aside.

Add the onions, carrots, garlic, bay leaves, and chile to the pot and sauté until nicely glazed by the pan drippings, about 5 minutes. Return the shanks to the pot. Add the orange zest and juice, chicken stock, hot sauce, vinegar, and bitters. Bring to a boil, cover, and transfer to the oven. Braise the lamb shanks until falling-apart tender, 2½ to 3 hours. Remove the pot from the oven. Uncover, skim the fat from the top, and discard.

To make the couscous: In a medium saucepan, heat the olive oil over medium heat. Add the couscous, salt, allspice, and cinnamon stick and stir to combine. Toast the couscous and the spices in the oil until the couscous is lightly browned, about 3 minutes. Stir in the chicken stock. Bring to a boil, reduce the heat to a simmer, and cook until the couscous is tender, about 15 minutes. Stir in the lime juice, butter, and ½ cup of the parsley.

Transfer 2 cups of the cooking liquid from the pot with the shanks to a sauté pan. Simmer the juices over medium-high heat until they reach the desired consistency for the sauce.

Scoop the couscous onto individual plates. Top with some vegetables and chunks of lamb, dividing it evenly. Spoon the sauce over. Garnish with the remaining parsley and serve at once.

Makes 6 to 8 servings

The Great Gumbo Controversy

There are at least three theories of where gumbo came from, and that in itself explains a lot. Different restaurants in New Orleans serve wildly different dishes they call "gumbo." Sometimes I think it's just marketing—give the tourists what they want, and they want gumbo. So that leftover pork loin, those last few mushrooms, that stray piece of brisket? Put it in a pot and call it "gumbo du jour." That actually happens, and it doesn't have to. When they make soup of these odds and ends, they should just call it "soup" instead of dragging the good name of gumbo into the mix. Tourists don't come to New Orleans for soupe de leftovers; they come for gumbo.

When you look at the origins of the word "gumbo," you get a better sense of why there are legitimate reasons gumbo varies so widely from pot to pot and from parish to parish. Depending on what word your version of gumbo derives from, you could be cooking something totally in your tradition and totally outside of someone else's.

There's an old drawing of Indians selling "gumbo" in a market back in the 1870s. They are selling this "gumbo" from a tray. No gumbo I have ever seen could possibly be kept in a flat tray. The "gumbo" they were selling was ground sassafras leaves; today we refer to this as "filé," and use it to thicken gumbo and provide an added subtle seasoning. The Creoles in New Orleans used filé to thicken gumbo in the winter when okra was out of season. Even when there was okra gumbo, people often added a spoonful of filé to their bowl of gumbo at the table. (It's odd that this practice is still widespread in homes, but I don't know of any restaurant that offers extra filé when a diner orders gumbo.) Sometimes the Indian version of gumbo is spelled "kombo," but in either case, it's easy to see how this word could be the origin of the emblematic food of Louisiana. Gumbo in Cajun country tends to be thicker than gumbo in New Orleans, and most of the time it does contain filé and doesn't contain okra. It's thickened with a dark roux, and while the flour

and oil of the roux is French in origin, no traditional French chef ever served a roux as dark and rich as the ones his Cajun cousins serve.

Another theory about how gumbo got its name comes from the Bantu languages in West Africa, in which the word for okra is "ochingombo." For a lot of New Orleanians, gumbo means, in essence, okra soup. For lots of folks all over Africa, various kinds of okra soup are common. As okra is an African vegetable, it stands to reason that the African word for this dish would be the one Americans ended up using. And since most of the cooks in the early days of New Orleans were West African, it makes sense that a lot of what was being cooked and enjoyed and handed down was West African food. Traditional gumbo in New Orleans is usually a combination of shrimp, crabs, oysters, and sausage. Creoles also use roux to thicken and flavor their gumbo, though they tend to use less of it and brown it less than the Cajuns do.

The most popular theory of where gumbo came from is the one that makes the least sense to me. People claim that gumbo is just a New Orleans version of bouillabaisse. The thinking goes that, since the Creoles of New Orleans couldn't find the right ingredients to make bouillabaisse, they improvised gumbo as a substitute. The problem is that the Gulf of Mexico provides plenty of suitable substitutes for the main ingredient in bouillabaisse—fish. Redfish, snapper, flounder, drum, croakers, tuna, and trigger fish may not be exactly the same as the Mediterranean fish they use in Provence, but they're close. Gumbo, however, never contains fish like that. The seafood in gumbo is always shellfish—shrimp, crabs, oysters, and the occasional crawfish. Another definitive ingredient in bouillabaisse, the slice of bread covered in rouille that is served on top of the soup, could easily have been made in New Orleans. There's no shortage of bread, garlic, red peppers, and lemons here. If New Orleanians had wanted to make bouillabaisse, they could have. But they didn't. They wanted to make gumbo.

Pie Crust

1 cup all-purpose flour, plus more for dusting

½ teaspoon salt

7 tablespoons cold unsalted butter, cut into ½-inch cubes

¼ cup ice water

½ cup pecan pieces, coarsely chopped

⅓ cup pine nuts

⅓ cup raw macadamia pieces

⅓ cup raw Brazil nuts, cut in half

4 large eggs

1 cup sugar

1 cup dark corn syrup

2 tablespoons unsalted butter, melted

1 teaspoon vanilla extract

2 tablespoons dark rum or bourbon

⅛ teaspoon salt

Two chefs inspired this dish. Frank Brigtsen makes the world's best pecan pie. He's the first person I ever saw use a grater to cut the butter into the pie dough. Mr. Lou, the pastry chef at Emeril's, would occasionally do a three-nut pie as a dessert special. It's basically a pecan pie using a couple of extra kinds of nuts. So this recipe adds a few of my own twists to the dishes these men created. I use pecans, pine nuts, Brazil nuts, and macadamia nuts. But feel free to substitute walnuts, cashew nuts, hazelnuts, or whatever nuts you like.

Preheat the oven to 375°F.

To make the pie crust: Sift together the flour and salt into a bowl. Using your fingertips, lightly pinch and toss the butter and flour mixture until the texture is like coarse cornmeal. Be careful not to overwork the dough.

Add the ice water and stir until thoroughly incorporated and a rough mass begins to form. Gather the dough into a ball, transfer to a lightly floured cutting board, and pat into a disk about 5 inches in diameter. Dust a rolling pin with flour and roll out the dough into a circle about ⅛ inch thick, adding flour to the board as necessary to prevent sticking. Place an 9-inch pie pan face down on the dough and cut the dough to fit the pan, leaving a border of about 1 inch. Line the pan with the dough, trim the edges, and refrigerate until ready to use.

In a small skillet over medium heat, toast all of the nuts until fragrant and nicely browned, about 5 minutes. Immediately pour onto a plate to cool. Set aside. In a bowl, using an electric mixer fitted with the wire whisk attachment, beat the eggs on high speed until frothy, about 1 minute. Add the sugar, corn syrup, melted butter, vanilla, dark rum and salt. Beat on medium speed until well blended. Stir in the toasted nut pieces.

Pour the filling into the pie shell. Bake for 40 minutes. Reduce the oven temperature to 350°F and bake until the filling is browned on top and the crust is light golden brown, 35 to 40 minutes longer. Remove from the oven and let cool for 1 hour. Cut into wedges and serve.

Makes 6 to 8 servings

POUND CAKE PAUL TREVIGNE

Alverda Smith, my friend Arthur's mother, made a wonderful pound cake one day and gave me a big slice. When I told her how much I liked it, she gave me a photocopy of the recipe she had used. She thought it came from the New Orleans Public Service Inc. cookbook, affectionately known as the NOPSI cookbook. Maybe it came from the original printing, because when I bought a copy of the new edition, the recipe wasn't there. I've tweaked the old recipe a little to make it my own. But I want to give credit to Mrs. Catherine Bouis in Kenner. It was her recipe for Southern Chocolate Chip Pecan Pound Cake that Mrs. Smith gave me. It inspired my sweet tribute to Paul Trevigne, editor of the original New Orleans *Tribune* and one of the great heroes of Faubourg Treme.

1 cup unsalted butter, at room temperature

1½ cups sugar

1 teaspoon vanilla extract

6 large eggs

¼ cup whole milk

¼ teaspoon salt

2½ cups cake flour

2 cups semisweet chocolate chips

1 cup pecans, chopped

Preheat the oven to 325°F. Butter an 8- or 10-inch Bundt pan.

Combine the butter with the sugar in the bowl of a stand mixer and beat on high speed until pale and fluffy, about 7 minutes. Stop the machine, scrape down the sides of the bowl, and add the vanilla. Beat on medium speed for another 2 minutes.

Add the eggs, 1 or 2 at a time, mixing on medium speed until well blended after each addition. Add the milk and salt and beat briefly to mix. Reduce the speed to low and add the flour, a little at a time, mixing until just incorporated. Remove the bowl from the mixer and fold in half of the chocolate chips.

Sprinkle the pecans into the prepared pan. Pour the batter over the pecans. Evenly distribute the rest of the chocolate chips over the top. They will sink as the cake bakes.

Bake until a toothpick inserted into the center comes out clean, about 65 minutes. Transfer to a wire rack and let cool, then invert and unmold the cake onto a platter. Cut into wedges and serve.

Makes 10 servings

LADONNA BATISTE-WILLIAMS

They tell me this is how it used to go: The Italian man would front the black man the money to open a barroom. He would give him his liquor on credit, and rent him the jukebox and the slot machines. The black man might not ever pay back all the money. Sometimes he would. Sometimes he ended up owning the bar and maybe even some rental property or another little business. Whether that's how Johnnie Flowers did it, I don't know. But as he got older, my grandfather talked about Johnnie Flowers all the time.

Johnnie Flowers had the Dixie Tavern Uptown in Black Pearl, right in the Riverbend, at Cherokee and Ann. (I know. They changed the name to Garfield Street. But the old timers always call it Cherokee and Ann, and they still have that name on the blue street marker in the banquette.) He had as much money as the preachers and the undertakers. Diamond tie pin. Pinky ring to match. Shiny Caddy out front. Not a pretty man, but a real man who could look at you and suck his teeth just so and you would know what he was talking about. I never saw a picture of him, but I could see that.

"Johnny Flowers's place was a lounge. It wasn't no barroom." That's what my granddaddy said. That was in the '40s and '50s when he was going there. They had Wynonie Harris, Joe Liggins, Ruth Brown, Amos Milburn—them kind of singers on the jukebox.

He stopped going there during World War II. That was when a lot of the men were working with white men building ships for the war. It got so the white men would bring their black women to the bar. It was illegal, just like it was illegal for blacks to be in a whites-only place. Granddaddy told Johnnie Flowers that if he wasn't gonna let black men bring white women in the place, he ought not let nobody break the law. But Johnnie Flowers was a businessman, not no activist.

Just like some businesses had signs on the door, "Closed for the duration," my grandfather boycotted Johnnie Flowers for the duration of the war. Eventually he went back, though.

When I got grown, I passed over there one time. It had long since been closed. I could see from the outside it wasn't a big place. It didn't seem big enough to hold all the dancing and the gambling and the smoking and the couples in the dark. But memory, you know. . . .

That's where I think my daddy got the idea from to buy Gigi's, hearing his daddy talk. He had just come back from Vietnam. He was mad at the world in general and white people in particular. He didn't want to work for any white man. He wasn't political. Not no black power militant. But all that was in the air and he had to hear it. When he saw Gigi's was for sale, he bought it and started fixing it up. He built the shelves and everything himself.

My mother never really liked the bar, but she got used to it. She used to send me or my brother over there with my daddy's supper. That's why it was always important to my daddy that there wasn't no whole lot of cursing or disrespect happening in there. Children weren't allowed except to come in and buy a bag of potato chips or a cold drink. But he wanted it so your mama didn't have to worry if she sent you there to get your daddy or to buy her a bottle of beer or whatever.

I liked it. I used to sit around, pretending that I had to wait to bring daddy's plate home. I liked hearing the men talk grown-folks' business. Soon, I was putting ice in the glasses and handing the beer bottles to my daddy to open. Then on Thursdays, mama would make a pot of something to sell, and I would dish that up. It was fun 'til I started getting a few curves and my daddy wouldn't let me hang out there any more. When I got out of school, I had a little job at the phone company, and he let me help him out on weekends. Then, eventually, I took over.

Because I grew up in it, I never thought about Gigi's. It was just Gigi's. And even when I opened back up after the storm, it was just what I was supposed to do. I didn't have a philosophy about it.

But you know, ain't but three places people go all the time, really. Maybe four. Home, work, their barroom, and church. Home is always some drama. Either you have to worry about setting an example for the kids or you have to argue with your wife or your husband about the money or the new carpet or the in-laws. At work, you better be on your best behavior if you want to keep your little job. So where can you go and just do you? Where can you go and not be responsible for anybody but your own damn self? Where can you go where people love you and know you, but don't expect anything from you?

It's not just Gigi's. It's all the little corner, neighborhood barrooms where people go to remember what they want to remember and forget what they want to forget. One time, I was in a place up in Chicago, and a photographer wanted to take some pictures. The bartender told him, "No pictures. Some of these people not who they supposed to be."

You can make out of that what you want. But we all need a place to go where we can not be who we supposed to be.

These are great places. These are good places.

CREOLE GUMBO

1 dozen fresh crabs
(about 2 pounds total weight)

2 pounds medium to large
shrimp, heads and tails intact

5 quarts water

1 pound andouille sausage

1 pound smoked sausage

¾ pound **Creole hot sausage**

2 tablespoons vegetable oil,
plus ¾ cup

2 pounds fresh or thawed frozen
okra, trimmed and cut crosswise
into ½-inch pieces

¾ cup all-purpose flour

2 large yellow onions, coarsely
chopped

2 tablespoons unsalted butter

1 bunch green onions, white and
tender green parts, chopped

5 celery stalks, chopped

1 large bell pepper, seeded and
chopped

6 cloves garlic, chopped

1 bunch fresh flat-leaf parsley,
chopped

4 bay leaves

1 tablespoon Basic Creole
Seasoning Blend (page 228)

2 tablespoons filé powder

1 pound fresh crabmeat, white,
lump or claw, picked over for
cartilage and shell fragments

Salt and freshly ground pepper

Hot cooked rice for serving

Makes 10 servings

They have so many different kinds of gumbo these days. Looks like they just put the word "gumbo" on the menu so tourists will buy it. But this is real New Orleans Creole gumbo, not that old Cajun stuff with the burned roux. On restaurant menus these days, they tell you what's in the gumbo—chicken and andouille gumbo or seafood gumbo. A real Creole gumbo always has shrimp, crab, and some kind of sausage. The rest is up to who's cooking it. But you don't never have tell people all the meat you have in there. If they know it's Creole gumbo, they already know what's in it.

I'll never forget I walked into Bachemin's meat market on St. Bernard to buy me some hot sausage and pickle meat. I guess the sign had always been there, but look like I was reading it for the first time. "We make our hot sausage just like our forefather's did. All beef." It never occurred to me that Creole hot sausage was made with beef. It's a fresh sausage, it's not smoked. It's like Italian sausage in terms of how it will naturally crumble apart if you take it out of the casing. But the seasoning is totally different. It's real red, so it must have a lot of cayenne and paprika in it. Probably a lot of garlic powder too. I've never seen it outside New Orleans. But now, since the storm, maybe you can find it in the places our people got exiled to. I know Vaucresson is back in business selling sausage, even though their store hasn't opened back up.

When you serve it, it's like a soup. Don't pick the meat out and just spoon a little gravy on top. That's what out of town folks do and I hate it. You're supposed to eat it with a spoon because the juice and all the ingredients have flavor.

Clean the crabs, removing the lungs, hearts, and glands and other parts so that only the parts of the shell containing meat (including the legs, swimmers, and claws) remain. Refrigerate the meaty parts of the crab. Put the portions of the crab that have been removed in a stockpot.

Peel and devein the shrimp, adding the heads and shells to the stockpot, along with the water. Put the shrimp in a covered bowl and refrigerate. Bring the stock to a boil over high heat, then reduce the heat to medium and simmer the stock for 30 minutes. Remove from the heat and let cool. When the stock has cooled, strain it into a bowl and discard the solids. Return the stock to the stockpot and set aside.

Cut all the sausage into 1-inch rounds. Working in batches, cook them in an ungreased skillet over medium-high heat, turning occasionally, until the pieces are slightly brown and some of their fat has been rendered, about 8 minutes per batch. Drain and discard the excess fat before putting the next batch of sausage into the skillet. As each batch is complete, put it in the seafood stock.

In a 12-inch skillet over high heat, heat the 2 tablespoons vegetable oil. Add the okra, reduce the heat to medium, and sauté the okra until slightly browned and much of the slime has dried out, about 45 minutes. Put the okra in the seafood stock.

In a large (12-quart) soup pot or clean stockpot, heat the ¾ cup vegetable oil over medium heat. When the oil is hot, add the flour slowly, 1 tablespoon at a time, stirring constantly. When all the flour has been added, continue cooking and stirring the roux until it gets to a medium brown color, somewhere between the color of caramel and milk chocolate. Add the yellow onions to the roux, stirring constantly. When the onions are wilted and slightly browned, 5 to 8 minutes, add the seafood stock to the roux along with the sausage and okra and bring to a simmer, still over medium heat.

continued

In a skillet over medium heat, melt the butter. Add the green onions, celery, bell pepper, garlic, and parsley and cook, stirring, until the vegetables wilt but don't brown, about 5 minutes. Add the vegetables to the pot and toss in the bay leaves. Return to a simmer and cook for 30 minutes to allow the flavors to blend. Add the reserved crab pieces and shrimp and cook for another 15 minutes. Remove the gumbo from the stove, add the Creole seasoning, and let rest for 15 to 20 minutes. As it cools, oil should form on the top. Skim it off. Add the filé powder and stir. Add the crabmeat and stir gently. Taste the gumbo and adjust the seasoning with salt and/or pepper, if needed.

Serve hot in shallow soup bowls or large rimmed plates, over the steamed rice.

SMOTHERED TURNIP SOUP

When somebody invites you to their house for gumbo, you are supposed to arrive ready to eat gumbo. That's pretty simple, right?

I was trying to be nice to my in-laws and invite them over for my gumbo. Larry's brother, Bernard, and his wife, Victorine, showed up. Now I had told Miss Thang what was on the menu in advance. All of a sudden, she doesn't eat meat this week. No, it wasn't Lent, but apparently it was free-pass day at the crazy house, so her loopy ass was roaming the streets free. These days, I wouldn't put up with it. But that wasn't long after I had gotten married, so I was trying to be accommodating.

I had some turnip bottoms in the ice box that I had smothered. I hadn't even put any pickle' meat in them. I figured that would make a nice soup for her while we were eating gumbo. The problem was, I had used all my milk for the pound cake. I just came up with this recipe on the fly, with what I had in the house. It was so good, everybody wanted to get some of it after they finished their gumbo.

½ cup (1 stick) unsalted butter, plus 1 tablespoon butter for finishing

3 yellow onions, chopped

4 pounds turnips, peeled and cut crosswise into ¼-inch-thick slices

1 cup white or brown rice

3 cloves garlic, minced

¾ teaspoon dried basil

¾ teaspoon dried thyme

¼ teaspoon cayenne pepper

4 cups vegetable broth or Basic Chicken Stock (page 230)

About 6 cups water

Salt and freshly ground black pepper

Finely chopped green onions for garnish

In a heavy 7-quart saucepan or large Dutch oven, melt the ½ cup butter over medium-high heat. Add the onions and turnips, stirring to coat each slice of turnip with the melted butter. Spread the vegetables evenly over the pan bottom and cook, without stirring, until all the vegetables are lightly to moderately browned, about 10 minutes. Next, stir thoroughly to allow more unbrowned vegetables to touch the pan bottom, and let these cook without stirring for another 5 to 10 minutes. Continue cooking the vegetables until they are all well browned, about 30 minutes longer, stirring thoroughly every 5 to 10 minutes. Toward the end of the browning process, stir more often and scrape the pan bottom clean as you stir to prevent burning.

Once the vegetables are finished browning, add the rice, garlic, basil, thyme, cayenne, and broth to the pan, stirring and scraping up any browned bits from the pan bottom. Cover the pan, raise the heat to high, and bring the liquid to a boil. Reduce the heat to low and cook until the vegetables are very tender, about 50 minutes, stirring occasionally.

Stir 4 cups of the water into the soup and raise the heat to medium. Re-cover the pan and continue cooking until the turnips and rice are tender, about 1 hour longer. Add the 1 tablespoon butter and stir until melted into the soup. Remove the pan from the heat and, while still hot, purée the soup in small batches in an electric blender. Thin with 2 cups or more water, if needed, for the desired consistency. Season with salt and black pepper.

Ladle into large soup bowls and sprinkle with the green onions. Serve at once.

Makes 12 to 14 appetizer servings or 6 to 8 main-course servings

JALAPEÑO CORNBREAD

2 large fresh jalapeño chiles
(about 2 ounces total weight)

2 teaspoons vegetable oil

2¼ cups all-purpose flour

1 cup yellow cornmeal

Scant 1 cup sugar

3 tablespoons baking powder

2 tablespoons kosher salt

Heaping ¼ teaspoon freshly
ground pepper

2 large eggs plus 1 large egg
white, lightly beaten together

1½ cups whole buttermilk, well
shaken

¾ cup (1½ sticks) unsalted butter,
melted and cooled

2 medium yellow onions, finely
chopped (about 1½ cups)

2 tablespoons bacon fat or
unsalted butter

Pure Cane Syrup Butter

½ cup unsalted butter, at room
temperature

2 tablespoons pure cane syrup,
preferably Steen's

2 teaspoons kosher salt (optional)

I get a lot of compliments on my cornbread. I don't like that old rough, dry, country cornbread. This is almost like a cake, it's so light. It's good alongside some greens. But, if you whip up some Steen's cane syrup with butter, it's a great snack or even dessert. If you put the kosher salt in the cane syrup butter, it's not going to melt. But I like that little crunch you get.

You'll see I prefer to use whole-fat buttermilk and bacon fat instead of butter in the bread. You can substitute lighter ingredients, but really, it's not that bad for you. Those fats sneak in a nice extra layer of flavor.

Position a rack in the middle of the oven and preheat to 450°F.

Put the jalapeños on a 5-inch square of aluminum foil and fold up the edges of the foil to form a shallow bowl. Pour the oil evenly over the peppers and bake for 15 minutes, turning once. Remove from the oven and seal the foil tightly to let the peppers steam for about 15 minutes. Set aside. Leave the oven set at 450°F.

In a large bowl, whisk together the flour, cornmeal, sugar, baking powder, salt, and pepper. Add the eggs and egg white, buttermilk, and melted butter and mix just until all the ingredients are incorporated; do not overmix. Set the batter aside.

Peel the jalapeños, remove and discard the membranes and seeds, and finely chop the flesh. Stir the jalapeños and onions into the batter.

Heat a 10-inch cast-iron skillet over high heat for 30 seconds. Add the bacon fat and rub with a paper towel to grease the sides and bottom of the skillet. Heat the skillet for 1½ minutes longer, then pour the batter into the pan. Immediately transfer the skillet to the middle shelf of the oven and bake until the cornbread is golden brown and a toothpick inserted into the center comes out clean, about 30 minutes. Remove from the oven and let cool for 30 minutes.

Meanwhile, make the cane syrup butter: In a small serving bowl, combine the butter, cane syrup, and salt, if using. Stir, mashing the mixture with the back of a spoon to blend well.

When the cornbread has cooled, turn it out onto a round serving platter. Cut into wedges and serve. Pass the cane syrup butter at the table.

Makes 10 to 12 servings

YEAST CALAS

When I was coming up, we always had calas (rice fritters) when somebody made their First Communion. My mama tells me women used to walk all around the 6th and 7th Wards selling calas from baskets, like Mr. Okra does from his truck nowadays. People don't celebrate First Communion with the calas so much anymore. I don't even make them as much as I used to. But the boys love them whenever I do.

In a small bowl, dissolve the yeast in the lukewarm water and set aside.

In a medium bowl, using a wooden spoon or rubber spatula, combine the rice and eggs. Add 1 cup of the flour, the brown sugar, the salt, and the nutmeg; mix well. Mix in up to 1 cup additional flour, just enough to make a batter that is thick but liquid enough to be dropped easily from a spoon. Add the yeast mixture and stir to mix thoroughly. Cover with a clean dish towel and let stand overnight at room temperature.

Pour the oil into a deep fryer or Dutch oven and heat to 350°F on a deep-frying thermometer. Drop heaping tablespoons of the batter into the oil a few at a time, being careful not to crowd the pot, and fry until nicely browned, 2 to 3 minutes. If the batter doesn't hold together in the oil, stir in a little more flour, 1 tablespoon at a time, until it does. Drain on a double thickness of paper towels.

Dust with powdered sugar and serve hot.

Makes 24 calas; serves 6 to 8

1 envelope (2¼ teaspoons) active dry yeast

½ cup lukewarm water

2 cups cooked and cooled medium-grain white rice (real rice, not instant or parboiled)

3 large eggs, beaten

1 to 2 cups all-purpose flour, or as needed

½ cup firmly packed light brown sugar

½ teaspoon salt

½ teaspoon freshly grated nutmeg

1 quart peanut oil

Powdered sugar for dusting

POTATO SALAD

8 red potatoes
(about 3 to 4 pounds total
weight), peeled and quartered

6 large eggs

¼ cup prepared yellow mustard

½ teaspoon cayenne pepper

2 tablespoons minced yellow
onion

3 large green onions, white and
tender green parts, minced
(about 5 tablespoons)

¼ cup chopped green bell pepper

1 cup mayonnaise

1 to 2 tablespoons fresh lemon
juice

1½ teaspoons Basic Creole
Seasoning Blend (page 228)

1 teaspoon finely ground black or
white pepper

2 tablespoons chopped fresh
flat-leaf parsley

1 teaspoon paprika

I don't eat potato salad from just anybody.

I don't like celery in my potato salad. It makes it too watery.

I don't like pickles in my potato salad, sweet neither dill.

I just like plain potato salad. A lot of people put potato salad in their gumbo these days. You can do that if you want to. My husband does, but I never do.

Place the potatoes in a Dutch oven and add cold water to cover. Bring the water to a boil over medium heat. Boil the potatoes until tender but not mushy, about 15 minutes.

Meanwhile, in a large saucepan, combine the eggs and add enough cool water so that there is at least 1 inch between the top of the eggs and the surface of the water. Bring the eggs to a boil over high heat. As soon as the water comes to a boil, reduce the heat to medium-high and simmer for another 10 minutes. Pour off the hot water and fill the pot with cool water to stop the eggs from cooking. Set aside at room temperature to cool, then refrigerate.

Drain the potatoes in a colander and let sit in the sink until all the excess water has drained, about 5 minutes, then transfer the potatoes to a deep bowl. Add the mustard and cayenne and mix with a large fork, taking care not to mash the potatoes. Peel the eggs and put them into the bowl with the potatoes. Refrigerate the eggs and potatoes until thoroughly cooled, about 30 minutes.

In a bowl, combine the yellow onion, 2 tablespoons of the green onion, the bell pepper, ⅔ cup of the mayonnaise, and about half of the lemon juice. Remove the potatoes and eggs from the refrigerator. Chop 5 of the eggs and set aside. Place the potatoes on a cutting board, and chop into small cubes, then return to the bowl and gradually stir in the mayonnaise mixture until thoroughly blended. Add the Creole seasoning, pepper, and chopped eggs and stir gently. Fold in the remaining ⅓ cup mayonnaise, remaining 3 tablespons green onion and the remaining lemon juice.

Smooth the top of the salad with a spoon or spatula, then slice the remaining egg and place as a garnish on top, along with the chopped parsley and paprika. Serve at once, or cover and refrigerate for up to 3 days.

Makes 12 servings

Oven-Braised Turkey Necks

You have to have something tasty but inexpensive to bring the after-work crowd into a bar. It has to be salty enough to make them thirsty, but you can't oversalt it. I have different specials on different days, but the one my crowd mostly seems to love is these turkey necks.

A lot of people boil their turkey necks in the pot right alongside crabs or crawfish, just letting the crab-boil season it. I prefer this method. You just set them in the oven and forget about them. It's not quick, but it is easy. Serve with hot rice or greens or both.

Preheat the oven to 350°F.

Season the turkey-neck pieces all over with the 1½ tablespoons Creole seasoning as you spread them in the bottom of a large heavy-bottomed, ovenproof saucepan or large Dutch oven. Add the onions, celery, bell pepper, garlic, and bay leaf, but no liquid. Cover the pan and bake for 2 hours without

stirring. Stir well, then continue cooking until the meat is close to falling off the bone, 1½ to 2 hours more, stirring every 30 minutes. A few minutes before the necks are done, taste and add more Creole seasoning, if desired.

Serve at once with the rice on the side, and pass the hot sauce.

5 pounds turkey necks, cut into 4- to 5-inch pieces

1½ tablespoons Basic Creole Seasoning Blend (page 228)

3 medium yellow onions, coarsely chopped

2 celery stalks with leaves, coarsely chopped

½ large green bell pepper, seeded and coarsely chopped

6 large cloves garlic, chopped

1 bay leaf

Hot cooked rice for serving

Hot sauce for serving

Makes 4 servings

Cajun v. Creole (v. Alan Richman)

Defining Creole food can be tough. And defining Cajun food can be tough. But trying to define each of them in such a way that the distinctions are clear is a whole other magnitude of toughness. Cajun and Creole are like Siamese twins: there are parts that obviously belong to one or the other. But I would hate to be the surgeon given a scalpel and the job of separating them without losing either patient. The two cuisines share the same major dishes—gumbo, red beans, jambalaya, étouffée. And whether you're in a Cajun house or a Creole house, you're going to find some of the same dishes and main ingredients that you'll find all over the South—grits, cornbread, fried catfish, fried chicken, okra, black-eyed peas.

We were getting along just fine down here, despite our murky differences. Then Alan Richman came to New Orleans after the federal flood and inserted himself in the discussion. He then proceeded to do a hatchet job for *GQ* on New Orleans food.

"Supposedly, Creoles can be found in and around New Orleans. I have never met one and suspect they are a faerie folk, like leprechauns, rather than an indigenous race," Richman wrote. "The myth is that once, long ago, Creoles existed. Certainly there was a Creole cuisine, a fancified amalgamation of French (mainly), Spanish (just a little), Italian (even less), and African-Caribbean (unavoidable). The African-Caribbean influence was the kind of fortuitous culinary accident that occurs when the swells eating the food don't come from the same background as the workers cooking the food."

The African-Caribbean influence "unavoidable?" It sounds like he's talking about yellow fever rather than one of the building blocks of American food.

He confessed in the beginning of the piece that he never really liked our food ("I'm not certain the cuisine was ever as good as its reputation") and nothing he ate on that trip changed his mind. But neither he nor his editors seemed to think that his admitted prejudgment disqualified him from rendering new judgments. New Orleanians were not amused. "Richman seems genuinely convinced that discovering schmaltz in a tourist-heavy culture amounts to breaking news," Brett Anderson wrote in the *Times-Picayune*. "And he devotes endless ink to the Cajun vs. Creole thing, a topic he has mastered roughly as well as Rush Limbaugh has Parkinson's. (According to Richman, Cajun food was 'brought down from Canada.')"

No shrinking violet, Richman did a podcast interview expounding on the foolishness he put in his essay. "New Orleans shouldn't exist. Let's start with that premise. New Orleans has no business existing, certainly not as it is now," he said.

My blood simmers just remembering the moment when I read the transcript. I would have calmed down eventually. But then that son of a bitch came into Brulard's while I was working there. Between Brulard's tortures and Richman's insults, I had no choice: I had to throw a drink in his face. A Sazerac, the state cocktail of Louisiana.

But though it pains me to, I've got to admit something. Richman was "right," at least to this extent: it is really hard to define Cajun or Creole, and most New Orleanians can't. But that's probably because they are so confident they know what the word means, that they haven't bothered to study it. Probably a lot of us human beings couldn't define "air," though we know what it is.

Cajuns are easily distinguished by geography and history. They are descendants of the Acadians, French Canadians who settled in southwest Louisiana after the French lost the French-Indian War in the 1700s; "Cajun" is a contraction of the word "Acadian." But Cajun country is not monolithic. The proportions may vary; you have the same mix of white, black, and Native American in that area as you do in much of south Louisiana. Some of the food traditions were certainly brought down from Canada, as Richman asserts. But, as chef Donald Link (of famed New Orleans restaurants Herbsaint and Cochon) makes a point of reminding us, many Cajun sausage traditions have their roots in the food of our German immigrants. By now, Cajun recipes and traditions have been so thoroughly integrated into Louisiana cuisine as to no longer be particularly Canadian.

The word Creole is a lot less specific.

In New Orleans, the rough translation of "Creole" is "ours." We celebrate Creole tomatoes down here, but nobody claims that the tomatoes grown here are of a genetically different variety. Creole tomato merely means a tomato grown in certain parishes in southern Louisiana, Plaquemines Parish being the most important in this regard. They get their favored "Creole" status just because they are grown in our soil.

In her book *Africans in Colonial Louisiana*, Gwendolyn Midlo Hall says that the word "Creole" was first applied in South America by African slaves to their children, who, unlike their parents, were born in the Americas, not in Africa. What remains consistent between that definition and the definitions people use today is this idea of the Old World and New World coming together. These days, you find "Creole" or its Spanish equivalent, "Criollo," on menus all over the Caribbean and Latin America, as if to say the food is not quite Spanish or French or Cameroonian or Senegalese or Taino, but a little bit of them all.

Creole also has a specifically racial definition. Sometimes people use the term when they are referring to people of mixed race or people who are tan or light brown, as if they by definition had parents of different races.

In terms of food, there are a few obvious differences between Cajun and Creole. The emblematic Cajun sausage is andouille, a coarse-ground smoked sausage. The emblematic Creole sausage is chaurice, a fresh, not smoked, sausage. The emblematic Cajun seasoning meat is tasso, spicy smoked pork shoulder. Tasso's Creole counterpart is pickled pork shoulder, or pickled meat or "pickle meat." Cajun gumbos tend to be meat based, generally andouille sausage joined by chicken, duck, or turkey in a dark, roux-based gravy, while Creole gumbo tends to be a mix of sausage and seafood—shrimp, crabs, and oysters specifically. The roux in a Creole gumbo is usually not as dark as a Cajun roux. And filé powder, the ground sassafras leaves used for thickening soups, stews, and gumbos around here, is much more often used in Cajun than in Creole gumbos, for which okra is usually the thickener of choice.

It's about a two-hour drive from New Orleans to Cajun country. Even in the days before everyone had a car, the distance between New Orleans, the Creole capital, and Lafayette, its Cajun component, wasn't great. As people traveled, so did their ideas about cooking techniques and ingredients. So Cajun and Creole food certainly influenced each other. Paul Prudhomme, one of the most influential American chefs of the 1980s hailed from Cajun country, but he cooked at Commander's Palace, the grand dame of Creole restaurants in New Orleans, before opening his own place, K-Paul's. A whole generation of chefs, including Greg Sonnier, Frank Brigtsen, and Emeril Lagasse, trained under Chef Paul before striking out on their own. How can you measure the degree of Cajun influence on these New Orleans chefs? Because Chef Paul and his blackened redfish craze swept the country by storm, Cajun became as much a way to market food as to describe it. Chefs around the country started adding pepper to their food and calling it "Cajun," as if pepper was the only difference between Cajun food and Amish food. Even in New Orleans, restaurants started promoting "Cajun" food because that's what the tourists wanted. You can be sure that the young man earning minimum wage to stand outside a French Quarter tourist trap and herd you inside isn't prepared to compare and contrast various Louisiana foods.

One final difference between Creole and Cajun cuisines could be the difference between rural and urban. New Orleans has been a sophisticated city for a long time. There are myriad fancy restaurants tailored to the well-heeled, be they natives or visitors. Restaurant chefs have embraced traditional New Orleans Creole cuisine for some time now; you'll see many a gumbo and jambalaya on the menu at white-tablecloth restaurants. Cajun country, by contrast, has long been off the beaten path. The fact that most of the residents spoke French until a few decades ago meant that it wasn't as attractive a tourist destination. So Cajun food is arguably less influenced by fine-dining chefs or out-of-town critics.

This is perhaps the point in this sort of essay when you're supposed to say, "It doesn't matter what you call it, as long as it tastes good." But it does matter. The ethnic origins of a dish shouldn't determine whether you like it. But if history and anthropology and food itself are worth studying, they are worth getting right. As Lolis Eric Elie pointed out in a column in the *Times-Picayune*, one of Alan Richman's great sins was confusing the unknown with the unknowable. I know what I'm writing here is not the last word on what's Creole and what's Cajun. I'm just saying that each of these words has meaning and, if you're willing to engage in even a little study, you can shed a little light on the big mystery.

MICROWAVE PRALINES

You would think I'd've been the one telling my mother about microwave pralines. But no—she was the one telling me. I guess after all those years of toil and trouble cooking from scratch, she was glad to see an easier way. These taste just as good as the ones we used to make on the stove, I promise you. But one thing you need to be aware of: if it's real humid, sometimes the pralines don't set right. Nowhere on Earth is more humid than New Orleans, and I make them here all the time. But don't think you can be inside making pralines on a day when it's hot and rainy outside.

In the unlikely event your first try produces a batter that comes out too runny to set up properly into distinct pralines, don't worry: It will still make a generous 3 cups of "praline sauce" to serve over ice cream or unfrosted cake, or even with the *calas* on page 127. And in case you want to make the praline sauce on purpose, the instructions are also in the recipe.

You don't have to have a handle on the dish you use. But if you don't want to burn the hell out of your hand, it'll help. In fact, I usually wear heavy oven mitts, too, when I'm doing this dish. Also, please note: chopped nuts are too small for pralines and pecan halves are too big. Cut the halves in half.

1 pound light brown sugar

1 cup heavy (whipping) cream plus 1 to 3 teaspoons cream or milk for thinning batter

2 tablespoons light corn syrup

2 cups pecan halves, cut in half again (in other words, not too big or small)

4 tablespoons unsalted butter, at room temperature, cut into 4 pieces

1 tablespoon vanilla extract

Line a heatproof surface like a countertop or 2 baking sheets with wax paper.

In an 8-cup microwave-safe glass measuring cup with a handle, combine the brown sugar, cream, and corn syrup, mixing until all the sugar lumps are dissolved and the batter is well blended.

Position the measuring cup in the microwave so you can see how the batter inside measures; the batter will be at or near the 2½-cup mark. Microwave on high without covering or stirring, watching it continuously, until the mixture slowly bubbles up to slightly higher than the 8-cup mark and then deflates to near the 4½-cup mark, 10 to 16 minutes (depending on how quickly your microwave cooks). Do not open the microwave during the cooking process and, if in doubt, cook for less time, not more.

(If you want to make praline sauce instead of pralines, let the batter cook as directed until it has expanded to slightly over the 8-cup mark and then has slowly deflated just to the 7-cup mark. Use warm or at room temperature. Refrigerate the leftovers, tightly covered, for up to 1 week.)

Carefully remove the very hot measuring cup from the microwave and, using a sturdy metal mixing spoon, gently stir in the pecans, butter, and vanilla, being careful to not splash any of the hot mixture on your skin. Continue stirring until the mixture is noticeably less glossy, about 3 minutes.

Working quickly, and using two spoons, scoop rounded tablespoonfuls of the mixture onto the wax paper, about 1 inch apart and, using a second tablespoon to push the batter off the mixing spoon. If necessary, thin the batter with the remaining 1 to 3 teaspoons of cream as you reach the end of the batter and it thickens as it cools. Let the pralines cool to room temperature, about 20 minutes, then serve as soon as possible. Any leftovers can be stored in an airtight container at room temperature for up to 4 days.

Makes 24 to 34 two-inch pralines, or 3 cups of praline sauce

DAVIS MCALARY

Dude, for patriotism to have meaning, it has to have Tabasco sauce and a backbeat. In New Orleans, we pledge allegiance to the groove. Or, to paraphrase Aretha, you got to give the people something they can feel. That's why we love New Orleans. That's why as many of us as could, came back to the water-logged ruins and rebuilt. There's a here, here. You wake up in the morning and you smell the coffee roasting from out at the coffee plants in New Orleans East. You leave the gig late at night and you smell the grits fries frying on the Purple Bus food truck parked outside the club. What we have here is a country you can be loyal to.

Our foreign food policy is strictly free trade. Most of those caffeinated Americans who wake up early to talk about how lazy and shiftless we are have no idea that their morning coffee probably came into the country right here. The Port of New Orleans processes more coffee than any other port in the country. You want to talk tomato paste? The Uddo family, genuine New Orleans Sicilians, damn near created the imported tomato paste business before World War I. They joined with the Taormina family, their padrinos in New York, to make the Progresso Italian Food Corporation, a major player across the nation. Bananas? Look up the Standard Fruit and Steamship Company (more local Sicilians). They were putting bananas in American lunch boxes for decades before Dole bought the company in the '60s.

You know what makes our food so great? We're egalitarian about it. It doesn't cost you a fortune unless you want it to, and you'll get your money's worth regardless. The best deal on the planet is a shrimp po-boy and a Barq's from Captain Sal's. You get your gumbo at a mom-and-pop place like Fay's Honey Whip Donuts across the river (yes, gumbo from a donut shop) or from Frank Brigtsen's place in the Riverbend, it's going to be good regardless.

This is a noble thing Janette is doing, trying to put all of this in a book. She talks about how much she learned in New York, but she could cook before she left here. I think she taught those stuck-up New Yorkers a thing or two about proper seasoning and the nutritional benefits of deep-frying (it intensifies the protein).

Amen, Janette! The church of good food. Now that's a religion I can believe in.

WAFFLES (OR PANCAKES) LAFON

2 cups all-purpose flour, sifted

4 teaspoons baking powder

1 tablespoon sugar

½ teaspoon kosher salt

3 large eggs, separated

1¼ cups milk

½ cup (1 stick) unsalted butter, melted and cooled

2 tablespoons bourbon or dark rum

Maple syrup, preserves, or whatever topping you like.

There are few things in life that can't be improved with a judicious jolt of brown liquor. These waffles have bourbon (or dark rum, if you prefer) and an extra egg for a dish so rich I named it after Thomy Lafon, the great Creole philanthropist that Rodolphe Desdunes writes about in his book, *Our People, Our History*. The secret to all good waffles is whipping the egg whites into stiff peaks so that resulting waffles are light and fluffy. If you don't whip the egg whites, you just have pancake batter, which is really good too.

I like my waffles with real maple syrup. But they're also good with fig preserves, fresh fruit, powdered sugar . . . whatever grooves you.

Preheat the waffle iron according to the manufacturer's instructions.

In a large bowl, combine the flour, baking powder, sugar, and salt, stirring with a fork until thoroughly mixed.

In a medium bowl, combine the egg yolks, milk, melted butter, and bourbon and whisk until well blended. Pour into the flour mixture, stirring just until incorporated and no longer, or you will overmix the batter.

In another medium bowl, beat the egg whites with a hand mixer until stiff but not dry. Fold the egg whites into the batter until barely blended.

Bake in the hot waffle iron according to the manufacturer's instructions. Be careful not to use too much batter for each waffle or it will overflow. Serve at once.

Note: This batter can be frozen in an airtight container for up to 1 month.

Makes 6 servings

Bourbon House Trio of Oyster Shooters

CHEF DARIN NESBIT

I was in the Ferry Plaza Building in San Francisco once and saw something I couldn't believe: Gulf oysters from Louisiana were cheaper than the West Coast oysters that, presumably, had been harvested a few hundred miles closer to the market. We're spoiled here. Oysters on the half shell are everyday food for us. But Chef Darin Nesbit's trio of raw oyster recipes from Bourbon House are Gulf oysters at their royal best.

This is obviously an extravagance, but a delicious one. Unless you happen to have 72 shot glasses in your cabinet, I suggest you serve these at the beginning of a party, as the guests are milling around. You can serve the first shooter, collect and clean the glasses; serve the second shooter, collect and clean the glasses; then serve the final round. Or serve in little disposable paper cups. Or pick one or two of these that you especially like, and just make those.

To make the granité: Combine all of ingredients in a 9-by-13-inch pan, preferably metal, and stir to mix well. Place the mixture in the freezer for about 90 minutes. Remove and break up any frozen parts with the tines of a fork. Return the mixture to the freezer. Repeat every hour until the granité has the consistency of shaved ice, about 4 hours total.

While the granité is coming together, shuck the oysters. Using an oyster knife and a shucking glove or thick kitchen towel to protect your hand, shuck all the oysters, transferring the meats and their liquor to a bowl as you work. Cover and refrigerate while you prepare the rest of the shooter accompaniments. (You can also pay your oyster purveyor a fee to shuck for you.)

To make the salad: Peel the fruit, being careful to remove all of the white pith between the peel and the flesh, even if it means leaving a little of the flesh to be discarded with the peel. Cut along the membrane on the side of each section to remove the citrus supremes, transferring the flesh and any juice to a bowl as you work and discarding seeds. Stir in the vodka, zest, and pepper. Refrigerate until ready to serve. Have the mint ready in the fridge.

To make the cucumber salad: In a small bowl, combine all of the ingredients except for the seaweed salad and set aside. Have the seaweed salad handy in the refrigerator.

To make the mignonette: In a small bowl, whisk together the Champagne, vinegar, shallot, mustard, and parsley. Slowly whisk in the olive oil until smoothly emulsified. Season with salt and pepper. Set aside and have the caviar handy in the refrigerator.

When the granité is ready and all of your accompaniments—and guests—are ready, assemble the shooters as directed.

For citrus shooters, divide the citrus salad evenly among 24 shot glasses. Top each with a shucked oyster and 1 teaspoon of the granité. Garnish with the mint.

For cucumber shooters, place 1 teaspoon of the cucumber salad in the bottom of each of another 24 shot glasses. Top with an oyster, top that with another teaspoon of cucumber salad, and garnish with the seaweed salad.

For caviar shooters, place 24 oysters in another set of shot glasses. Spoon in 2 tablespoons of the mignonette and top each with a small spoonful of caviar.

Place the shooters on trays and serve at once.

Makes 4 to 12 appetizer servings

Granité

1 cup dry white wine

1 cup fresh satsuma juice or other citrus juice such as navel or blood orange juice

Dash of lemon juice

Freshly ground pepper

6 dozen raw oysters

Citrus Salad

1 ruby red grapefruit

1 blood orange

1 navel orange

½ cup citrus-flavored vodka

2 teaspoons lemon zest

Freshly ground pepper

Julienned fresh mint for garnish

Cucumber and Tobiko Salad

1 medium cucumber, peeled, seeded, and cut into ¼-inch dice (about 1 cup)

½ cup rice wine vinegar

½ teaspoon red pepper flakes

½ teaspoon minced fresh chives

½ cup wasabi tobiko

½ cup seaweed salad (available in Asian and gourmet markets and delis)

Champagne Mignonette

½ cup Champagne or sparkling wine

¼ cup rice vinegar

1 shallot, minced

1 tablespoon Creole mustard

1 tablespoon chopped fresh flat-leaf parsley

1 tablespoon olive oil

Kosher salt and freshly ground black pepper

6 ounces bowfin or other caviar

BOUCHERIE'S COLLARD GREENS
WITH FRENCH FRIED GRITS

3 bunches collard greens
(2 to 2½ pounds total weight)

8 ounces thick-sliced bacon, cut
crosswise into 1-inch pieces

1 medium yellow onion, chopped

¼ cup minced garlic (about
1 head)

1½ tablespoons chopped fresh
thyme

1½ teaspoons red pepper flakes

2 quarts Rich Chicken Stock
(page 230), Basic Chicken Stock
(page 230), or store-bought rich
chicken or turkey broth

2 cups water

French Fried Grits

1 quart whole milk

4 cloves garlic, minced

1 cup stone-ground grits

½ cup grated Cheddar cheese

½ teaspoon Tabasco sauce or
other hot sauce

¾ teaspoon salt

Freshly ground pepper

3 tablespoons unsalted butter

2 tablespoons apple cider vinegar

1 teaspoon Worcestershire sauce

1 teaspoon soy sauce

Salt and freshly ground pepper

Vegetable oil for deep-frying

Basic Creole Seasoning Blend
(page 228)

Makes 4 to 6 servings

Back before he had a restaurant, Nathaniel Zimet used to park his purple Que Crawl bus outside of nightclubs. Late at night, after hearing music and imbibing herb, you'll eat anything. But Que Crawl set the bar so high for good food, we'd go looking for that bus rather than eat anywhere else. Nathaniel's not from here, he's from North Carolina, and this isn't really a New Orleans kind of dish. I used to see the recipe for fried grits on the back of the box when I was a kid, but I never actually tasted them until chefs started putting them on menus around here. This version has a lot more flavor than the plain Jane recipe they used to have on the box.

Discard any wilted, yellow, or damaged collard leaves. Wash the remaining leaves by swirling them in a sink full of cool water, separating the leaves and giving them plenty of room to soak for a few seconds. Lift the leaves out of the water before emptying the sink, then rinse the sink, refill with fresh water, and repeat the washing process as needed until all the dirt and grit have been removed. Drain the greens briefly in a colander, then trim and discard the tough stems and spines. Chop or tear the leaves into rough 3-inch squares and set aside. Leave the colander in the sink.

In a large heavy-bottomed saucepan or Dutch oven over medium heat, fry the bacon until crispy, about 10 minutes, stirring occasionally. Add the onion, garlic, thyme, and red pepper flakes. Reduce the heat to low and cook, stirring occasionally, until the onions are translucent, about 4 minutes. Add the stock and bring to a boil over high heat. Continue boiling the liquid until reduced by about half, 15 to 20 minutes.

Meanwhile, bring the 2 cups water to a boil in a large saucepan over high heat. Add the reserved greens, cover, and boil for 2 minutes. Remove from the heat and immediately drain the greens in the colander.

When the stock mixture has finished reducing, add the drained greens to the pan. Reduce the heat to medium and cover. Cook until the greens are tender, about 2 hours, stirring occasionally.

Meanwhile, to make the grits: Have ready an ungreased 8-inch-square baking pan. In a heavy-bottomed 3-quart saucepan, combine the milk and garlic. Bring to a boil over medium-high heat, whisking occasionally. Whisk in the grits, reduce the heat to medium-low, and cook until the grits have

thickened enough to stick to the whisk for several seconds when you lift the whisk out of the grits, about 1 hour 15 minutes. Be sure to whisk often during the cooking process and almost constantly toward the end to prevent the grits from sticking to the pan bottom.

When the grits have thickened enough to stick to the whisk as described above, whisk in the cheese until it melts into the grits. Whisk in the hot sauce, salt, and season with pepper. Immediately remove from the heat and pour the mixture into the baking pan, using the back of a spoon to spread the grits into an even layer about ¼ inch thick. Let cool at room temperature for at least 30 minutes or up to about 1½ hours.

When the collards are tender, stir in the butter, vinegar, Worcestershire, and soy sauce and season with salt and pepper. Keep the greens warm over low heat while deep-frying the grits.

Just before deep-frying the grits, pour at least 2 inches of oil into a 12-inch sauté pan or deep skillet and heat to 350°F on a deep-frying thermometer. Meanwhile, cut the grits into the shape of French fries about ½ inch by ¾ inch thick and 2 inches long. Next, lightly roll the pieces between your palms to make the fries slightly thinner and about 3 inches long. (Don't worry if the fries don't all look exactly alike.) Fry the grits in batches in the hot oil until golden brown all over, about 3 minutes total, carefully turning them at least once with a spatula. Drain briefly on paper towels, then sprinkle fries very lightly with Creole seasoning.

Serve the greens with some of the broth in large shallow soup bowls, garnished with the fried grits.

ELEVEN 79'S
PASTA BOLOGNESE

One #10 can (6 pounds 6 ounces, or 102 ounces) whole plum tomatoes, preferably San Marzano

½ cup olive oil

1 pound ground beef

1 pound ground veal

1 pound ground pork

½ pound Italian sausage, removed from the casing and chopped

2 ounces guanciale or pancetta, chopped

½ pound veal sweet breads, chopped (optional)

2 or 3 chicken livers, chopped (optional)

1 large yellow onion, finely chopped

1 bunch green onions, white and tender green parts, chopped

6 cloves garlic, chopped

3 carrots, peeled and finely chopped

½ cup dry white wine

1 cup Basic Chicken Stock (page 230) or store-bought chicken broth

½ teaspoon ground sage

1½ teaspoons dried oregano

2 tablespoons chopped fresh basil

Pinch of red pepper flakes

½ teaspoon sugar

Salt and freshly ground black pepper

½ cup milk

2 pounds dried bucatini

½ cup freshly grated Parmesan cheese, preferably Parmigiano-Reggiano

Joe Segreto is a New Orleans institution. He managed the great Louis Prima; he revived Broussard's restaurant after Joe Broussard's death; and he opened that standard bearer of Sicilian Creole cuisine, Restaurant Eleven 79. Why has this man never been elected mayor?

The recipe calls for a #10 can of tomatoes. Of course, most home cooks will just use three and a half of those 28-ounce cans. But calling it a #10 can is old school restaurant lingo. It's Joe Segreto's way.

Pour the tomatoes with their liquid into a large bowl and crush by hand. Set aside.

In a large pot, heat the olive oil over medium-high heat. Add the beef, veal, pork, Italian sausage, guanciale, and sweetbreads and chicken livers, if using. Cook, stirring often and using the spoon to break up the ground meats, until all the meats are browned, 10 to 15 minutes. Remove from the heat. Using a slotted spoon, transfer all the meat to a large bowl and set aside.

Return the pot to medium-high heat and add the yellow onion, green onions, garlic, and carrots. Sauté, stirring constantly, until the yellow onion turns transparent and is just starting to turn brown, about 5 minutes. Add the wine and stir to scrape up any browned bits from the pan bottom. Cook until the liquid is reduced by half, about 5 minutes. Add the chicken stock, bring to a simmer, and cook for 10 minutes.

Add the meats and any juices accumulated in the bowl and stir to blend. Stir in the tomatoes and all of their liquid. Add the sage, oregano, basil, red pepper flakes, sugar, and season with salt and pepper. Stir to mix

all the ingredients evenly. Reduce the heat to low and cook for 1½ hours. Stir in the milk and cook until thickened and flavorful, about 30 minutes longer. Taste and adjust the seasoning.

While the Bolognese sauce finishes cooking, bring a pot three-fourths full of water to a boil and stir in 1 tablespoon salt. When the water is boiling, add the bucatini and cook until al dente, 10 to 12 minutes or according to the package directions. Drain and rinse briefly, but leave most of the cooking water clinging to the noodles.

Using tongs, divide the pasta among individual plates, or pile on a platter family style. Spoon the sauce over the pasta. (If serving family style, toss to coat the noodles evenly with the sauce.) Sprinkle the cheese on top and serve at once.

Makes 12 to 14 servings

Signature Sandwiches:
Po-Boys, Poor Boys, and Muffalettas

Philly is triply blessed with hoagies, cheesesteaks, and roast pork sandwiches. Chicago double-dips its Italian beef. Buffalo places its beef on weck. Louisville broils its hot browns. Memphis mounts its barbecue shoulder sandwiches with coleslaw (but so do many places in the smoky pork kingdom of the Southeast). Boston rolls its lobster cold and fries its clams hot. The Coney Island hot dog is native, ironically, to Detroit. Grouper sandwiches are the standard in much of Florida (though some doubt whether all that "grouper" really comes from grouper, if you catch my drift).

In New Orleans, "sandwich" usually means po-boys (or poor boys) and muffalettas. Poor boys take you way back to the days when streetcar drivers were represented by Local 194. Bennie and Clovis Martin moved from Raceland, Louisiana, in the nineteen-teens and worked as streetcar conductors. In 1922, they opened Martin Brothers' Coffee Stand and Restaurant in the French Market. Seven years later the streetcar motormen and conductors were out on strike and things got heated. Management called in strikebreakers from New York. The Martin brothers wrote an open letter to their union brothers:

New Orleans, La. Aug.6th.1929,

To the Striking Carmen, Division 194,
Dear Friends,

We are with you heart andSoule, at any time you are around the French Market, dont forget to drop in at Martin's Coffee Stand & Restaurant, Cor. Ursuline & North Peters Sts,,our meal is free to any members of Division 194.

We have thirty nine employees , all riding Jitneys to help win the strike.

We are with you till h--l freezes , and when it does, we will furnish blankets to keep you warm,

With best wishes for your cause, We are,

Your friends & Former Members of Division 194

Clovis J. & Bennie Martin.

Bennie Martin would later recall, "We fed those men free of charge until the strike ended. Whenever we saw one of the striking men coming, one of us would say, 'Here comes another poor boy.'" Hence the name of the sandwich.

Po-boys, as they are more commonly known now, are served on long loaves of New Orleans French bread. The local version of the bread is much lighter than a traditional baguette and, while it won't win any points from artisan bread purists, its light, crisp crust is perfectly suited to its purpose. Roast beef, fried shrimp, and fried oysters are the three mainstays of the po-boy family, but everything from ham and cheese, fried catfish, liver cheese, and even French fries can be made into a po-boy. When you order a sandwich "dressed," it comes with mayonnaise, pickles, sliced tomatoes, and lettuce (iceberg, of course.) When you add catsup and hot sauce to the mayonnaise on a seafood po-boy, it's like creating your own special cocktail sauce.

If you're trying to make a po-boy and you don't have access to New Orleans French bread, I'd recommend substituting ciabatta. That Italian bread is a bit less dense than a traditional French baguette.

The muffaletta is like a cousin to the hoagie. Both combine cured meats, cheese, and pickled peppers. The muffaletta's signature features are its flat, seeded, oversize Sicilian roll and the salad of pickled olives and olive oil that are spread on in a generous layer before the sandwich is closed up. Muffalettas tend to vary only in temperature. They're traditionally served cold, but the Napoleon House and Cochon buck that tradition.

Li'l Dizzy's
Trout Baquet

2 to 3 teaspoons vegetable oil (optional, unless your skillets are not well seasoned)

4 skinless, speckled trout fillets (each 4 to 5 ounces and about ½ inch thick at the thickest part)

Kosher salt and freshly ground pepper

3 to 4 tablespoons all-purpose flour

Crabmeat Topping

4 tablespoons unsalted butter (more if you like—Wayne says more!)

1½ teaspoons fresh lemon juice

3 cloves garlic, minced

8 ounces fresh lump crabmeat, picked over for cartilage and shell fragments

Kosher salt and freshly ground pepper

Minced fresh flat-leaf parsley for garnish

My city council candidacy was aborted at Li'l Dizzy's Café when Judge Bernard Williams engaged me in some old fashioned political horse trading. In exchange for bowing out of the race, I got a get-out-of-jail-free card and, since the judge was paying, an order of the best (and most expensive) dish on the menu. Crabmeat and trout are pretty easy to get down here. But I've also made this dish with red snapper, flounder, or redfish. Use whatever flaky, sauté-able fresh fish you can get.

Place 2 heavy skillets over medium heat. If your skillets are not well seasoned, wipe their inside surfaces with a paper towel moistened with the vegetable oil. Heat simultaneously until very hot, 7 to 10 minutes.

Meanwhile, season each fish fillet on both sides with salt and pepper, then dust both sides very lightly and evenly with flour, shaking off any excess; set aside.

To make the topping: In a separate heavy skillet over medium heat, melt the butter. Add the lemon juice and garlic and cook until the garlic is soft, 1 to 2 minutes, stirring almost constantly. Add the crabmeat, reduce the heat to medium-low, and cook just until the crab is heated through, 1 to 2 minutes, stirring gently to avoid breaking up the lumps. Remove from the heat and season with salt and pepper. Cover the pan to keep warm while you cook the fillets.

When the skillets are very hot, carefully add 2 of the fillets to each. Cook, turning once, just until both sides of the fillets are golden brown and cooked through at the thickest part, about 1½ minutes per side. (If you are only using 1 skillet to cook the fish, keep the first batch of fillets covered loosely with aluminum foil while cooking the second batch.)

Serve at once on heated individual plates, dividing the crabmeat topping and sprinkling all with the parsley.

Makes 4 servings

Prejean's Pheasant-Quail-Andouille Gumbo

If you were to list all the dishes that go by the name "gumbo" in Louisiana, you'd have a collection of recipes that, in many cases, would have nothing in common but the spelling. There are at least a dozen different legitimate kinds of gumbo in and around New Orleans, and that's not including all the other soups and stews that misappropriate the name.

Prejean's Restaurant's gumbo is one of the best gumbos I've ever had. It's also one of the most popular dishes every year at Jazz Fest. That's quite a feat. A hot soup selling like hot cakes in 90-degree weather? It's got to be good.

In a large cast-iron pot or Dutch oven over medium-low heat, heat the oil. Adjust the heat to maintain a hot, but not smoking, pot while you brown the other ingredients.

In a large heavy, nonstick skillet, sauté the andouille sausage until browned, about 5 minutes, and add to the hot oil in the pot. Repeat this process with the Cajun sausage, yellow onion, bell pepper, celery, quail, and pheasant, sautéing each ingredient individually and transferring each to the Dutch oven once browned.

Add the paprika, black pepper, white pepper, cayenne, and bay leaf to the pot and stir. Stir in the stock. Stir in the roux until well blended. Raise the heat to medium-high and bring to a boil, then return the heat to medium-low and simmer gently, stirring attentively, until the meats are tender and the broth is slightly thickened, about 40 minutes.

Add the Kitchen Bouquet, hot sauce, and green onions and stir well. Simmer for 5 minutes longer to allow the flavors to blend. Serve hot over the rice.

Makes 6 to 8 servings

¼ cup corn oil

½ pound andouille sausage, cut into ¼-inch slices

¼ pound **Cajun** smoked sausage, cut into ¼-inch slices

1 small yellow onion, coarsely chopped

½ bell pepper, seeded and coarsely chopped

1 small celery stalk, finely chopped

3 boneless quail (about 4 ounces each)

2 boneless pheasant breasts or chicken breasts (about 6 ounces each)

2 tablespoons paprika

¼ teaspoon freshly ground black pepper

¼ teaspoon freshly ground white pepper

¼ teaspoon cayenne pepper

1 bay leaf

2½ quarts Rich Chicken Stock (page 230) or store-bought rich chicken or turkey broth

½ cup plus 1 tablespoon Dark Roux (page 175)

2 teaspoons Kitchen Bouquet

3 dashes of Tabasco or other hot sauce

3 green onions, tender green parts only, thinly sliced

Hot cooked rice for serving

ALBERT LAMBREAUX

You can't get good food in New Orleans nowadays.

That stuff they call "gumbo" is thick as molasses in the wintertime. The roux is so dark, it looks like the people put it on the stove and forgot it. If it wasn't for Jiffy, there wouldn't be cornbread in New Orleans. And people have the nerve to say they're cooking from scratch just because they opened the box themselves.

Even if people could still cook, they couldn't get the ingredients. You go to the market and all the food is already cooked and packaged; just waiting for you to heat it and eat it. You don't need pots; just a microwave.

When I was coming up, we used to buy our chickens at Steve's Poultry House right there on North Claiborne Avenue. The chicken was fresh and you could taste it. Don't even get me started on these city eggs. The Dupre family had Pecan Grove Dairy. They used to deliver real milk in the bottle and Creole cream cheese, uptown and down. Now, you can't hardly find real cream cheese, except if you go out to Dorignac's in Metairie.

Mulé's used to make the best hot sausage sandwiches, but they *been* closed. The few good places they had left, the storm took them out. Miss Davis at Chicken Deluxe behind Dillard University used to serve fresh greens, not that frozen mush people usually sell. Barrow's catfish up in Hollygrove was so good, that's all they sold: catfish, potato salad, and bread. But I remember when they served plate food too.

They used to have two butcher shops on St. Bernard Avenue, Vaucresson and Bachemin's. Vaucresson had this crawfish sausage everybody goes crazy for over at the Jazz Fest. I liked the pickle' meat Bachemin sold, because they made their own, right there in the shop, and it made the best cabbage and the best red beans. Vaucresson's still selling sausage, but neither one of them opened their stores back up.

These days, if you try to do things the right way, you feel like you're in a cage at the zoo. People come by to see it because they know nobody else is doing it this way. But some things you have to do for yourself and don't care who's watching. Like I tell Davina and all of my kids, everything you do, you making you. If you want to be out-the-box, off-the-rack, seen-it-before, then you just do like everybody else do.

Like when I sew. I'm not just trying to be the prettiest. I'm trying to do it like it was taught to me back when people wasn't trying to get on television or in a museum. And when I cook, you better believe this: no boxes, no cans, no bullshit. It's old-time cooking.

Carrot Casserole

8 tablespoons all-purpose flour

2 pounds carrots, peeled

6 tablespoons unsalted butter

1 cup firmly packed light brown sugar

1½ cups evaporated milk

¼ teaspoon salt

3 large eggs

My wife's Auntie Odette taught her to make this dish. It's kind of sweet, so you serve it instead of candied sweet potatoes. But it's not all syrupy like some people make things. Auntie Odette used to work for the Goldsteins on Prytania Street, fancy white folks. So she cooked some things you wouldn't just get every day. I've never seen anybody else make this exactly like she did. Usually they grate the carrots too small and they come out the consistency of mashed potatoes. Serve this warm as a vegetable side dish, much as you would sweet potatoes or pumpkin.

Preheat the oven to 350°F. Grease a 9-inch Bundt pan generously, then lightly dust it with 2 tablespoons of the flour.

Grate the carrots on the largest section of a box grater so they come out in short strips, not mush. Put the grated carrots in a 3-quart saucepan and add water to cover. Bring to a boil over high heat. Reduce the heat to medium and cook for 15 to 20 minutes, or until the carrots are just slightly soft, not at all mushy. Remove from the heat and put the carrots into a large colander to drain.

In a 3-quart saucepan, melt the butter over low heat. When the butter is melted, add the brown sugar and stir to dissolve. Remove from the heat and a little at a time, add the remaining 6 tablespoons flour, stirring to blend. Add the evaporated milk, ½ cup at a time, stirring between each addition. Add salt and stir.

Put the eggs in a small bowl and beat until well blended. Add the eggs to the milk and sugar mixture and stir gently to mix. After all ingredients are well blended, add the drained carrots and stir well.

Pour the carrot mixture into the prepared pan. Bake for 45 minutes, or until the edges are lightly browned and starting to pull away from the sides of the pan. Remove from the oven and let cool for about 30 minutes. Loosen the edges with a small, thin-bladed knife or spatula. Place a large flat plate or serving dish upside-down on top of the pan. Invert the pan and plate and unmold the casserole. Serve at once.

Makes 10 to 12 servings

VEGETARIAN MUSTARD GREENS

I never did like collard greens. Too tough. Give me some turnip greens, or either some mustards. And since my doctor's been trying to get me to eat healthy, I came up with this recipe for mustard greens that tastes good even though it doesn't have pickle' meat or pigtails or anything in it. Of course, the greens taste better alongside a fried pork chop, but you don't need to tell that to your doctor unless he asks.

Discard any wilted, yellow, or damaged mustard leaves. Wash the remaining leaves by swirling them in a sink full of cool water, separating the leaves and giving them plenty of room to soak for a few seconds. Lift the leaves out of the water before emptying the sink, then rinse the sink, refill with fresh water, and repeat the washing process as needed until all the dirt and grit have been removed. Drain the leaves briefly in a colander, then trim and discard the tough stems and spines. Tear the leaves into large bite-size pieces.

Put the mustard greens in a large heavy-bottomed saucepan or large Dutch oven along with the butter, onions, salt, cayenne, and habanero, if using. Add just enough water to reach one-fourth of the way up the leaves. Bring to a boil over high heat. Reduce the heat to medium-low, cover, and cook until the greens are tender, about 1 hour, stirring occasionally; if you like your greens very tender, cook them longer. Season with habanero pepper sauce, if using, and serve at once.

Makes 8 servings

3½ pounds mustard greens

½ cup (1 stick) unsalted butter

4 small to medium yellow onions, peeled but left whole

2 teaspoons salt (I use more)

¼ teaspoon cayenne pepper

1 habanero chile, left whole (optional), or ½ teaspoon habanero pepper sauce, or to taste (I use more) (optional, if not using a habanero pepper)

LAMBREAUX'S CORNBREAD

1 cup yellow or white cornmeal, plus 2 tablespoons

1 cup all-purpose flour

1 tablespoon plus 1 teaspoon baking powder

1 tablespoon sugar
(if you like sweeter cornbread, use 2 tablespoons sugar)

½ teaspoon salt

1 cup whole milk

1 large egg

2 tablespoons unsalted butter, melted

¼ cup vegetable oil

These days, people seem to confuse their cornbread with their cake. I guess maybe sugar is so cheap, people figure they just as soon use it as don't. This is old-fashioned cornbread made the right way: just enough sugar to season it, and not enough to sweeten it.

Preheat the oven to 425°F. Grease a 10-inch cast-iron or other heavy ovenproof skillet with oil and place the skillet in the oven to preheat. In a large bowl, whisk together the 1 cup cornmeal, the flour, the baking powder, the sugar, and the salt. Add the milk, egg, melted butter, and vegetable oil and stir with a spoon or whisk just until well mixed and smooth; do not overbeat.

Remove the hot skillet from the oven. Sprinkle the 2 tablespoons cornmeal over the bottom and return to the oven for 2 minutes. Remove from the oven again and gently pour the batter into the hot skillet, being careful not to disturb the cornmeal in the bottom too much. Bake until the cornbread is nicely browned and bounces back when lightly pressed in the center with your fingertips, about 20 minutes. Remove from the oven and turn out the bread onto a platter. Serve immediately.

*Makes 6 to 8 servings
(or 5 cups crumbled)*

CORNBREAD–FRENCH BREAD DRESSING

The secret to making good dressing is to mix French bread and cornbread. That's the only way to get the right texture. Not too smooth, not too rough. My wife's friend Cat Tanner taught her that. Now, thanks to her, this is our family recipe.

The turkey necks can be cooked and the meat from them shredded a day ahead; refrigerate the unstrained stock from cooking the necks until called for in the dressing recipe. The cornbread can be made hours in advance. You can make the whole dressing up to 1 day ahead; assemble, cover, and refrigerate, then bake just before serving.

To make the stock: Peel the skin and any fat from the turkey neck pieces and discard. Put the necks in a large heavy-bottomed saucepan or Dutch oven and add the water, yellow onion wedges, celery, bell pepper, green onions, and garlic. Bring to a boil over high heat. Reduce the heat to medium-low, stir in the bay leaves, Creole seasoning, salt, pepper, and poultry seasoning. Cover and simmer, stirring occasionally, until the turkey neck meat is so tender it is starting to fall off the bone, about 1½ hours. Remove from the heat. Using tongs, transfer the necks to a bowl. Set aside the unstrained stock at room temperature until cool.

When the necks are cool enough to handle, pull all the meat from the bone with your hands and shred. Then roughly chop the meat. Discard the bones. Cover the cooled unstrained stock and the chopped turkey meat and refrigerate separately until ready to assemble the dressing.

To make the dressing: Preheat the oven to 350°F. In a large heavy-bottomed saucepan or Dutch oven, melt the ½ cup butter over medium-high heat. Add the yellow onion, reduce the heat to medium, and cook, stirring occasionally, until the onion starts

to soften, about 3 minutes. Add the garlic and cook and stir for 2 minutes. Stir in the celery, bell pepper, green onions, and parsley and cook until all the vegetables are softened, about 15 minutes, stirring occasionally.

When the vegetables are softened, reduce the heat to low and stir in the crumbled cornbread, the French bread crumbs, and 2 cups of the turkey neck meat. Add 2 cups of the reserved unstrained turkey neck stock (including some of the vegetables), mixing until all the bread is moistened. (Save any leftover turkey neck meat and stock for another use.)

Transfer the dressing to an ungreased 1½-quart glass casserole dish and spread the 2 tablespoons softened butter over the dressing with a knife. Cover and bake until the dressing is heated through, about 50 minutes; this also gives the flavors time to blend. Serve warm.

Makes 8 to 10 servings as a side dish

Turkey Stock

2½ to 3 pounds turkey necks, cut into 4- to 5-inch lengths

5 cups water

1 medium yellow onion, cut into 8 wedges

2 celery stalks with leaves, coarsely chopped

½ green bell pepper, seeded and coarsely chopped

2 green onions, white and tender green parts, coarsely chopped

10 cloves garlic, chopped (about ⅓ cup)

3 bay leaves

1 tablespoon Basic Creole Seasoning Blend (page 228)

1 teaspoon salt

1 teaspoon freshly ground pepper

½ teaspoon poultry seasoning

Dressing

½ cup unsalted butter, plus 2 tablespoons at room temperature

1 yellow onion, chopped

10 cloves garlic, chopped (about ⅓ cup)

3 large celery stalks, chopped (about 1½ cups)

½ green bell pepper, seeded and chopped

4 green onions, white and tender green parts, very finely chopped (about ½ cup)

1 cup finely chopped fresh flat-leaf parsley

3½ cups crumbled Lambreaux's Cornbread (facing page)

½ loaf day-old French bread, crusts and all, broken into small crumbs (about 3½ cups)

How Do You Explain New Orleans' "French" Bread?

It isn't French, first of all. Well, not really. It's shaped like a French baguette, but it's fatter and wider. The inside of the bread is lighter and the outside is flakier. It's not artisanal in the sense that people usually talk about these days. It's regular white bread. It's not all whole grain or made with some yeast that's been kept around since the days of Charlemagne. In fact, the bread's connections to France are a bit specious. French bread in France is nothing like French bread in New Orleans. Many if not most of the bakers specializing in making New Orleans bread since the 1830s have been Germans—George Leidenheimer, George Reising, Alois J. Binder. Angelo and John Gendusa weren't German, but they weren't French either. In fact the late Joe Logsdon, the full-time historian and part-time gourmand, said New Orleans French bread reminded him of some of the softer breads he tasted in Germany and Austria. Like almost everything else here, the bread is Creole, a mix of all the folks whose hands help knead the dough.

Sandy Whann, the current owner of Leidenheimer's and the great-grandson of George Leidenheimer, explained it in an essay by Michael Mizell-Nelson in the book, *New Orleans Cuisine: Fourteen Signature Dishes and their Histories*: "New Orleans French bread evolved based on the variety of ingredients used to make poor boys. The delicate balance of thin, crisp crust with enough firmness to stand up to brown and red gravy and a lightness that would not compete with Gulf seafood made the poor boy loaf the perfect base. Restaurants needed a loaf that diners could readily bite into without cutting the roof of their mouth as might happen with traditional French bread; however, the loaf had to be strong enough to hold up to gravy, mayonnaise, and other dressings."

Trying to make a po-boy without New Orleans French bread is like trying to make gumbo outside of south Louisiana. You can find sausage and crabs and okra and shrimp almost anywhere. But unless most of those ingredients come from around here, it just doesn't ever taste right.

Even fancy, fine-dining chefs know not to mess with a good thing. A lot of the best restaurants here—Upperline, Commander's Palace, Brigtsen's, Mr. B's Bistro, Palace Café—they all serve regular New Orleans bread. Ann Cashion, a Washington, D.C., chef friend of mine who won a James Beard Award for her restaurant, Cashion's Eat Place, serves po-boys at her new place,

Johnny's Half Shell. She's obsessive enough to fly in bread from New Orleans for her sandwiches and she's not even from here. She's from Jackson, Mississippi.

"We have always flown our bread up for our po-boys at Johnny's Half Shell, from the very first week we opened, twice a week, and the only exception to that was right after the levees broke," she told me. "For a couple of months after that, Leidenheimer was not producing and when they started back up, they didn't have the wherewithal to ship. That's when I would cajole my New Orleans boyfriend into picking up our bread and taking it to the UPS store on South Claiborne Avenue.

"Why go to all that trouble? I guess because it was impossible for me to conceive of a po-boy worthy of the name on any other bread. I'd had po-boys outside of New Orleans on various types of rolls and buns and frankly, whatever else might be wrong with the sandwich, it was the bread that was always in the way. And that's the way I would put it, 'in the way,' because New Orleans French bread is as distinctive for what it isn't as for what it is. It is understated and egoless. As the platform for a po-boy, it allows the flavors of the filling to shine, enclosing them in a light, crisp, absorbent, and delicate yet strong casing. I have always heard that it's the water that makes New Orleans French bread so unique. Since there's not much in the recipe other than flour, yeast, salt, and water, I'd say that's probably a good bet and would mean that it's the New Orleans 'terroir' that accounts for its distinctive qualities."

I could try to give you a recipe for French bread, but it wouldn't work. John Gendusa used to have a sign on the wall with the recipe for his bread. Visitors would ask him if they could copy down the recipe. He'd let them, knowing that it would take a lot more than a mere recipe to put some flour, yeast, and salt in the oven and have it come out like New Orleans French bread.

STUFFED MIRLITON

Davina Lambreaux: When my mother was alive, she and Miss Alice White had a standing arrangement. When the mirlitons got ready in the fall, Mama would send me or Delmond or Cheri, or sometimes all three of us, to go around the corner and pick all the mirlitons we could. It seems like there would be hundreds of them. I know it was dozens at least. Then Mama would boil them and scoop the meat out of them. She would stuff the meat back into their skins with some shrimp or some ham and some seasoning. We would keep about half of those for Sunday dinner and send some to Miss Alice. There was still plenty of mirliton left. So Mama would freeze the rest of the meat and cook it a little at a time until Christmas. That's when she cooked the last of it.

This is my favorite of my mother's recipes. (It's also my daddy's favorite.) My mother always hated it when people made ground beef the main ingredient in their oyster dressing or their stuffed mirliton. Why call it oyster dressing? Why call it stuffed mirliton? She would say it's really just beef seasoned with oysters or mirliton or eggplant whatever. I hear her voice echoing with that whenever I eat other's people's versions of one of these dishes. The mirliton and the shrimp are the stars here. Mostly, it's the mirliton.

My mama died years ago. Miss Alice never came back after the storm. The mirliton vine drowned in the flood. It wasn't until the year after Katrina that it hit me. We had us a little ritual. And as much as I used to hate picking mirlitons and helping Mama clean them and cook them, it was one of the things that we did together. When I would walk back to Miss Alice's house and see how happy she was to get the stuffed mirlitons, it all seemed worth it.

If you can't find a Miss Alice with a mirliton vine, then try to find a Miss Alice without one. When you buy the mirlitons from the store, get two or three extra ones and fix them for your Miss Alice. That's about the best advice I can give you to make your mirlitons taste like Mama's used to.

Put the mirlitons in a 3-gallon pot, or two large stockpots, and cover with water. Bring to a boil over high heat. Cover the pot(s) and continue boiling, just until the mirlitons are fork tender, 45 minutes to 1 hour. Remove from the heat and, using a slotted spoon, immediately transfer the mirlitons to a colander to drain and cool.

Once cool enough to handle, place the mirlitons on a cutting board or other flat surface. Cut them in half lengthwise. With a paring knife, shallowly trim away any spiny or blemished spots from the skin, and tough pulp from the end nearest to the seed. Remove and discard the seed and use a small spoon to carefully remove the pulp from the inside of each half, leaving a ¼- to ½-inch-thick shell. Drain the mirliton pulp in a colander, lightly squeezing it to release excess moisture, then chop the pulp. Set aside the pulp and shells.

continued

8 medium mirlitons (chayotes) (about 4½ pounds total weight)

Stuffing

¾ pound medium shrimp, peeled and deveined

1 teaspoon Basic Creole Seasoning Blend (page 228)

½ teaspoon cayenne pepper

½ cup (1 stick) unsalted butter, plus about 5 tablespoons

1 yellow onion, chopped

2 celery stalks with leaves, finely diced

¼ large green bell pepper, seeded and chopped

¼ cup minced fresh flat-leaf parsley

3 tablespoons finely chopped green onions, white and tender green parts

2½ tablespoons finely chopped garlic

½ cup very fine dried bread crumbs, plus about 5 tablespoons

1 teaspoon salt

½ teaspoon freshly ground pepper

1 large egg, lightly beaten

Makes 8 main-course servings or 16 appetizer servings

Preheat the oven to 350°F.

To make the stuffing: Season the shrimp with the Creole seasoning and cayenne, mixing well. Set aside. In a heavy 5-quart saucepan or large Dutch oven over low heat, melt the ½ cup of butter. Add the onions and cook until they start to soften, about 5 minutes, stirring occasionally. Stir in the celery, bell pepper, parsley, green onions, and garlic, and cook and stir for 2 minutes. Add the reserved mirliton pulp and cook for 6 minutes. Put ½ cup of the bread crumbs into a small bowl.

Once the mirliton pulp mixture has cooked for 6 minutes, add 2 tablespoons of the reserved bread crumbs, mixing thoroughly, then continue adding 2 tablespoons at a time until you have added all of them, stirring thoroughly between additions.

Cook the mixture over low heat, until it is noticeably dryer but still moist, about 3 minutes, stirring as needed. Next, add the seasoned shrimp, salt, and pepper.

Continue cooking until the shrimp turn pink, about 1 minute more, stirring almost constantly. Remove from the heat and stir in the egg, blending well.

Mound the stuffing in the 16 mirliton shells, using it all. Place the stuffed shells in a baking pan, such as a 12-by-17-inch baking pan, that will hold the shells in a single layer touching each other lightly to help support their shapes as they cook. Sprinkle about 1 teaspoon more bread crumbs evenly over the top of each stuffed shell and center a scant 1 teaspoon butter on the top of each. Cover tightly with aluminum foil and bake in the hot oven for 10 minutes. Remove the foil and continue baking until the tops are browned, about 1 hour more. Serve at once.

Note: To make ahead, prepare through the point of stuffing up to 1 day in advance. Cover the stuffed mirlitons tightly and refrigerate. Bake as directed when ready to serve.

CUSHAW PIE

Cushaw is a type of pumpkin. It's green-and-white striped and has a curved neck. Tell you the truth, it looks almost like an oversize, striped zucchini. Look through the supermarket around Halloween or Thanksgiving time; you'll probably see a few of them. Before she died, my wife used to make cushaw all the time. It was special because her Aunt Stella taught her to make it. When everyone else was having pumpkin for Thanksgiving, we always had cushaw. Sometimes my wife would make it in a pie; sometimes she would make it in a pone.

If you make them the same way, cushaw and pumpkin don't taste that different. But sometimes even a word can be special. Cushaw makes me think of my wife and my family more than any other dish. One day, my daughter Davina brought me one of these pies that Frances Chauvin sells in the farmers' market. It doesn't taste exactly like my wife's pie . . . it's more of a custard consistency. In fact, I call it cushaw custard pie. But it's not my recipe, so you might as well call it what the lady wants it called.

1 cushaw squash (3½ to 4 pounds), cut into about 12 pieces and seeded

¾ cup sugar

1 tablespoon unsalted butter, melted

1 tablespoon McCormick pumpkin pie spice

¼ teaspoon ground cinnamon

Pinch of salt

3 large eggs

1½ cups heavy (whipping) cream

Pie Crust

2½ cups all-purpose flour, plus more for dusting

1 teaspoon salt

1 cup butter-flavored shortening

¾ cup ice water

Preheat the oven to 350°F.

Arrange the cushaw pieces on a baking sheet, cut-side down, and bake for 1½ hours, or until tender when pierced with a fork. Or, cook in a microwave oven for 20 to 30 minutes, until fork-tender. Let cool slightly and peel. Leave the oven on.

Put the squash flesh in a food processor and process to the consistency of mashed potatoes. Measure 1 heaping cup of the cushaw mash and put in a large bowl. (Save the rest of the cushaw for another use. Chauvin freezes it by the heaping cup.)

Add the sugar, melted butter, pumpkin pie spice, cinnamon, and salt to the mashed squash and stir to mix thoroughly. Using a hand-held electric mixer set on low, beat in the eggs, 1 at a time. Add the cream and beat until smooth.

To make the pie crust: Sift the flour and salt together into a bowl. Add half of shortening and cut in with a pastry blender, then cut in the rest of the shortening until it has a few marble-size chunks. Add the ice water all at once. Do not stir. Instead, pick at the mixture with a fork until it forms a big glob. Using your hands, gather into a big ball. Divide the dough in half and pat each half into a disk about 5 inches in diameter and ½ inch thick.

Dust a work surface and a rolling pin with flour. Place one of the dough disks on the work surface. Roll from the center out, first one way, then the other way. By that time the pie crust should be full size and ⅛ inch thick. The less you roll it, the better. Transfer the crust to a 9- or 10-inch pie pan, fitting it into the pie pan and fluting the edges.

Use the second dough disk to make "shoe soles" (see Note), or wrap tightly in plastic wrap and freeze for another use, up to 2 months.

Scoop the pie filling into the crust and bake until the filling is set and a toothpick inserted into the center comes out clean, 60 to 70 minutes. Transfer to a wire rack and let cool, then cut into wedges and serve.

Note: Since this is an open-face pie, you don't need the second half of the crust dough. I like to use the extra pie dough to make my version of "shoe soles." Unlike the usual version of the confection, which is made with puff pastry and sugar, this one is made with pie dough and sugar. Roll out the second half of the dough the same way you did the first. Rub with room-temperature butter and sprinkle with cinnamon and sugar. Cut into rough rectangles. Bake alongside the pie, but only for 30 minutes, or until lightly browned and the pastry starts to puff and bubble a bit. Remove from the oven and let cool slightly, then snack on them.

Makes one 10-inch pie; serves 8 to 10

DOOKY CHASE'S GUMBO Z'HERBES

1 bunch mustard greens

1 bunch collard greens

1 bunch turnip greens

1 bunch watercress

1 bunch beet tops

1 bunch carrot tops

1 bunch spinach

½ head crisp green lettuce such as romaine

½ head green cabbage

2 yellow onions, chopped

6 cloves garlic, finely chopped (about 2 tablespoons)

1 pound smoked sausage

1 pound boneless smoked ham

1 pound well-trimmed beef stew meat

1 pound boneless brisket

1 pound chaurice sausage or chorizo

Vegetable oil (if needed for making the roux)

⅓ cup all-purpose flour

1 tablespoon salt

1 teaspoon dried thyme

1 teaspoon cayenne pepper

1 tablespoon filé powder

Hot cooked rice for serving

Hot sauce for serving

The Thursday before Easter Sunday is a day of holy obligation. You have to eat at Dooky Chase and you have to have some of Mrs. Chase's gumbo z'herbes. If the Pope tasted this, he'd make gumbo z'herbes part of the communion ritual. One year, Jessica Harris, this food historian from New York, stood up in the dining room and talked about how gumbo z'herbes probably came from a green leaf stew you find in a lot of places in West Africa. She wrote a whole book called *Beyond Gumbo*. I was moved by what she said that day:

"Africans and Indians meet up in the gumbo pot in New Orleans. Some are thickened with African okra, others with Native American–pounded sassafras. Everyone has a different favorite. On Holy Thursday, however, there's only one gumbo to have and that is Leah Chase's thick, rich, green gumbo z'herbes at Dooky Chase restaurant. One taste of the verdant soup reminds us of the green sauce gumbos of Benin and the soupikandia of southern Senegal. Two tastes, and the culinary connections between Africa and America come together in your mouth. Sip, savor, and enjoy the taste of history in a bowl."

My daughter Davina points out that this gumbo is a very pretty green color if served within a few hours after it's made, so don't make it any further ahead than that if you can help it. You can, however, prepare the vegetables and meats, render the chaurice, and make the roux a day in advance. This recipe makes a feast. Be prepared either for leftovers or company.

Mrs. Chase says you have to use an odd number of greens, but she's not a stickler for using these exact greens. If you need to substitute or use twice as much of one and none of another, that's fine. And, now that my children are monitoring my every bite, sometimes I make it with less meat in it. That's up to you.

Discard any wilted, yellow, or damaged parts from all the greens. Wash the leaves by swirling them in a sink full of cool water, separating the leaves and giving them plenty of room to soak for a few seconds. Lift the leaves out of the water before emptying the sink, then rinse the sink, refill with fresh water, and repeat the washing process as needed until all the dirt and grit have been removed. Drain the leaves briefly in a colander.

Put all of the greens in 2 very large pots, such as 12-quart stockpots, in which the leaves won't be overcrowded as they cook. Divide the onions and garlic between the pots. Add enough water to each pot to cover the greens and bring to a gentle boil over medium-high heat. Reduce the heat to medium and continue boiling, uncovered, for 30 minutes, stirring occasionally. Remove from the heat.

Meanwhile, cut the smoked sausage, ham, stew meat, and brisket into bite-size pieces and combine them all in a large bowl. Cut the chaurice into bite-size pieces and spread in a single layer in a large skillet; set aside.

When the greens have boiled for 30 minutes, strain through a colander set over a large heatproof bowl or a saucepan, reserving both the greens and the cooking liquid separately.

In another 12-quart pot, combine the reserved meats with 2 cups of the reserved cooking liquid from the greens. Bring to a simmer over medium heat and cook, uncovered, for 15 minutes, stirring occasionally. Remove from the heat and set aside.

Meanwhile, place the skillet of chaurice over medium-high heat and cook until most of the fat is rendered from the meat, 15 to 20 minutes, turning the pieces at least once. Remove from the heat and use a slotted spoon to transfer the chaurice to paper towels to drain. Pour the fat in the skillet into a heat-proof glass measuring cup; if the fat doesn't measure about ⅓ cup, add vegetable oil to make up the difference, or if it is more than about ⅓ cup, pour off until there is ⅓ cup in the measuring cup.

Now make the roux: Return the ⅓ cup fat to the skillet and heat over medium heat for about 1 minute. Add the flour, stirring until thoroughly blended with the fat. Let the roux cook gently for 3 to 4 minutes, stirring and scraping the pan bottom almost constantly. (This will cook the raw flour taste out of the roux but should not be enough to brown the roux, although it's okay if it browns slightly.) Remove from the heat and stir for another minute or 2 more to help the roux cool without browning from the residual heat. Set aside.

Working in batches, put the drained greens in a food processor and process to a smooth purée. Add some of the reserved cooking liquid if needed to thin the purée for ease of processing. Make sure to reserve 2 quarts of the cooking liquid for finishing the dish. Set aside the puréed greens.

Return the pot of meats to a simmer. Gradually add the roux to the pot, stirring until completely dissolved into the liquid. Add the puréed greens and 2 quarts of the reserved cooking liquid. Bring to a simmer, stirring often and scraping the pan bottom clean as you stir.

Simmer for 20 minutes, then add to the gumbo the browned chaurice, the salt, thyme, and cayenne, stirring well. Continue simmering until all the flavors have married, until the grease separates and starts to float to the top, about 40 minutes more, adding more cooking liquid from the greens (or water) if needed. Stir in the filé powder and remove from the heat. (If making ahead, don't add the filé powder until you are reheating the gumbo just before serving.)

Spoon the rice into large individual bowls. Spoon the gumbo over the rice and serve at once. Pass the hot sauce at the table.

Makes 16 to 24 servings

ANNIE TALARICO

You know all those movies where the Italian mother is telling her kids, "Mangia! Mangia! Eat! Eat!"? If you want to understand how I grew up, you have to forget that image. My mother was all about music. She was more concerned that I practice than that I eat. Well, maybe she wasn't that bad, but she was more serious about music than she was about food. When other families were eating at fancy restaurants we were going to hear the New York Philharmonic.

My father's Filipino-American. My mother's Italian-Italian. They met in America, so most of what we ate was kind of typical American. And we lived in New York, so most of that was takeout, and a lot of that was, of course, Chinese. My mother had a few rudimentary staples she could prepare, but there were no big multi-course Italian banquets at my house. This did not make my Filipina grandmother happy. Her house is where I got stuffed with *pancit* (Filipino noodles), *ensaymada* (sweet bread), *bibingka* (rice cake with coconut), and, of course, chicken adobo.

I guess I always associated that food as much with my grandmother's house as with my grandmother. I would never come home and ask my mother if she could cook like that, any more than I would go to my grandmother's house and ask her to play something by Sibelius.

My life was compartmentalized from early on. In New York, I could never figure out how to break down those barriers and bring all the sides together. Leaving the conservatory, traveling around Europe—I was trying to figure out how the pieces of my life could fit together.

New Orleans seems to have a niche for everybody. Either you find a crowd that does what you do and believes how you believe, or you create your own. Musically, that means I can play Gottschalk one night with Joe Krown, play standards the next night with David Torkanowsky, and play my own music the next night with Bayou Cadillac. You can be a "serious" musician here, even if you aren't playing the classical repertoire.

In terms of food, it's been a smorgasbord. When Sonny and I first moved here, I had my places I would go to that were good and cheap. La Spiga in the Marigny was a bakery that would serve sandwiches and brunch and biscuits to live for. I used to like the jambalaya at Coop's on Decatur Street and the sandwiches at Verti Mart. Then La Spiga changed ownership and became NOLA Cake Cafe. I would get the breakfast panini, and I would try (unsuccessfully) not to get a red velvet cupcake, but I always ended up getting it.

Living with Davis showed me another side of New Orleans life. He thinks nothing of taking a night's pay and going to a nice restaurant. Eating at Eleven 79 and at Tommy's Cuisine with him was like having the Italian dining experience I didn't get at home. Restaurant One, Vizard's, Irene's Cuisine. It's not that these places are necessarily better than the casual places. It's just nice to be able to do both sometimes.

I guess what I've learned living here is that it doesn't have to be either/or. A lot of times, it can be both/and.

La Spiga's Buttermilk Biscuits

1¼ cups (2½ sticks) cold unsalted butter

5¼ cups unbleached all-purpose flour, plus more for dusting

2 tablespoons plus 2 teaspoons baking powder

¾ teaspoon salt

2 teaspoons sugar, plus more for sprinkling (either is optional; use in a sweet context or to help satisfy a sweet tooth)

2 cups cold, well-shaken buttermilk, plus more for brushing

Jam or honey for serving (optional)

Makes 2½ to 3½ dozen biscuits

I had my first biscuit ever at La Spiga, a bakery in the Marigny, not too far from where Sonny and I lived. La Spiga's biscuits spoiled me for any others. They are flaky and buttery but not greasy. It's easy to peel them open and make a sandwich with them. I always assumed that Dana Logsdon, the bakery owner, created the recipe. When she gave me this recipe, she told me to be certain to give credit to "Julia Carter and all the biscuit rollers at La Spiga." That means you too, Will.

Preheat the oven to 400°F.

Cut the chilled butter into ½-inch cubes and freeze or refrigerate. In the large bowl of an electric mixer fitted with the paddle attachment (or in a large bowl, using a mixing spoon), combine the flour, baking powder, salt, and 2 teaspoons sugar, if using. Beat on low speed until well blended, then turn off the mixer and add the reserved chilled butter cubes to the bowl all at once, separating them with your fingers. With the mixer on low speed (or with a pastry blender, the blades of 2 knives or the tines of 2 forks, or your fingertips), blend the butter into the dry ingredients until most of the cubes are reduced to pea-size and the rest of the mixture resembles meal, scraping down the sides of the bowl with a rubber spatula if needed. After about 3 minutes of beating, turn off the mixer periodically to check for what appear to be large chunks of butter, but are actually butter mixed with dry ingredients that can readily be crumbled apart with your fingers. Once these chunks start appearing, immediately stop beating the mixture and crumble the chunks by hand, or your biscuits will end up less flaky. Add the buttermilk and mix on low speed or with a spoon just until a rough dough forms, only 30 seconds to 1 minute; do not overmix. The finished dough will be somewhat sticky and messy.

Turn the dough out onto a large, lightly floured work surface. (If your surface is small, roll out and cut biscuits from half the dough at a time, refrigerating the other portion until needed.) Form the dough into a 12-by-18-inch rough-looking rectangle about 1 inch thick, using a combination of rolling out the dough with a floured rolling pin and gently shaping it with floured fingertips. As you work, use only enough flour to keep the dough from sticking to the work surface, rolling pin, and your fingers.

Using a broad, thin-bladed spatula or pastry scraper, peel one of the short ends of the rectangle from the work surface and fold it over half the dough, just as you would fold up the bottom third of a business letter, then loosen and fold the other short end over the first fold to end up with a "letter" folded in more-or-less even thirds. Turn the dough a quarter turn, then roll and shape the letter into a rectangle that is 1 inch thick. Repeat folding the short ends into a letter, turning a quarter turn, then rolling it out and shaping it into a 1-inch-thick rectangle at least 3 more times, and once or twice more, if needed, until the dough is noticeably smoother (keeping in mind that the fewer times the dough is rolled out, the flakier the biscuits will turn out). The dough will get easier to roll as you repeat this process, which is key to producing the flaky layers of the biscuits. After the final folding, roll out the dough to a thickness of ½ to ¾ inch. If the dough starts sticking excessively while you work, scrape the rolling pin and work surface clean and lightly reflour.

To cut out the biscuits, using a floured large-bladed knife or dough scraper, make a quick, clean motion to cut straight down through the dough on the four edges to make the rectangle neat. Then use this same motion, without twisting or mashing the dough, as you cut the dough into 2-inch squares. The biscuits may also be cut into rounds with a floured 2-inch round metal cutter, though square biscuits are preferred to reduce the amount of scraps you produce. Wipe the edge of the knife, scraper, or cutter clean as needed. Gather the scraps to make additional biscuits, but don't knead them together or

continued

turn them on their sides; instead, lay the scraps on top of each other as they were rolled out to preserve their layering, pat them out to a ½- to ¾-inch thickness, and cut out more biscuits.

Arrange the biscuits on ungreased baking sheets so they are close together but not quite touching. Use a pastry brush to brush the tops, but not the sides, with buttermilk, and let the biscuits sit for 5 minutes to allow the baking powder in the dough to activate longer. Bake on the middle shelf of the oven, or on the 2 middle shelves simultaneously, if desired, until puffed and golden brown on both tops and bottoms, 20 to 25 minutes; turn the pan(s) a half turn after 10 minutes of baking so the biscuits brown evenly, or if baking the biscuits on 2 oven shelves, alternate the shelf each pan is on as well as rotating back to front.

Remove the biscuits from the oven and loosen with a spatula. If making sweetened biscuits for strawberry shortcake (or if you just prefer sweet biscuits), sprinkle them lightly with sugar while hot. Let the biscuits cool for 5 minutes before serving as is or with jam or honey, or use them for strawberry shortcakes. If not using the biscuits the same day as baked, let them cool completely, then double-bag them in self-sealing plastic bags and freeze for up to one month. To reheat, arrange the frozen biscuits on an ungreased baking sheet, and cook, uncovered, in a 350°F oven for about 15 minutes.

Beignets and Calas

Beignets have a lot going for them—Café Du Monde is a must-stop in the French Quarter, it doesn't matter if you're playing tourist with the family in daytime or sobering up with college buddies in the wee hours. Morning Call is a powerful draw for true students of beignet history. They've followed it from the Decatur Street location, where Joseph Jurisich founded it in 1870, to its thirty-four-year-old strip mall location in the suburbs. Cafe Beignet, a relatively new entrant in the beignet field, is located right by the 8th District police station, where I worked.

The only people championing *calas* are the octogenarians who remember how to make them, the baby boomers who remember how to eat them, and a small band of preservationists who are trying to revive them.

I've got a soft spot for the underdog. So when the New Orleans food maven Poppy Tooker told me about calas, I couldn't wait for a taste.

Calas are rice fritters, made with leftover rice, eggs, sugar, flour, and yeast or baking powder. Unlike beignets, which are made from dough, calas are made from batter. I like them with yeast. You get a rumlike flavor from the yeast, whereas I don't think the baking powder adds anything but leavening. Poppy and Frank Brigtsen both make savory calas with crawfish and other ingredients. But calas are usually served sweet and topped with some powdered sugar just like beignets.

Beignets are thought to have arrived with the Ursulines nuns when they came to New Orleans in 1727. The term means "fritter" in French, so it covers a wide variety of options. The ultra-airy dessert beignets at Coquette, a New Orleans restaurant newcomer, are a world away from the traditional square donuts. But they still fit comfortably under the beignet rubric. I've had great beignets at Chez Panisse in Berkeley, The Modern in New York City, and Jackson's Bar & Oven in Sonoma, California. How can you go wrong with fried dough?

Once they arrived in New Orleans, calas proved to be much less mobile. Just like a lot of New Orleans dishes, calas have origins in both West Africa and France. Food historian Jessica Harris traces the recipe back to the Vai people of Sierra Leone and Liberia. But there's also a nearly identical recipe for *beignets de riz* in a French cookbook from 1653, even though French cuisine generally doesn't include a lot of rice.

For more than a century, *les calas* were sold by vendors who plied New Orleans streets, calling out, "*Belles calas, toutes chaudes!*" ("Calas, nice and hot!"). After World War II, consumption declined, and calas came to be associated almost exclusively with African-American Catholics, who traditionally ate them for breakfast on Carnival Day and on the Sunday of a child's First Communion. Those traditions are dying out. But you can create your own traditions with these recipes.

Boiled Shrimp

1 lemon, halved

6 cups water

¼ cup chopped yellow onion

5 cloves garlic, smashed

2 bay leaves

2 teaspoons fennel seed

¾ teaspoon red pepper flakes

¼ teaspoon black peppercorns

1¾ teaspoons hot sauce

2 tablespoons salt

2 pounds large shrimp, peeled and deveined

Extra-virgin olive oil for drizzling

Olive Salad

2 tablespoons minced anchovies (about 10 anchovies)

2 cloves garlic, minced

2 teaspoons chopped fresh oregano or ½ teaspoon dried oregano

2 teaspoons chopped fresh basil or ½ teaspoon dried basil

1½ teaspoons salt

½ teaspoon freshly ground pepper

¼ teaspoon whole celery seed

¼ teaspoon red pepper flakes

½ cup dry red wine vinegar

¾ cup extra-virgin olive oil

½ cup pimiento-stuffed green olives, halved

½ cup pitted Kalamata olives, halved

1 small carrot, peeled and cut into ¼-inch slices (about ½ cup)

½ cup thinly sliced red onion

¼ cup drained pepperoncini slices

1 cup cauliflower florets

3 hearts of Romaine lettuce, torn into bite-size pieces

2 medium ripe tomatoes, cored and cut into wedges

Finely grated Pecorino Romano or Parmesan (preferably Parmigiano-Reggiano) cheese for sprinkling

When my Italian-American mother heard that WOP Salad was a New Orleans specialty, she couldn't wait to try it. That side of the family is from Italy, Italy. Not Ellis Island. So they are not easily insulted by the word "wop." Wop as in "without papers," a derogatory term for Italian immigrants. Some restaurants in New Orleans still have it on the menu by name. Others are a little more politically correct. A neighbor of mine, who lived around the corner from where Davis and I lived in Treme, helped me come up with a fancified home version of the dish. I decided that this salad is different enough from the original to warrant a new name.

To make the shrimp: In a medium pot, squeeze the juice from the lemon, and then add the lemon rind. Add the remaining ingredients except the shrimp and olive oil. Bring to a boil, reduce to a simmer, and cook for 20 minutes to allow the flavors to blend. Add the shrimp to the pot and remove it from the heat.

Let the shrimp sit in the boil for 2 to 3 minutes, or until pink and cooked through. Meanwhile, line a baking sheet with aluminum foil. Remove the shrimp from the boil with a skimmer or sieve and spread out on the prepared baking sheet, discarding the liquid from the boil. Drizzle olive oil over the shrimp and refrigerate until cool. If not using immediately, transfer to a small container, discarding remaining aromatics such as peppercorns, and cover and refrigerate for up to 2 days.

To make the salad: In a bowl, stir together the anchovies, garlic, oregano, basil, salt, pepper, celery seed, and red pepper flakes. Whisk in the vinegar and olive oil. Stir in the olives, carrot, red onion, pepperoncini, and cauliflower. Set the olive salad aside and let it marinate at room temperature for 4 hours, stirring occasionally, or cover and refrigerate for up to 2 days before serving.

Divide the romaine lettuce among six individual salad bowls. Top each portion with about ½ cup of the olive salad, a few tomato wedges, and the chilled shrimp, dividing it evenly. Sprinkle with the cheese and serve.

Makes 6 servings

SHRIMP BISQUE

4 pounds large shrimp, heads and tails intact

8 tablespoons (1 stick) unsalted butter

1 cup chopped yellow onion (save trimmings for stock)

¼ cup chopped shallots (save trimmings for stock)

1 cup peeled and diced carrots (save trimmings for stock)

2 tablespoons chopped fresh flat-leaf parsley (save trimmings for stock)

½ cup brandy

½ cup canned plum tomatoes in their juices

1 teaspoon dried tarragon

Salt

Cayenne pepper

¼ cup all-purpose flour

⅔ cup dry white wine

Crystal or other hot sauce (optional)

4 cups heavy (whipping) cream

¼ cup Madeira wine

I've realized there are two kinds of bisque in New Orleans. The famous one is crawfish bisque, which usually has no cream and features crawfish heads stuffed with crawfish meat dressing. Other kinds of seafood bisques are creamy soups like this one. Davis's mother made this dish at Thanksgiving, and it was amazing. It's so rich and so good. I actually made it with her one day. The plan was for me to learn to make it myself. So far all I have is the recipe and good intentions.

Peel the shrimp, setting aside the heads and shells to make the stock. Cover the peeled shrimp and refrigerate until needed.

Melt 2 tablespoons of the butter in a stock-pot. Add all the vegetable peelings and discards (onion and shallot peels, carrot root ends, tips, and peels, parsley stems; see whole ingredients list) along with shrimp shells and shrimp heads to the pot. Cook over high heat, stirring constantly, until shrimp peels are pink, about 5 minutes.

Pour ¼ cup of the brandy into a skillet or small saucepan. Using a match, carefully light the brandy to flambé. Pour over the stock mixture, stirring until the flames die out. Add ¼ cup of the tomatoes and add water to cover all by about 2 inches, 7 to 8 cups. Bring the shrimp stock to a boil over high heat and simmer briskly for about 10 minutes. Strain and set aside.

In a soup pot, melt the remaining 6 table-spoons butter over medium heat. Add the peeled shrimp and sauté until just barely cooked, about 3 minutes. Using a slotted spoon, transfer the shrimp from the pot to a cutting board, chop coarsely, and set aside.

Add the onion, shallots, and carrots to the butter in the pot. Sauté until the onion and shallots are translucent, about 4 minutes. Add the parsley and tarragon, and season with salt and cayenne. Add the remaining ¼ cup tomatoes. Cook for another 3 minutes to allow the flavors to blend. Flambé the remaining ¼ cup brandy, pour over the contents of the pan, and stir until the flames die out.

Sprinkle the flour over the mixture and cook to remove the raw flour taste, about 5 minutes. Add 5 cups of the shrimp stock and the white wine and raise the heat to high. Bring everything to a boil, then reduce the heat to low and simmer until slightly thickened and very fragrant, about 45 minutes longer.

Purée the soup in the pot with an immersion blender until smooth. Taste and adjust the seasoning, and add a little hot sauce, if desired. Stir in the shrimp and cream and cook until heated through, but do not let boil. Stir in the Madeira. Ladle the bisque into warmed soup bowls and serve at once.

Makes 4 to 6 servings

Chilean Adobo

This is the national dish of the Philippines. I hadn't given it much thought until I got into a conversation with Christina Quackenbush at Riomar. She's a server there, but she's also a Filipina and a helluva cook. One thing led to another, and she invited me to her house for some home food. It was like visiting my grandmother.

Fill a stockpot three-fourths full with water and add the chicken, garlic, vinegar, bay leaf, and peppercorns. Bring to a boil over high heat, then reduce the heat to medium-low and simmer, without stirring, until the chicken flesh is very tender, about 20 minutes. (You will fry to crisp up the skin later.) Skim off any impurities that float up to the top of the stew. Add the salt and simmer for another 10 minutes.

Using tongs, transfer the chicken to a large plate and allow any excess liquid to drain off.

Continue simmering the stock until reduced to about ¼ cup. Add the soy sauce and coconut milk when the reduction is almost complete.

Heat the oil in a wok or large saucepan. When the oil is hot, add the chicken pieces and fry, turning as needed, until the skin is golden brown and crispy all over.

Arrange the chicken pieces on a serving platter. Make sure the stock is hot, and then pour it over the chicken. Serve at once, over the rice.

1 frying chicken (about 3 pounds), cut up into serving pieces, or 3 pounds chicken pieces of your choice

9 large cloves garlic, minced (about 3 tablespoons)

1 cup apple cider vinegar

1 bay leaf

1 tablespoon crushed peppercorns

1 tablespoon salt

2 tablespoons soy sauce

1 cup unsweetened coconut milk

3 tablespoons vegetable oil

Hot cooked jasmine rice for serving

Makes 4 servings

TERRY COLSON

Jack and Peter got me into this. I had parked the car and walked back to Café du Monde just in time to hear my oldest boy say, "Our dad's are better."

They were sitting in Café du Monde, the St. Peter's Basilica of beignets, saying that their dad's beignets are better than the most famous ones in the world. I was very embarrassed. But I was more proud than embarrassed. You spend so much time telling your kids to do their homework, wash behind their ears, and turn off the video games, that you can only hope they think of you as something other than an ogre. At worst, it turns out, I'm an ogre who makes good doughnuts.

It also turns out, the woman they were talking to was a chef, Janette Desautel. She was fascinated to find a cop who was serious about his doughnuts. Next thing you know, I'm agreeing to contribute recipes to her book.

I don't mean to brag—it's not about me, it's about the doughnuts—but a book like this needs doughnuts in it. Specifically beignets. The doughnut is blue-collar food. It's not fancy French liver or beer-fed beef. A doughnut is the last thing an expense-account journalist is looking for. That's why all the reporters have been focused on the rebirth of fancy restaurants in New Orleans. For a reporter, writing about fancy restaurants in New Orleans is like finding a terrorist cell on the French Riviera: good story, great location. But they would laugh you away from the water cooler if you went back to the *New York Times* with doughnuts on your expense account.

But New Orleans doughnuts almost died.

They weren't done in by Hurricane Katrina or the levees or gangbangers with guns. Still, a few years ago, you had a hard time finding decent doughnuts in this town, especially if you wanted local ones instead of Krispy Kreme or Dunkin'. When I was coming up, you walked into the corner grocery store, they'd have Cloverleaf doughnuts, made at a funky little place uptown, right off Oak Street. You walked a few blocks more, there was a Tastee Donuts or a MacKenzie's. If you were working the late shift, Picou's had hot donuts at all hours. And, if you were near Broadmoor, Gambino's on Washington Avenue could accommodate you. Then, in the '80s, you could go to National/Canal Villere chain or just about any of the supermarkets and get good doughnuts made with potato flour right there in the store.

Then McKenzie's closed. Cloverleaf closed. Tastee hit hard times. Gambino's moved. And the supermarkets started serving Krispy Kreme. Historically speaking, this was the New Orleans doughnut's dark ages.

Once I had my two boys, I started experimenting with my own doughnuts. At first it was just me messing around with the beignet mix from Café du Monde. Then I started fiddling around with making beignets from scratch. The boys loved it. They started looking forward to breakfast on Saturday because Dad was cooking. When things didn't work out between me and Kay, I got even more serious about the doughnut thing. For a time, it seemed like the only thing that made the boys want to come over.

Since I'm a cop, I'm not allowed to have a serious doughnut discussion, until after I wade through all the doughnuts and cop jokes, some of which are really sick, like the "bad cop, no donut" bumper stickers that appear after a bad shoot or something. People forget that it used to be soldiers, not cops, who were the doughboys.

I read this book called *The Donut Book*. It's light reading, but it's pretty good. Sally Levitt traces the history of the term "doughboy" all the way from when it meant pastries to when it meant English soldiers to when it meant American soldiers fighting in Mexico in the 1850s. But it was in World War I, one of the good wars, that the Salvation Army flew over to France and fried doughnuts for the boys in uniform. Yes, that Salvation Army, the same one John T. Edge refers to as "kindly white-bread Protestants who dressed in grand bell hop regalia" in his book, *Donuts: An American Passion*. World War I is the recent reason soldiers and donuts are connected. But you never see a cartoon with a fat soldier stuffing his face with doughnuts. That caricature is reserved for the doughboys in blue.

There's a simple explanation for why cops hang out at doughnut shops. Before Starbucks and PJ's, there weren't many places open late where a cop on the night shift could go for a bite or a jolt of caffeine or even a clean, well-lighted place to sit down and write a report. So we went to doughnut shops. Tastee, in particular, in New Orleans. It also helps that doughnuts are cheap. Cops could afford them. You, dear reader, don't pay us much.

Cops and doughnuts do have something else real in common: the public both loves us and hates us. Whenever somebody wants to talk about expanding crime rates, they blame cops. When they want to blame some food for widening America's waistline, they point to doughnuts. Paul R. Mullins offers the best examination of this in *Glazed America: A History of the Doughnut*. It's the most scholarly work on the subject. "The attack on doughnuts, though, often overinflates their actual capacity to kill or isolates doughnut consumption from other unhealthy foodways," Mullins writes. Perhaps "capacity to kill" was a bit strong, but you get the point. Mullins then traces doughnut prejudice all the way back the 1840s and William Alcott's book, *The Young Housekeeper: or Thoughts on Food and Cookery*.

Doughnuts make good reading too.

But I digress.

The thing that I've learned is that doughnuts connect people. Everybody likes doughnuts, whether they're an anthropology professor in Indiana or a cop on the beat in New Orleans. Doughnuts don't need an explanation; they're just good. And if doughnuts can help a divorced father connect with his two boys, they are worth every drop of cholesterol and every ounce of sugar.

BEIGNETS

In French, "beignet" is a generic word for fritter. But in New Orleans, beignets are anything but generic. They've gotten to be our signature doughnut. Café du Monde serves hot beignets 24 hours a day. That's enough to make it one of the biggest tourist attractions in town. You can buy the beignet mix, and there's nothing wrong with it. But I kind of like my own recipe.

1 cup evaporated milk

1 envelope (2¼ teaspoons) active dry yeast

6 tablespoons granulated sugar

¼ cup vegetable shortening

4 cups all-purpose flour, plus more for dusting

2 large eggs, lightly beaten

1 teaspoon salt

Vegetable oil for frying

Powdered sugar for dusting

In a small saucepan over medium heat or in a glass cup in the microwave, warm the milk until no hotter than 110°F. Transfer to the bowl of an electric stand mixer (or medium bowl if mixing by hand) and stir in the yeast. Let stand until the yeast begins to bubble, about 5 minutes.

Add the granulated sugar, shortening, flour, eggs, and salt. Beat on low speed for 1 minute until well combined, or stir with a wooden spoon. Transfer the dough to a lightly floured work surface and knead gently to form into a ball. Put the dough in a lightly greased bowl and turn to coat with the oil. Cover and set aside at room temperature until doubled in bulk about 4 hours; or refrigerate overnight.

Turn the dough out onto a lightly dusted work surface and roll out to a ¼-inch thickness. Using a pizza cutter or knife, cut into 2- to 3-inch squares. Let the dough rest for 15 minutes.

Fill a deep cast-iron pot or Dutch oven with 4 to 6 inches of oil and heat over medium-high heat to 350°F on a deep-frying thermometer. Meanwhile, line a baking sheet with parchment paper and set a wire rack on top.

Working in batches to avoid crowding the pan, fry the beignets in batches, turning once, until puffed and golden brown on both sides, 1½ to 2 minutes per side. (Another method is to drop a few dough pieces into the pot and then use a spoon to drizzle the hot oil over the top of each piece, like basting, instead of having to turn them. But mind you don't get burned!)

Transfer the beignets as they are finished to the wire rack. Generously dust with powdered sugar. (The parchment will catch the excess sugar so you can reuse it.) Serve at once.

Makes about 3 dozen beignets

Restaurant Stanley's Chili-Prawn Po-Boy with Asian Slaw

Asian Slaw

2 teaspoons sesame oil

½ napa cabbage, cored and thinly sliced

½ red bell pepper, seeded and thinly sliced

2 teaspoons rice wine vinegar

1 teaspoon sugar

4 teaspoons soy sauce

¼ teaspoon Sriracha hot chili sauce

½ teaspoon sesame seeds

Shrimp Mix

12 jumbo shrimp, peeled and deveined

Salt and freshly ground pepper

2 tablespoons olive oil

6 cloves garlic, chopped

2 cups dry white wine

¼ cup red pepper flakes, preferably Korean

2 teaspoons Sriracha hot chili sauce

4 teaspoons sugar

Pinch of salt

6 tablespoons unsalted butter, cut into small cubes

Two 7-inch pieces New Orleans French po-boy bread, split lengthwise

Sliced green onion for garnish

Stanley was one of the first restaurants to serve food after Hurricane Katrina. In those days, the chef, Scott Boswell, would buy hamburger meat and other stuff at the supermarkets in the suburbs. Then he would drive to New Orleans and cook everything on a barbecue pit for cops and journalists and French Quarter residents who never left the city. I was working out of the 8th District then, right on Royal Street in the French Quarter. I fell in love with those burgers. That is until they added this sandwich to the menu and my loyalties shifted.

To make the slaw: Heat the sesame oil in a skillet over high heat. Add the cabbage and bell pepper and sauté quickly to wilt, about 2 minutes. Add the rice wine vinegar, sugar, and soy sauce and cook until the liquid has reduced to a sauce that lightly coats the cabbage mixture, about 3 minutes. Stir in the Sriracha, mix well, and transfer to a container. Refrigerate until well chilled, about 2 hours. (The slaw can be made up to 2 days ahead.)

In a small skillet over low heat, toast the sesame seeds until golden brown, about 3 minutes. Pour onto a small plate and set aside until ready to serve.

To make the Shrimp Mix: Season the shrimp with salt and pepper. In a medium sauté pan or skillet, heat the olive oil over high heat until smoking, then carefully add the shrimp, one by one to avoid splattering. Sauté the shrimp just until pink, about 1 minute per side. Add the garlic and continue to sauté and stir until the garlic begins to brown, about 30 to 45 seconds. Add the wine, red pepper flakes, chili sauce, sugar, and salt and stir carefully to combine all ingredients. Bring the contents of the pan to a vigorous simmer. Reduce the heat to medium and cook until the shrimp are cooked through, 1½ to 2 minutes longer. Using tongs or a slotted spoon, transfer the shrimp to a warmed plate and set aside.

Continue to simmer the liquid in the pan until reduced to by three-fourths. Add the butter and swirl the pan to melt it and thicken the sauce. When all of the butter is incorporated, remove the pan from the heat and add the shrimp, stirring just to reheat.

Open each French bread piece like a book. Carefully spoon the Shrimp Mix on the bottom of each bread, dividing it equally. Drizzle the sauce over the top. Stir the toasted sesame seeds into the Asian Slaw and mound over the shrimp. Garnish with the green onion. Press the sandwiches closed and serve at once.

Makes 2 servings

Kitchen Witch's
Hot and Cold Redfish Salad

Seasoning Mix

4 teaspoons sea salt or kosher salt

2 teaspoons paprika

1 teaspoon cayenne pepper

1 teaspoon freshly ground black pepper

½ teaspoon freshly ground white pepper

½ teaspoon granulated garlic

½ teaspoon dried thyme

½ teaspoon dried basil

½ teaspoon dried oregano

½ teaspoon dried dill

4 boneless, skinless redfish, Louisiana crappie, red snapper, or any other firm white flaky fish fillets (about 6 ounces each)

2 tablespoons olive oil

¼ cup dry white wine

Juice and finely diced zest of ½ lemon

Dash of Worcestershire sauce

Salad

Juice and zest of ½ lemon

6 tablespoons extra-virgin olive oil

1 teaspoon minced fresh herb of your choice (I recommend thyme)

½ head romaine lettuce, washed well, spun and torn into pieces

½ head butter lettuce, washed well, spun and torn into pieces

½ head green leaf lettuce, washed well, spun and torn into pieces

Pinch of Seasoning Mix (above)

4 plum tomatoes, diced

1 cucumber peeled, seeded, and diced

1 small red onion or 4 green onions, white and tender green parts, finely diced

8 artichoke hearts (optional)

½ cup jarred thinly sliced roasted red peppers, drained (optional)

1 cup croutons (optional)

Around the corner from the 8th District Station, there's a used cookbook store. That's just about all they sell, cookbooks. I went in it just because I couldn't imagine that there would be that big of a market for used cookbooks. Philipe La Mancusa runs it. He's a former chef who used to cook at Commander's Palace and Peristyle. When I told him I didn't cook, he told me he had a delicious recipe that was healthy and so simple that even I couldn't mess it up. At first I told him he underestimated my inability. Then I tried this dish and realized he was right. Philipe recommends serving it with crusty garlic bread and a chilled Alsatian Riesling.

You can substitute any good-quality store-bought version for the spice mixture, such as Chef Paul Prudhomme's Seafood Magic.

To make the seasoning: Whisk together all the ingredients in a bowl and set aside.

Preheat the oven to 350°F. Place four individual plates in the refrigerator to chill.

Arrange the fish on a baking sheet and let come to room temperature. In a bowl, combine the olive oil, wine, lemon juice and zest, and Worcestershire. Pour over the fish. Sprinkle the fish with the Seasoning Mix, reserving a pinch for the salad. Bake for 6 to 9 minutes for medium-rare to medium. You'll know that they're done when you press them with your finger and you can feel the flakes of the fish beginning to separate.

While the fish is baking, make the salad: For the dressing, whisk together the lemon juice and zest, olive oil, and fresh herb. Set aside.

In a large bowl, combine all the lettuces and toss to mix. Drizzle in the dressing and a pinch of seasoning mix and toss to coat the lettuce lightly with the dressing. Arrange the dressed lettuce on the chilled plates and compose the remaining salad ingredients nicely on top.

Lay a fish fillet on each salad, pour some of the pan juices over the fish, and serve at once.

Makes 4 servings

CHICKEN ÉTOUFFÉE

CHEF POPPY TOOKER

Étouffer means "smother" in French. In a real New Orleans restaurant, you might see either term, but a tourist trap would never have smothered chicken on its menu. It doesn't sound exotic enough. By either name, it's a standard Louisiana cooking technique.

One thing that our resident expert, Poppy Tooker, told me was something I'm sure a lot of local cooks would disagree with. But, here goes: "I cook my roux fast and hot—so it takes maybe five to seven minutes max. I get the oil hot, add the flour, and cook it over that high heat the whole time. There's no need to slow cook a roux, unless you're trying to make one with butter, which really doesn't work for our kind of cooking."

A bachelor has to have one dish he can make when he invites a young lady to dinner. My ex-wife, Kay, isn't from New Orleans, so this one really knocked her out the first time I made it.

In a deep cast-iron skillet or Dutch oven, heat the bacon fat over medium heat. When the fat is hot, add the flour slowly, 1 tablespoon at a time, stirring constantly to help it dissolve and incorporate. When all the flour has been added, continue cooking the roux, stirring almost constantly, until it turns a rich dark brown color, similar to the color of dark chocolate, about 7 minutes. Add the onion and cook, stirring constantly, until it softens and darkens, about 3 minutes. Add the celery, bell pepper, and garlic and cook until the vegetables are tender, about 5 minutes longer.

Whisk three-quarters of the beer into the pan, stirring to incorporate. Drink the rest of the beer. Stir in the thyme and bay leaf. Bring to a brisk simmer and cook for 10 minutes, then add the chicken breasts. Reduce the heat to maintain a low simmer, cover tightly, and cook until the chicken is tender, about 20 to 25 minutes. You may have to open another beer to add more liquid as the chicken cooks—a little more for the cook and a little more for the pot! Season with hot sauce, salt, and pepper.

Scoop the rice into individual bowls or plates and spoon the étouffée over. Serve at once.

½ cup bacon drippings or olive oil

¾ cup all-purpose flour

1 yellow onion, chopped

3 celery stalks, chopped

1 bell pepper, seeded and chopped

3 cloves garlic, minced

One 12-ounce bottle of beer or 1 cup Basic Chicken Stock (page 230) or store-bought chicken broth

2 teaspoons minced fresh thyme

1 bay leaf

6 boneless, skinless chicken breast halves (about 6 ounces each)

2 tablespoons hot sauce

Salt and freshly ground pepper

Hot cooked rice for serving

Makes 6 servings

Oyster Farmers: Croatian, Black, Vietnamese, and Cambodian

On the surface, New Orleans can be explained in black and white. I'm from Alabama. I can understand that. But as you dig deeper into the culture of this city, all sorts of other colors and complications start popping up. I learned that when I asked a simple question about the oyster industry.

A lot of the big restaurants here use P&J Oysters. The oysters are great and the people are reliable. But I had gotten to be friends with Captain Pete Vujnovich (pronounced VOY-no-vich) at his place on St. Claude Avenue near Rampart. He was just as serious about his oysters as the guys at P&J's. So before Hurricane Katrina destroyed his business, my menu proudly featured Captain Pete's oysters.

When I started asking about oyster suppliers after the storm, it seems every name that came up in the discussion ended in i-c-h or v-i-c and often started with something unpronounceable—Cvitanovich, Jurasich, Popavic, Tesvich.

Turns out Croatians have been coming to the Louisiana coast since the 1840s and '50s. Many of them had fished in the Adriatic Sea along the Dalmatian Coast before coming here aboard sailing ships. In his book, *Yugoslavs in Louisiana*, Milos Vujnovich credits these immigrants with virtually inventing the oyster farming business in Louisiana. Contrary to what most people think, oysters are farmed, not just fished. Oystermen take small "seed" oysters, often from public grounds, and "plant" them miles away in the waters they have leased from the state. When the oysters mature, they are harvested by ships with special rakelike implements

that dredge the sea floor for the bivalve mollusks. Lots of Croatians still work the waters off St. Bernard Parish.

Still others have started some of the city's iconic restaurants like Uglesich's, Drago's and Crescent City Steak House. Before Ruth Fertel bought the steak house on which she would build her empire. Ruth's Chris Steak House was just Chris Steak House and was owned by the Matulich family.

Croatians aren't the only ones working Louisiana's oyster waters. In the aftermath of the hurricanes, Byron Encalade emerged as spokesman for the black oystermen working off the coast on the eastern side of Plaquemines Parish. I met

him at one of the many community meetings we had after Katrina, when we talked about the impact of the storm on the food supply. His family has been on the water for generations. He told me, "When I was a little boy, I remember handing cotton to my grandfather while he built boats in the yard, underneath the oak tree." He added, "My dad bought me my first boat when I was thirteen years old. One side of my family was mostly oystermen and shrimpers, and the other side was mostly farmers and shrimpers."

In New Orleans, we keep trying to tell people that Hurricane Katrina, in and of itself, was not such a big deal. By the time it arrived in the city it was a strong storm, but not a devastating one. Our problem was that the floodwalls and levees that the federal government built leaked as a result of the storm, even though they were supposed to be able to withstand a hurricane of that magnitude. Plaquemines is a coastal parish. It got the brunt of the impact.

"We got devastated by Katrina. We had twenty-five feet of water. There was nothing left," Byron said.

Boats were thrown a mile inland by the storm. So far, FEMA won't pay to have them moved back on to the water, where they could be towed to be repaired. Where houses used to be, you see stairs to nowhere, since the only thing remaining of the structures are the cement stairs. For a long time, there was no ice machine in the area, so that even if fishermen were able to get out to sea and work, they didn't have a way to safely keep their catch. Funny thing is, it wasn't FEMA's job or the government's job necessarily to replace a damaged ice machine. But unless the ice machine and other parts of the infrastructure were replaced, nothing else mattered. People would not be able to go back to earning a living.

Two other immigrant groups have managed to re-create their Old World fishing lives off Louisiana waters: the Cambodians and the Vietnamese. While Vietnamese fishermen have focused largely on the shrimping business, there are many Cambodian oystermen, especially in south Plaquemines Parish. Now roughly a third of the fishermen working in Louisiana waters are from Southeast Asia. If you go shopping for fresh seafood, you'll see that a lot of the old places have been bought by Vietnamese. They serve pho and fried rice alongside boiled crabs and fresh shrimp.

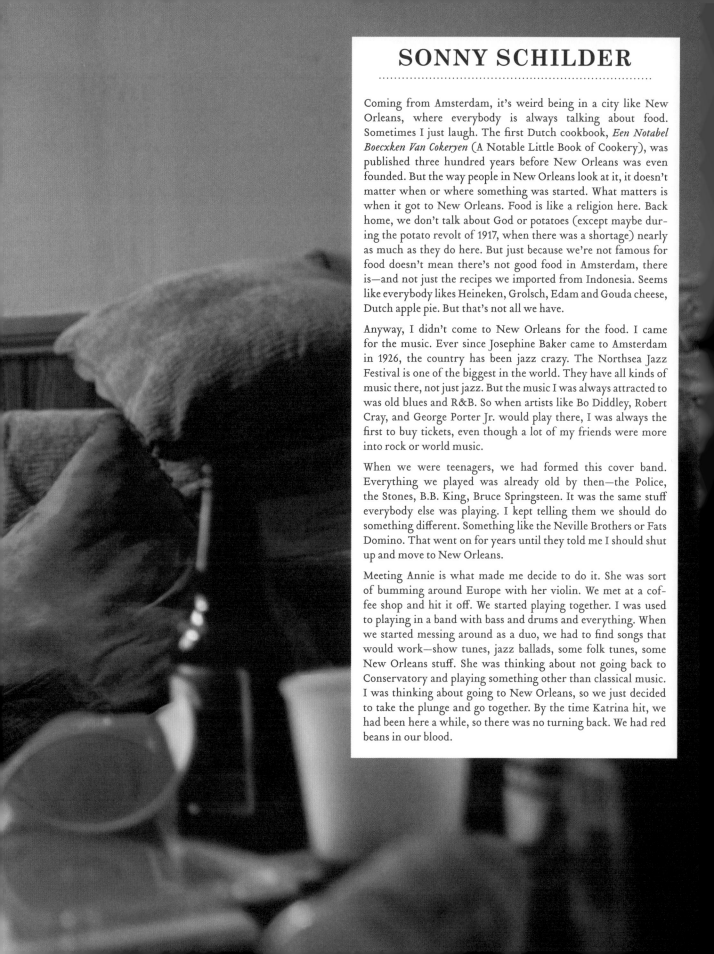

SONNY SCHILDER

Coming from Amsterdam, it's weird being in a city like New Orleans, where everybody is always talking about food. Sometimes I just laugh. The first Dutch cookbook, *Een Notabel Boecxken Van Cokeryen* (A Notable Little Book of Cookery), was published three hundred years before New Orleans was even founded. But the way people in New Orleans look at it, it doesn't matter when or where something was started. What matters is when it got to New Orleans. Food is like a religion here. Back home, we don't talk about God or potatoes (except maybe during the potato revolt of 1917, when there was a shortage) nearly as much as they do here. But just because we're not famous for food doesn't mean there's not good food in Amsterdam, there is—and not just the recipes we imported from Indonesia. Seems like everybody likes Heineken, Grolsch, Edam and Gouda cheese, Dutch apple pie. But that's not all we have.

Anyway, I didn't come to New Orleans for the food. I came for the music. Ever since Josephine Baker came to Amsterdam in 1926, the country has been jazz crazy. The Northsea Jazz Festival is one of the biggest in the world. They have all kinds of music there, not just jazz. But the music I was always attracted to was old blues and R&B. So when artists like Bo Diddley, Robert Cray, and George Porter Jr. would play there, I was always the first to buy tickets, even though a lot of my friends were more into rock or world music.

When we were teenagers, we had formed this cover band. Everything we played was already old by then—the Police, the Stones, B.B. King, Bruce Springsteen. It was the same stuff everybody else was playing. I kept telling them we should do something different. Something like the Neville Brothers or Fats Domino. That went on for years until they told me I should shut up and move to New Orleans.

Meeting Annie is what made me decide to do it. She was sort of bumming around Europe with her violin. We met at a coffee shop and hit it off. We started playing together. I was used to playing in a band with bass and drums and everything. When we started messing around as a duo, we had to find songs that would work—show tunes, jazz ballads, some folk tunes, some New Orleans stuff. She was thinking about not going back to Conservatory and playing something other than classical music. I was thinking about going to New Orleans, so we just decided to take the plunge and go together. By the time Katrina hit, we had been here a while, so there was no turning back. We had red beans in our blood.

Rodekool met Appels
(Braised Red Cabbage with Apples)

CHEF DIRK-JAN ZONNEVELD

Two things you need to accompany Hachee (page 182): some potatoes and some red cabbage. For the potatoes, use whatever boiled, baked, or mashed potato recipe you like. Potatoes are a staple in the Netherlands even though they come from this hemisphere. When I was growing up, I ate a lot of potatoes, but I didn't bother putting a potato recipe here. Our mashed potatoes aren't that different from anybody else's.

For the cabbage, use this recipe from my friend, Dirk-Jan Zonneveld, who wrote a Dutch cookbook and mailed me a copy. (Thanks, buddy!) It's the best.

Peel off the outer leaves of the cabbage and discard. Quarter the cabbage and trim away the core. Cut the quarters into ¼-inch slices. In a medium heavy-bottomed saucepan or large Dutch oven over medium heat, melt the butter. Add the onion and sauté until soft, about 2 minutes, stirring occasionally. Stir in the cabbage, mixing well, then stir in the flour.

Add the wine, water, vinegar, brown sugar, bay leaf, cloves, ½ teaspoon salt, and ¼ teaspoon pepper. Bring to a boil over high heat. Cover and reduce the heat to maintain a simmer. Cook until the cabbage is tender, about 1 hour and 15 minutes, stirring occasionally. If you stew the cabbage this long, all the aromatics mingle and the cabbage still has a bite; however, if you prefer your cabbage very crunchy, simmer for only 30 to 45 minutes and add more brown sugar if you like.

Add the apples and continue cooking, uncovered, until the apples are soft and most of the liquid has cooked away, about 2 minutes more. Remove from heat and season with more brown sugar, salt, and pepper if desired.

1 red cabbage (about 2 pounds)

2 tablespoons unsalted butter

1 yellow onion, halved and cut crosswise into ⅛-inch slices

1 teaspoon all-purpose flour

1 cup dry red wine

1 cup water

¼ cup red wine vinegar

1½ tablespoons dark brown sugar, plus more to taste

1 bay leaf

3 whole cloves

Salt and freshly ground pepper

2 apples, peeled, cored, and cut into ¼-inch dice (use your favorite variety)

Makes 6 to 8 servings

HACHEE MET LEFFE BIER
(BEEF ONION STEW WITH DARK BEER)

1½ pounds beef stew meat, cut into 1-inch cubes

Sea salt and freshly ground pepper

3 tablespoons olive oil

3 yellow onions, coarsely chopped (about 4 cups)

2 tablespoons unsalted butter

2 tablespoons all-purpose flour

2 cups store-bought beef broth

One 12-ounce bottle dark beer such as Guinness

2 tablespoons red wine vinegar

Pinch of freshly grated nutmeg

1 bay leaf

1 whole clove

1 teaspoon Dijon mustard

1 teaspoon tomato paste

½ teaspoon dark or light brown sugar

1 tablespoon finely chopped fresh flat-leaf parsley for garnish

1 tablespoon finely chopped fresh tarragon for garnish

When I left Amsterdam, the only thing on my mind was New Orleans music. I didn't imagine how homesick I would be for Dutch food. Hachee (pronounced hah-shay), that's real Dutch cooking—simple, full of flavor, full of the feeling of home. It's one of the classic Dutch dishes we all grew up with. The minute the weather turns cold, I think of my mother and my grandmother and I start to crave this dish. I got this recipe from Dirk-Jan Zonneveld. The dark roux he uses reminds me of the essential ingredient in a good gumbo. This stew is even better if made a day ahead. It is wonderful with mashed potatoes and Rodekool met Appels (Braised Red Cabbage with Apples, page 181).

Season the stew meat all over with 1½ teaspoons salt and 1½ teaspoons pepper. In a large heavy saucepan or large Dutch oven over medium heat, heat 1 tablespoon of the oil until hot, about 2 minutes. Working in batches if necessary to prevent overcrowding, add the meat to the hot oil and cook until all the pieces are nicely browned, about 15 minutes total. (It's important not to overcrowd the pan as the meat browns so the meat doesn't boil in its own juices instead of browning.) During the browning process, stir occasionally and add 1 tablespoon more oil if needed. Using a slotted spoon, transfer the meat to a bowl, leaving drippings in the pan.

If the pan of drippings looks very dry, add 1 tablespoon oil to the pan. Place pan over medium heat and add the onions, slowly sautéing until nicely browned but not burned, about 30 minutes, stirring often. Remove from the heat and set aside to add to the roux immediately after made.

Preheat the oven to 375°F.

Meanwhile, prepare the roux: In a heavy 10-inch skillet over medium heat, melt the butter. Using a long-handled metal whisk or wooden spoon, stir in the flour until smooth. Continue cooking until the roux turns dark chocolate brown, about 10 minutes, stirring constantly and scraping the skillet bottom as you stir, to keep the roux from burning. (If it burns, you will need to make a new batch of roux; cook roux over

lower heat to have better control of it.) Once the roux is the right color, immediately remove the skillet from heat and stir the reserved browned onions into the roux to help cool it more quickly. Continue stirring constantly for about 2 minutes, or until the roux is no longer darkening.

Transfer the roux and onion mixture to the pan used for browning the meat. Stir in the reserved meat, then add the stock, beer, vinegar, nutmeg, bay leaf, clove, mustard, and tomato paste, blending thoroughly. If necessary, add just enough water so that all ingredients are covered with liquid. Bring to a boil over high heat, then cover and bake in the oven until the meat is fork tender and the juices have reduced to a nice smooth sauce, about 2 hours, stirring occasionally (the sauce will be fairly thin).

Remove the pan from the oven and stir in the brown sugar. Add more salt and pepper if needed. Serve at once or reheat for serving if made ahead. Garnish with parsley and tarragon just before serving.

Makes 4 servings

BUN (VIETNAMESE VERMICELLI SALAD WITH BEEF)

I learned this dish from Linh and it's become one of my favorites. Vietnamese dishes are always designed for balance. With this dish you have the warm cooked beef and the cold raw vegetables. The fish sauce is salty, but the dressing is kind of sweet. The noodles are soft, but the vegetables are crunchy. It's a good lesson.

To make the marinade: In a medium bowl, whisk together the fish sauce, chopped cilantro, chopped onion, vegetable oil, sugar, and garlic. Slice the steak crosswise into ⅛-inch slices and add to the marinade, mixing well so each slice is coated with marinade. Cover and refrigerate for at least 2 hours or up to 8 hours ahead.

About 1½ hours before serving time, put the noodles in a large heat-resistant mixing bowl and cover with boiling water. Allow the noodles to soak for 45 minutes, until tender. Drain and pat dry with a clean kitchen towel. Set aside at room temperature until ready to serve. (Or you may cook the noodles for 6 to 7 minutes in boiling water until tender, drain, pat dry, and set aside at room temperature.)

While the noodles are soaking, arrange the lettuce leaves in four large individual serving bowls. Divide the bean sprouts, cucumber, tomatoes, carrot, sliced onions, mint leaves, cilantro leaves, basil leaves, and sliced jalapeño among the bowls. Cover each bowl with a damp paper towel and refrigerate until ready to serve.

To make the Nuoc Mam: In a small bowl, whisk together the sugar and hot water until sugar is completely dissolved. Add the fish sauce, lime juice, minced jalapeño, garlic, and chili sauce. Twenty minutes before ready to serve, stir in the carrots. (The sauce can be made up to 1 week ahead and stored, covered tightly, in the refrigerator. Add the carrots just before serving.)

Preheat a grill or grill pan until hot. Remove the steak from the marinade and pat dry; discard the marinade.

Remove the serving bowls from the refrigerator, uncover, and add a portion of the noodles on top of each salad.

Grill the steak slices until nicely charred and medium-rare, about 1 minute per side. Divide the still-hot steak slices among the salad bowls, add 2 tablespoons of Nuoc Mam to each, and garnish with peanuts. Serve at once.

Makes 4 servings

Marinade

½ cup **Vietnamese fish sauce**

½ cup chopped fresh cilantro, stems and leaves

¼ cup chopped white onion

3 tablespoons vegetable oil

1 tablespoon sugar

2 cloves garlic, minced

1 pound **strip steak**

One 6-ounce package rice stick noodles

Boiling water for soaking

Leaves from 1 head red leaf, romaine, or green lettuce, rinsed and well dried

1 cup fresh mung bean sprouts

1 medium cucumber, peeled and seeded, halved lengthwise and cut into ¼-inch-thick half moons

½ cup wedges or slices fresh ripe tomatoes

1 medium carrot, peeled and coarsely shredded

¼ cup thinly sliced white onion (optional)

½ cup fresh mint leaves

½ cup fresh cilantro leaves

½ cup fresh basil leaves, torn

1 large fresh jalapeño chile, not seeded, cut crosswise into ⅛-inch slices

Nuoc Mam

5 tablespoons sugar

⅓ cup hot water

¼ cup **Vietnamese fish sauce**

2 tablespoons fresh lime juice

1 teaspoon minced fresh jalapeño chile

1 clove garlic, minced

½ teaspoon Sriracha hot chili sauce

2 tablespoons peeled and coarsely shredded carrot

¼ cup roasted and chopped peanuts for garnish

Madame Bégué and the Invention of Brunch

"Brunch is a New Orleans tradition born from the heart of Catholic faith. Until the mid-twentieth century, Catholics were prohibited by church law from eating or drinking anything after midnight on Saturday if they intended to go to communion on Sunday morning. After mass, those who had been fasting were hungry and ready for a meal, though in many cases it was too late for breakfast and too early for lunch. Hence, brunch became a favorite Sunday meal for Catholics in New Orleans."
—John Folse, *Hot Beignets and Warm Boudoirs*

"Madame Bégué is dead. No more Epicurean breakfasts in the Quartier Latin for the bon-vivants of the nation. No more snails a là Creole, or artichokes a la Begue, or the thousand-and-one curious palate-ticklers that one could get nowhere else west of Paris. Madame Bégué is dead, and the queer little two-story structure on the French Market-place, with concrete over the bricks, and painted on that in Creole fashion, the single word 'Bégué's' is silent and desolate."
—Felix J. Koch, *The Boston Cooking School* magazine, Volume 11, June/July 1906, May 1907

Every Sunday at 11 a.m., the hotel owners and tourism marketing people of New Orleans fall to their knees, giving thanks and praises to the dearly departed Elizabeth Kettenring Dutrey Bégué. They pray for good weather. They pray that their restaurants do a lot of brunch business. And they pray that their devotion will undo all the curses the chefs, cooks, dish-washers, and waitstaff have heaped on this same long dead woman hours before as these poor working stiffs brushed the bourbon from their breath and sleep from their eyes and rushed to prep for Sunday brunch.

Madame Bégué was a German immigrant. She and her husband, Louis Dutrey, opened a coffee shop near the French Market in 1863. After Dutrey died, the widow married Hypolite Bégué, one of her bartenders. As the story goes, French Market shop owners and tradesmen might grab only a snack in the morning en route to opening up and preparing for the start of that day's business. But around eleven o'clock in the morning, when things slowed down, they would be looking for a more substantive meal. Madame started serving a "second breakfast" that was as impressive as any brunch you've ever seen or read about.

The *Boston Cooking School* magazine took two pages to describe the meal. There was a bottle of wine for each person at the table. The first course was boiled crawfish. Then an omelette. Then a crudité course of celery and radishes. Then tripe in a yellow sauce. Then the fried chicken and "fried boiled potatoes." That concluded the first hour's offerings. Then there was beef steak and broiled tomatoes. Then the cheese course with apples. Then the café brûlot. At other times gumbo, crawfish bisque, jambalaya, and *pain perdue* (French toast) were part of the plated parade. The meal could go on for four hours and cost a whole dollar.

In his book *Southern Food*, John Egerton wrote, "Nobody serves breakfasts like that any more, not even in New Orleans." I think he was sad.

Not me.

Even though no one does it exactly like Madame Bégué, this is the meal on which the New Orleans reputation for Sunday brunch is built. These days, every Sunday Brunch in New Orleans is a "jazz brunch." It's kind of like a jazz funeral. For the chefs, it's the same sort of sad occasion, only with music.

The problem is, the cooks probably got off late Saturday night and "unwound" until early in the morning. Then they have to turn around and be back at work around sunrise. Most brunch food is pretty straightforward. But even simple cooking requires you to be awake and alert.

Having said all that, we have some recipes in this book that are a win-win. You can cook them at home and I and the rest of the cooks can sleep in.

Appeltaart (Dutch Apple Pie)

CHEF DIRK-JAN ZONNEVELD

The three things everyone knows about Dutch food are Gouda cheese, Heineken beer, and Dutch apple pie. The beer and cheese you should buy. And if you were in Amsterdam, I could tell you where to buy the pie. They serve it at just about every restaurant, café and bar in town. As Dirk-Jan says, after you taste this pie, you'll wish your grandmother had been Dutch so you could have had it every Sunday.

To make the pie crust: In a large mixing bowl, use a large spoon to combine the flour, brown sugar and salt. Add the diced butter, vanilla, and half of the beaten egg, stirring until all the ingredients are starting to blend. Reserve the remaining egg. With the dough still in the bowl, knead the dough with your hands until the butter is thoroughly incorporated and the dough has a smooth cookie-dough texture, 6 to 8 minutes.

Transfer the dough to a very lightly floured surface. Pinch off one third of the dough and shape it into a rectangle about 5 inches by 2 inches. Wrap well with plastic wrap and refrigerate for about 30 minutes, so that it cools but is still pliable.

Grease a 9-inch springform pan. Using your fingers, press the remaining two-thirds dough into the prepared springform pan to cover the entire bottom of the pan and extend up the sides 1½ inches. Set aside at room temperature.

In a small saucepan, place the currants and cover with the water. Bring the water barely to a simmer, then remove the pan from heat and set aside for at least 10 minutes. (You may do this several hours ahead.)

Drain the currants and dry them in a clean dish towel. Put them in a large mixing bowl. Peel and core the apples, cut them into large pieces, and add them to the bowl with the currants. Add the sugar and cinnamon, and mix by carefully shaking the bowl in an up and down motion until the apples and currants are coated evenly with the sugar and cinnamon. Pour the filling into the dough-lined springform pan, making sure the currants are well distributed in the filling. Arrange the apple pieces to make the filling a consistent thickness. Set aside.

Position a rack in the middle of the oven and preheat to 350°F.

Remove the dough rectangle from the refrigerator, unwrap, and place on a lightly floured work surface. Use a lightly floured rolling pin, roll out to a 10-by 4-inch rectangle. With a knife, cut this rectangle into strips that are 10 inches long and ½ inch wide. Use the blade of the knife to carefully loosen the dough strips from the work surface (they may be sticky since this is a soft dough). Lay half the strips over the filling in parallel rows about 1 inch apart. Then lay the remaining strips perpendicular to the first half to form a lattice of diamond shapes, through which you see some of the filling. Trim the ends of the dough or pinch them to fit the inside edge of the pan. Use any leftover strips around the outer edge of the lattice to make a smooth border.

Beat the remaining half egg in a small bowl, and use a pastry brush to brush the lattice and edge with the egg. (You may have a little egg left over.)

Bake until the crust is golden brown and the juices are bubbly, about 50 minutes. Remove from oven and place on a wire rack to cool completely before removing sides of pan, about 2 hours. As it cools, the pie will pull away from the sides of the pan.

Serve at room temperature, cut in wedges, and topped with generous dollops of whipped cream.

Pie Crust

2¼ cups all-purpose flour, plus more for dusting

⅔ cup firmly packed light brown sugar

⅛ teaspoon salt

1 cup (2 sticks) cold unsalted butter, cut into ¼-inch dice

½ teaspoon vanilla extract

1 large egg, beaten

¼ cup currants or raisins, or 2 tablespoons of each

½ cup water

2 pounds apples (use your favorite variety)

1½ teaspoons sugar, or more if using very tart apples

¼ teaspoon ground cinnamon

Whipped cream for serving

Makes one 9-inch pie; serves 8 to 10

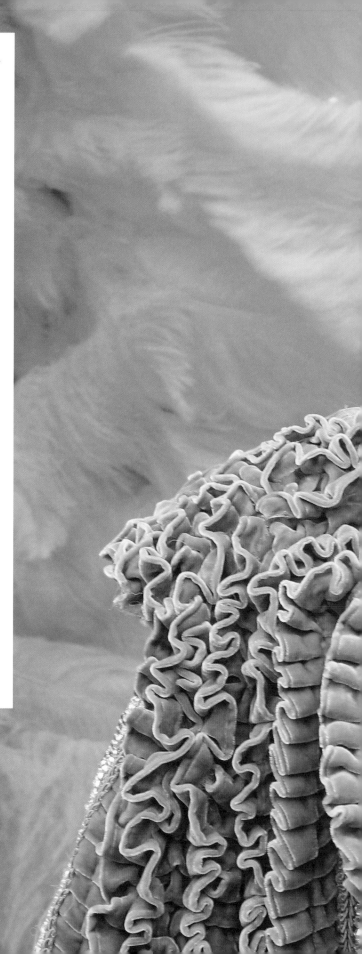

DELMOND LAMBREAUX

Picture this: You have a pig in a forest in France and an American jazz musician in the middle of Paris. The musician speaks no French and has never been outside the United States. What you think's gonna happen first? The pig's going to find the truffle, or the jazz musician's going to find the McDonald's? Take my word for it. Don't bet on the pig. Paris might be famous for good food, but back in the day you couldn't tell us that.

We were young guys, never been anywhere, never seen anything. If it didn't involve girls or music, we weren't getting too excited about it. We wanted home food, and I don't mean mama's cooking. I learned how to say "am-beur-guer" and then "Le McDo" real fast so there would be no mistaking what I was looking for. And, once I found it, I developed a two-Big Mac-a-day habit.

That was the first time I was in Europe. We had a week at this club in the Latin Quarter. On our night off, the club owner's wife invited us to their apartment for dinner. One thing led to another, and she started asking us about the food we ate at home. The other guys didn't have much to say. A lot of them were raised on fast food and microwave dinners. But I grew up on good Creole cooking. So I started telling them about my mom's red beans and rice, and shrimp Creole and smothered chicken. I was feeling all superior to the other guys. Then the wife asked me if I could cook some Creole food for them. Of course, I couldn't. So much for my superiority complex.

New Orleans food has an identity. You don't have to tell people where you from. You just start telling them what you eat and they know. New Orleans. It's like the music. The minute you play some brass band or some traditional jazz or some Nevilles or Dr. John, people know what passport you carry.

When I started seeing food in that musical context, I decided to at least learn some basic stuff about my home food. It's like, I don't think any New Orleanian should be allowed to move out of the city unless they have at least 10 classic New Orleans records with them to share with the world. Go where you want, but don't forget where you came from.

I don't carry beans and rice in my suitcase. But I have perfected red beans and merguez sausage, and some other recipes adapted for what I can find in Europe or South America. I still ain't no gourmet cook. But at least I can represent a little bit.

MUSCADINE WINE LEMONADE

One 750-ml bottle white muscadine wine

6 cups water

1½ cups sugar

2 cups fresh lemon juice, preferably from Meyer lemons

Seems like my father can never stop talking about the wine his grandfather used to make in Maringouin, Louisiana, back in the day. He would make it from whatever fruit was in season. When I brought back a bottle of wine from a gig I had in Italy, he just turned his nose up. All he could say was, "It's not like my grandfather's."

One Thanksgiving, I decided to surprise him. I bought some of Henry Amato's fruit wines in the farmers' market. Henry makes wine in Independence, Louisiana, in Tangipahoa Parish. I bought damn near every flavor they had—strawberry, orange, blueberry. He liked them. I actually bought something that pleased my father and met his Maringouin standard. Amazing. Finally there was only one bottle left, the white muscadine. My mother was still living then. She took that last bottle and made this lemonade with it. It was fantastic. Refreshing and not too strong. You can sip it all afternoon. For measuring, I just empty the wine into the pitcher, then refill the bottle twice with water.

Combine all the ingredients in a pitcher.
Stir vigorously until the sugar is dissolved.
Refrigerate until well chilled. Serve cold.

Makes 6 to 8 servings

Ruth's Garlicky
White Shrimp Remoulade

CHEF RUTH FERTEL

My parents used to take us to Ruth's Chris Steak House on Broad Street whenever one of us graduated from high school or college. They didn't have the money to do it, but they knew that achievements had to be observed and celebrated. Some kids in our neighborhood never made those milestones. The waitresses were always nice to my sisters and me, especially Miss Lainey, Miss Connie, Miss Robin, and even Miss Ruth. They didn't even turn their noses up when my father ordered his steak "on the well side of medium well." But it wasn't the steak I really remember; it was the shrimp remoulade appetizer. New Orleanians never get tired of eating boiled shrimp, but the remoulade at Ruth's was something special.

Years later, after Hurricane Katrina, I met Randy Fertel. He helped start Artist Corps, a program that sends professional musicians and other artists to teach in the schools. He wanted me to help him find some musicians who might like to teach. When I told him how much I loved the shrimp remoulade at his mother's restaurant, he told me that he had a recipe for me. This is the note he put in the e-mail he sent with the recipe:

"A family recipe from Plaquemines Parish with roots in France, this remoulade sauce was changed a bit for Ruth's Chris. In New Orleans there are two kinds of remoulade: the red remoulade, which is full of paprika, cayenne, lemon, and olive oil and served at famous restaurants like Galatoire's; and this more classically French one, the garlicky mayonnaise-based white remoulade. Best to make ahead of time so that the garlic marries with the other ingredients. I think Zatarain's Creole mustard is a key here, but if you must, substitute another grainy dark mustard. In my mind, you don't make enough remoulade to fit the quantity of shrimp, or vice versa. You make the remoulade and are very happy when there are leftovers, because it's great on roast beef and ham sandwiches . . . everything short of cheesecake. It will keep covered in the refrigerator for up to 2 weeks."

If you're in New Orleans, it's easiest to buy boiled shrimp from a seafood market. The second best option, no matter where you live, is to boil your own shrimp, using Zatarain's Shrimp & Crab Boil. For the purists, I'm including a from-scratch shrimp boil. You decide.

Garlicky White Remoulade

One 15-ounce jar Hellmann's mayonnaise

4 ounces Zatarain's Creole Mustard (use all but an ounce or so of a small 5 ¼-ounce jar)

2 or 3 cloves garlic

3 tablespoons fresh lemon juice

½ teaspoon Worcestershire sauce

¼ teaspoon Tabasco

3 tablespoons minced fresh parsley

2 green onions, white and tender green parts, minced

Boiled Shrimp

1 gallon water

6 cloves garlic, roughly chopped

3 stalks celery, roughly chopped

1 large yellow onion, roughly chopped

Juice of 1 lemon

½ teaspoon ground allspice

2 bay leaves

1 tablespoon salt

1 teaspoon cayenne pepper

4 to 5 pounds medium shrimp, unpeeled, heads intact

1 head iceberg lettuce, cored and chopped

To make the remoulade: In a bowl, combine the mayonnaise, mustard, garlic, lemon juice, Worcestershire, and Tabasco and whisk to blend. Add the parsley and green onion and stir gently to blend. Transfer to a serving bowl and refrigerate until ready to serve.

To make the shrimp: In a large soup pot or stockpot, combine all the ingredients except the shrimp. Bring to a boil over high heat. Fill a large bowl with water and ice cubes to make an ice water bath. When the liquid in the stockpot is boiling, add the shrimp. Let the water return to a boil, then remove from the heat and let the shrimp steep for 3 minutes. Using a slotted spoon or a skimmer, immediately transfer the shrimp to the water bath to stop the cooking. (Discard the boiling liquid, or continue to simmer until reduced to a shrimp stock, about 30 minutes. Let cool completely, then transfer to airtight containers for another use. Refrigerate for up to 3 days or freeze for up to 4 weeks.)

When shrimp have cooled, transfer to a strainer and drain thoroughly, then pat dry with paper towels.

Arrange the lettuce on a serving platter. Scatter the shrimp over the lettuce. Spoon the remoulade over the shrimp and serve at once.

Makes 6 to 8 servings

Dickie Brennan's Steakhouse Tomato Napoleon

CHEF ALFRED
SINGLETON

The state vegetable of Louisiana is the Creole tomato, even though tomatoes are actually fruit. On the East Coast, they're almost as crazy about Jersey tomatoes as we are about Creole tomatoes in New Orleans. I tried to take my father to a nice Christmas dinner at Dickie Brennan's. That was when he was having so much trouble getting insurance money to fix the house. I had the nerve to suggest he might want to get some counseling. He stormed out of the restaurant. And that was that. It was just as well, I guess. It wasn't Creole tomato season then anyway.

To make the remoulade: Blend all ingredients, except the vegetable oil and salt, in a food processor until smooth. With the food processor running, slowly add the oil until emulsified. Season with the salt, and set aside.

To make the Napoleon: place the lettuce strips in a bowl, add the cane vinegar, sprinkle with salt and pepper, and toss to coat evenly. Divide the dressed lettuce among eight salad plates. Place 1 slice of tomato on top of the lettuce on each plate and sprinkle with salt and pepper. Put about 2 tablespoons of blue cheese on top and layer with another slice of tomato. Pour ¼ cup of remoulade sauce over the tomato and top each with another 2 tablespoons of blue cheese. Garnish with shaved red onions.

Makes 8 servings

Remoulade Sauce

½ yellow onion

¼ cup Dijon mustard

½ cup Creole mustard

½ cup ketchup

¼ cup prepared horseradish

2 celery stalks, finely chopped

Leaves of 3 fresh flat-leaf parsley sprigs, finely chopped

2 large eggs

2 cloves garlic, chopped

1 tablespoon Crystal or other hot sauce

2 green onions, white and tender green parts chopped

¼ thin-skinned lemon, peeled and seeded

¾ cup vegetable oil

Salt

Tomato Napoleon

1 head green leaf lettuce, cored and cut crosswise into ½-inch strips

¼ cup cane vinegar

Salt and freshly ground pepper

2 large ripe tomatoes, cut into a total of sixteen slices about ½ inch thick

1 pound blue cheese, crumbled and divided into 8 equal portions

1 red onion, cut into thinly shaved slices

ZUCCHINI AND SHRIMP SEMPLICE

3 pounds zucchini, unpeeled

4½ tablespoons unsalted butter

1 yellow onion, coarsely chopped

1 green bell pepper, seeded and cut into ¼-inch strips the length of the pepper

2½ teaspoons Basic Creole Seasoning Blend (page 228)

3 cloves garlic, finely chopped

1 pound medium shrimp, peeled and deveined

Hot cooked rice for serving

The hardest thing for a New Orleanian to get used to in New York is the price of shrimp. Shrimp are cheap back home, but up here you have to take out a loan to get a pound of shrimp. Since zucchini is cheap, this dish balances out. It's a simple dish. "Semplice," as the Italian composers would say.

Cut the zucchini or squash crosswise into rounds ¼ inch thick. Melt 4 tablespoons of the butter in a heavy 5-quart saucepan or large Dutch oven over medium-high heat. Add the onion and sauté until soft and just starting to brown, about 5 minutes, stirring occasionally.

Add bell pepper strips and cook for 2 minutes, then add the zucchini and 2 teaspoons of the Creole seasoning. Cook for 1½ minutes, then cover the pan, reduce heat to medium, and cook until the zucchini is very tender, about 25 minutes, stirring occasionally.

Meanwhile, in a heavy 2-quart saucepan, melt the remaining ½ tablespoon butter over medium heat. Add the garlic and sauté for 1 minute. Remove from heat and set aside momentarily. Put the shrimp in a medium mixing bowl and season with the remaining ½ teaspoon Creole seasoning mix, stirring thoroughly. Add the shrimp to the pan with the garlic and cook and stir over medium heat just until the shrimp start to turn pink, about 2 minutes. Promptly remove from the heat.

Once the zucchini is very tender, stir the shrimp into the zucchini. Cover the pan and turn off the heat but leave the pan on the hot burner just until the shrimp are cooked through, about 5 minutes, stirring as needed.

Divide the rice among four plates. Spoon the zucchini and shrimp over the rice and serve.

Makes 4 servings

CHEF TENNEY FLYNN

GW Fin's Grilled Lemon Fish with Thai-Style Mirliton Slaw, Blue Crab Fritters, and Chile Oil

Citrus-Chile Oil

1 cup canola oil

2 tablespoons whole annatto seeds

Zest of 1 lemon

Zest of 1 orange

1 jalapeño chile, quartered and seeded

Mirliton Slaw

Juice of 4 limes

¼ cup fish sauce

2 tablespoons raw sugar

2 cloves garlic, finely minced

1 teaspoon diced chile such as jalapeño, Anaheim, or cayenne, seeds intact

1 red bell pepper, seeded and finely julienned

1 yellow bell pepper, seeded and finely julienned

2 medium carrots, peeled and julienned

2 mirlitons (chayotes), cut into matchsticks

2 tablespoons chopped fresh cilantro

2 tablespoons finely diced green onion

Cilantro Purée

Leaves from 1 bunch fresh cilantro

4 large leaves from romaine or iceberg lettuce

1 jalapeño chile, split and seeded

½ cup canola oil

Pinch of salt

Pinch of citric acid (optional) (see Note)

Makes 4 servings

I'd known about Tenney Flynn's work as executive chef with the Ruth's Chris Steak House chain. Until we talked late one night after dinner, I hadn't known his musical history. Back in the late seventies, he used to manage a club called Tom's Tavern in Stone Mountain, Georgia. People assume that jazz musicians live this debauched, out-all-night life. Maybe that was the case when Diz and Bird were out there, but it's not how it is now. It sounds like that's the life Tenney was leading back in the day, though. He doesn't drink or smoke now, but it wasn't always that way. "In those days, I rediscovered all my old bad habits and found a few new ones," he told me. "When you quit drinking, going into bars is not an interesting thing. When you're around people who are drinking and you're not, the conversation gets pretty boring after they've had three or four drinks."

Just as memorable as the conversation that night was the grilled fish with mirliton slaw.

Blue Crab Fritters

¾ cup all-purpose flour

1 tablespoon baking powder

1 tablespoon Chef Paul Prudhomme's Shrimp Magic Seasoning Blend

1 large egg

1 tablespoon seeded and finely diced jalapeño or poblano chile

½ cup milk

½ pound lump crabmeat, picked over for cartilage and shell fragments

Canola oil for frying

⅓ cup pepper jelly, warmed

Canola oil spray

4 skin-on pompano, cobia (lemon fish), king mackerel, swordfish, amberjack, redfish, or any other firm-fleshed white fish fillets (5 to 6 ounces each)

Salt and freshly ground pepper

4 teaspoons Chef Paul Prudhomme's Shrimp Magic Seasoning Blend

4 fresh cilantro sprigs

4 fresh Thai basil sprigs

To make the oil: Place all the ingredients in a saucepan and heat to 200°F on a deep-frying thermometer. Remove from the heat and let steep for 2 hours, then strain the oil into a bottle and discard the solids. (Store the remaining chile oil, tightly sealed, in the refrigerator for up to 4 weeks.)

To make the slaw: In a small bowl, whisk together the lime juice, fish sauce, sugar, garlic, and chile to make a dressing. In a bowl, combine the bell peppers, carrots, and mirlitons. Add the dressing to the vegetables and toss to mix. Add the cilantro and green onion, stir to mix well, cover, and refrigerate until ready to use.

To make the purée: Combine all the ingredients in a blender or food processor and process to a smooth purée. Transfer to a squeeze bottle or small bowl and refrigerate until ready to use.

To make the fritters: Sift together the dry ingredients into a large bowl. Mix in the egg and chile until incorporated. Add the milk and stir gently, just to loosen the mixture. Add the crabmeat and gently fold it into the batter just until incorporated. Cover the batter and set aside. Pour oil into a deep fryer or heavy-bottomed saucepan with tall sides to a depth of 2 inches. Spoon the jelly into a microwave-safe bowl. Set aside.

continued

When you have the Cilantro Purée and Citrus-Chile Oil prepared and have made the slaw and the fritter batter, it's time to prepare the fire. (It's also time to make anything else that might be accompanying the dish.) The rule in this regard is to have the rest of the meal prepared, really almost on the table, before cooking the fish.

You don't need much fire to cook 4 fish fillets—one layer of coals is plenty. Build a hot fire in a charcoal grill, preferably one that has a top. When the charcoal is coated in a white ash (about 30 minutes), you're ready to cook.

Preheat the oven to warm. Spray the grill rack with oil and also spray the fish. Heat the oil to 350°F.

Season each fillet with salt and pepper and the seasoning blend. Arrange the fillets, skin-side up, on the grill rack and grill for 2 minutes. Using a large spatula, carefully rotate the fish a quarter turn (to make crosshatch grill marks) and cook for another 2 minutes. Cover the grill and cook until the fish is tender and flaky, about 3 minutes longer.

When the fish is cooked, transfer to a baking sheet and place in the warm oven with four dinner plates while you fry the fritters. Place the pepper jelly in a small bowl and warm in the microwave until syrupy, 30 seconds or so.

Working in batches, scoop teaspoonfuls of the fritter batter into the hot oil, being careful not to crowd the pan. Fry until golden brown, about 3 minutes. Transfer each fritter as it is finished to the bowl with the warm pepper jelly and toss to coat, then transfer to a plate.

Squeeze most of the liquid out of the slaw and place about ½ cup in the center of each warmed plate. Drizzle a tablespoon or so of the Cilantro Purée around the slaw and 1 teaspoon of the chile oil in a circle closer to the rim of the plate. Place 3 fritters on each plate, close to the slaw. Finally, top each with a fish fillet. Garnish with the cilantro and Thai basil and serve at once.

Note: Citric acid occurs naturally in many fruits, especially citrus fruit. Citrus acid powder is very bitter and is often used as an additive in food to give added tanginess. It is widely available at gourmet shops, online, and at some health food stores.

COCHON'S BRAISED PIG
WITH STEWED TURNIPS AND CABBAGE

CHEF STEPHEN
STRYJEWSKI

I used to wonder why pigs dominated the dinner table in the South and then this professor broke it down for me. It's a matter of mathematics: Pigs give birth in three to four months and deliver several piglets each time. Cows take nine months to calve and they only deliver one. Goats and sheep both take longer than pigs and often deliver only one. You could starve to death waiting around to build a herd of cows, sheep, or goats. Breed pigs and you'll be putting bacon on the table and ribs on the grill in no time. At Cochon, Stephen Stryjewski takes full advantage of all the porcine bounty. This is his signature dish, though his ribs with watermelon pickles are hard to beat.

Preheat the oven to 350°F.

To make the pork: Put the pork butt in a roasting pan and add the garlic, herb sprigs, and bay leaves, distributing them evenly around the pan. Season with salt and black pepper. Add water to cover the meat and place in the oven. Braise until the meat is falling-off-the-bone tender, 8 to 12 hours. Remove meat from the pan, saving the braising liquid.

Place the roasting pan over medium-high heat on the stovetop and reduce the braising liquid until there are small bubbles on the surface and the liquid becomes lightly syrupy.

As the liquid reduces, pull the meat and fat off the bone. Discard the skin and bone.

Mix reduced braising liquid with pulled pork to keep it moist. Taste and season with salt, pepper, and red pepper flakes.

Once meat has cooled, form pork into thick patties (each about 5.5 ounces). Lightly dust the patties with flour. Place a skillet over medium-high heat. Add 2 tablespoons of oil and when hot, sear 2 to 3 patties at a time until lightly crisp on both sides. Repeat until all the patties have been seared.

To make the turnips and cabbage: Render the bacon lardons over medium heat. Add the turnips and continue cooking for 5 minutes, stirring occasionally. Add the onion and garlic, and cook until soft. Add the cabbage.

Add chicken stock to cover the vegetables about halfway, add a splash of apple cider vinegar, a dash of hot sauce, the sugar, and season with salt and pepper.

Simmer the stew until the cabbage is soft, then taste and adjust seasonings as needed.

To serve, spoon about one cup of hot cabbage stew per person into bowls and top each with a pork patty.

Makes 8 servings

Braised Pork

One 8- to 10-pound bone-in, skin-on pork butt

12 cloves garlic

4 fresh thyme sprigs

4 fresh sage sprigs

4 fresh rosemary sprigs

8 bay leaves

Salt and freshly ground black pepper

Red pepper flakes

1 cup all-purpose flour

½ cup canola oil

Stewed Turnips and Cabbage

8 ounces bacon lardons

4 turnips, peeled and cut into small triangles

1 yellow onion, chopped

4 cloves garlic, chopped

1 small head green cabbage (3 to 4 pounds), cored and diced

2 cups Basic Chicken Stock (page 230) or store-bought chicken broth

Splash of apple cider vinegar

Dash of hot sauce

Pinch or 2 of sugar

Salt and freshly ground black pepper

RED BEANS AND RICE
WITH SMOKED TURKEY WINGS

1 pound dried red kidney beans

6 cups water

1 pound smoked turkey wings

1 large yellow onion, chopped

2 stalks celery, chopped

½ green bell pepper, seeded and chopped

2 tablespoons chopped garlic

2 bay leaves

½ cup vegetable oil

Salt and freshly ground pepper

Hot sauce to taste (I use Matouk's West Indian)

Hot steamed rice for serving

My girlfriend, Brandi, has a funny diet. She doesn't eat pork, except for bacon and ham. (Don't ask.) Anyway, she made me these red beans one day and they were slamming. The truth is, this recipe will work with any dried beans—navy beans, black-eyed peas, pinto beans, you name it.

Pick over the beans for stones or grit. Rinse and drain well. In a large stockpot or Dutch oven, combine the water, turkey wings, onion, celery, bell pepper, garlic, bay leaves, and oil and bring to a boil over high heat. Reduce the heat to medium-low and cover the pot. Simmer, stirring every 15 to 30 minutes, until the turkey wings are tender, about 2 hours.

Remove the pot from the heat and discard the bay leaves. Transfer the turkey wings to a plate and let cool. When cool enough to handle, pull off the meat. Discard the bones and skin. Chop, shred, or pull the meat into bite-size pieces and set aside. Scoop about 1 cup of the bean mixture from the pot into a blender or food processor and process to a smooth purée. (Or scoop it into a bowl and crush it with the back of a spoon until it is a thick and creamy consistency.)

Return the crushed beans and the turkey meat to the pot. Season generously with the salt, pepper, and hot sauce. Stir the pot well. The whole beans should be totally tender and the broth surrounding them should be creamy. Taste and adjust the seasoning. Serve over or next to steamed rice, depending on which side of the red beans and rice debate you fall on.

Makes 6 to 8 servings

PORK AND BEANS WITH BACON AND ONIONS

Most of my mother's cooking was from scratch. But even she had a few dishes that she opened up cans for. This is one of them. Beans from a can ain't so bad. Beans from a can doctored up like this is fantastic. If you don't have bacon handy, you can use some smoked sausage. The important thing is to let those onions sweat till they get sweet.

4 bacon slices, cut into 2-inch pieces

1 medium yellow onion, chopped

One 28-ounce can pork and beans, not drained

1 bay leaf

1 cup water

1 tablespoon pure maple syrup or brown sugar (optional)

Hot cooked rice for serving

In a heavy 3-quart saucepan over medium heat, cook the bacon pieces until most of the fat has been rendered and the bacon is crisp, about 8 minutes. Saving the bacon fat, lower the heat and add the onion to the pan, cover, and cook until well browned, about 7 minutes, stirring occasionally.

Add the pork and beans, bay leaf, and water to the pan. Cover the pan and reduce the heat to low. Continue cooking until the flavors marry, about 20 minutes more, stirring occasionally. Stir in the maple syrup or brown sugar, if using. Remove from heat.

Serve at once (or prepare a day ahead and reheat for serving), placing equal amounts of rice and beans (about 1 cup of each per person) on large plates.

Makes 4 servings

The Mirliton Missionary

After the storm, a lot of us chefs tried very consciously to focus on New Orleans food. It sounds obvious. We were New Orleans chefs, cooking in New Orleans. What else would we focus on? Fair question. But before the storm, many of us felt the city didn't need another version of gumbo or bread pudding or remoulade. We had cooked elsewhere. We had studied other things, and we wanted to create our food, not our version of the Creole food canon.

But when the levees failed and we had senators and congressmen saying that we didn't deserve to exist, we decided that we had to be there for our city and our culture and to hell with anybody who wasn't with us. I still didn't want to do Desautel's oyster po-boy, or anything like that. But I had an idea. I'd do something with mirlitons.

Mirlitons are one of the great home dishes that you don't see on restaurant menus much. People in the Caribbean and Latin America eat them a lot. And you can find them in grocery stores in Latino neighborhoods in other parts of the country. They call them chayotes. But New Orleanians are the only Americans who have created their own recipes for mirlitons. Using that vegetable in and of itself was a statement of pride in this city.

With that in mind, I went to the supermarket and bought a bunch of mirlitons to play with in the kitchen. But no matter what I did, somehow they just didn't taste right. They were kind of bland. It really seemed like one of those situations where the old time home cooks knew something

the fancy restaurant chefs didn't know. I imagined myself standing in the supermarket line and having some older woman look at the mirlitons in my basket and say, "Darling, don't forget to put a pinch of baking soda in your water when you berl 'em." Whatever the secret was—baking soda, full moon, ten hail Marys—I didn't know it.

Then I read an article by the *Times-Picayune* food writer Judy Walker about Lance Hill. He's a history professor at Tulane; he also has a passion for mirlitons. So much so that he founded mirlitons.org, a website dedicated to "promoting the conservation and innovative uses of Louisiana heirloom mirlitons." I wasn't the only one lamenting the flavorlessness of modern mirlitons. Lance had noticed it, too. He sent me an e-mail that was a history lesson, a food lesson, and a science lesson all rolled into one. It turns out the mirlitons I had bought were probably not local. The local variety had all but died off.

"Up until 1995," he wrote, "almost all mirlitons in groceries were locally grown varieties and were seasonal (a small spring crop and a big fall crop). There were three major causes of the dramatic decline in backyard mirliton growing. First was the influx of imported commercial mirlitons. In the early 1990s, chilling techniques were developed that delayed 'sprouting' of the chayote (mirlitons) grown in Costa Rica and Mexico. Now they could ship chayote to the United States year-round and fairly cheaply, so people became accustomed to buying

them in a store rather than growing their own. Also, the imported mirlitons were grown at 4,000 to 5,000 feet and were adapted to a cooler and hazy high-altitude mountain environment. Agriculture agencies mistakenly advised people to use these imported varieties as seed; the outcome on the Gulf Coast was almost always failure. The solution was to find traditional heirloom varieties that had thrived in our environment for perhaps two hundred years (that's what we do at mirlitons.org).

"Second, mirlitons are pollinated almost exclusively by honey bees, and during this same period we lost 80 percent of our feral bee colonies due to colony collapse syndrome. (They are coming back, but we teach hand-pollination methods or bee-attracting flower plantings near the vine.)

"Finally, there was the shift of population of people from above sea-level neighborhoods (rich, alluvial soil along the river and ridges like Esplanade), which had natural soil drainage, to below sea-level suburbs built in drained swamps that had little natural drainage. Mirlitons can die from root damage if the soil gets too soggy, so suburban gardeners experienced failure even if they had heirloom varieties. (That's why we teach 'large hill planting' systems that elevate the plants' roots above the water table.) We have probably permanently lost some of our traditional locally grown varieties.

"Imported chayote are hybridized for uniform shape, color, and (I am not kidding) 'insipid flavor.' They are treated heavily with pesticides and fungicides

and, although there is no science on this, my guess is that they have had some of the natural resistance to plant disease bred out of them. Imported mirlitons are relatively small compared to the local varieties, with smooth skins, no furrows, no spines, and globular in shape. In the old days, 'stuffed mirlitons' were larger and had more mirliton flesh-to-stuffing ratio."

While I was soaking in all the culinary science this historian was able to churn out, he ended with a sentiment that reminded me of why I cared about mirlitons and New Orleans in the first place.

"I think a large part of what made home-grown mirlitons special is the way they helped build and sustain family, neighbor-hood, and social networks. What was special about them was that you waited all year for the vines to flower or for your relatives or neighbors to bring over that Schwegmann bag of mirlitons. I have written elsewhere that mirlitons are a 'sociable vegetable.' Their bountifulness breeds altruism. I still have old growers who supply us with seed heirlooms, who tell us that mirlitons.org will just have to wait until they've distributed their crop to the relatives and friends who have come to expect this fall ritual of community and sharing."

NELSON HIDALGO

When I would drive home to San Antonio from college, I would always stop at Bob's Smokehouse and get some of Bob's ribs and smoked lamb breasts before I came home. Bob used to have the barbecue sauce in plastic, electric coffee pots so you wouldn't be pouring cold barbecue sauce on hot meat. Details, Bob was about the details. The sauce and the fat from the lamb would be all over my face, so I'd have to use about a dozen of the moist wipes because I knew what was coming next.

I'd drive home stuffed like a tamale and mi abuela would say "Que te pasa mi hijo! No has comido. Tan flaquito. La universidad te va a matar!," ("Look at you! You haven't eaten. So skinny. College is going to kill you!") And I would have to eat again—deep fried puffy tacos or slow-roasted cabrito or, if it was Sunday morning, barbacoa de cabeza—beef cheeks and all the meat around it, the whole cow's head, roasted underground, the meat folded into a fresh made tortilla. Mama Mia, Jesus and Joseph!

Let me give you one example: Saturday morning, my cousin Arnie brought me to meet one of the guys he'd been working with. Ten in the morning, but it was already hot as a six-shooter out there. First thing out the guy's mouth, "Can I get you a beer?" This was a working man. This wasn't a skid row wino sharing his liquid breakfast. It was man welcoming another man into his home like they were old army buddies. What could I do but say yes? We sat there and talked business for a while, and I thought we were making some progress, coming to an understanding, then he just stopped the conversation. "You hungry? My old lady's not here but you know what I have a taste for? A ham and potato salad sandwich." So he went into the kitchen, sliced some baked ham and put it between two slices of white bread with a half of a slightly burned pineapple ring that the ham had been baked with. Who ever heard of a ham and potato salad sandwich with roasted pineapple? I was converted.

That's what New Orleans is about. Making people feel at home, making them feel connected to each other and to the city. These are the recipes I feel connected to. Most of them are from New Orleans, but one of them's even more special. It's a genuine San Antonio recipe for carne guisada. My gift to you.

RALPH'S ON THE PARK'S
CRABMEAT LASAGNA

RALPH BRENNAN

After I'd been in New Orleans for a few weeks, it seemed to me like half the restaurants in the city were owned by some guy named Brennan—Brennan's, Dickie Brennan's Steakhouse, Mr. B's Bistro, Commander's Palace. Turns out that these places are all owned by various branches of the Brennan family. It's a tough call, but I think Ralph Brennan's crabmeat lasagna may be my favorite Brennan dish. I guess this is what you would call an Irish-Sicilian-Creole dish.

The lasagna may be assembled a day in advance and baked just before serving. The sauce should be prepared within an hour of serving time or it might separate.

To make the béchamel: In a heavy, 2-quart saucepan over medium-high heat, melt 2½ tablespoons of the butter. Stir in the flour until smooth. Cook about 1 minute, stirring constantly and scraping the pan bottom clean. Do not let the roux start to brown.

Stir in the milk and raise the heat to high. Cook the béchamel, whisking or stirring constantly with a wooden spoon, until it thickens enough to leave a distinct trail on the back of the spoon when you draw a finger through it, about 3 minutes. Remove from heat.

Let the béchamel cool to warm room temperature, about 1 hour, so its heat won't curdle the egg yolk.

Meanwhile, in a heavy 12-inch skillet over medium heat, melt 1 tablespoon of the butter. Add the onions and cook for 15 minutes. Stir in the garlic and continue cooking until the onions turn medium-brown, about 5 minutes more, stirring often. Set the onions aside to let cool to room temperature; if prepared ahead, let cool and refrigerate in a covered container.

In a heavy 5½-quart saucepan over high heat, warm the olive oil until hot, about 1 minute. Add half the spinach and cook just until it wilts enough to make room for the remaining spinach, about 1 minute, tossing constantly with tongs. Add the remaining spinach and continue cooking just until all the spinach is wilted, 1 to 2 minutes more. Drain the spinach in a colander and set aside until cool enough to handle, about 30 minutes.

Wrap the cooled spinach in a lint-free cloth napkin or dish towel (one that you don't mind getting stained) and wring dry to extract as much liquid as possible. Coarsely chop the spinach and set aside; if prepared ahead, let cool and refrigerate in a covered container.

In a large bowl, combine the ricotta, crab claw meat, browned onions, cooked spinach, Parmigiano-Reggiano, egg yolk, ½ teaspoon of the salt, ¼ teaspoon of the pepper, and 1 cup of the cooled béchamel. Stir the filling gently to mix thoroughly while keeping the crabmeat as intact as possible, and refrigerate while you cook the lasagna noodles.

In a large pot over high heat, bring salted water to a boil. Add the lasagna noodles and cook until al dente, about 12 minutes. Drain the noodles, rinse with cool tap water, and drain well again.

Preheat the oven to 350°F.

Cut the noodles into 9-inch lengths to fit a 9-by-9-by-2¼-inch baking pan. Generously grease the bottom and sides of the pan.

To assemble the lasagna, arrange 4 cooked lasagna noodles on the bottom of the pan, and spread half of the filling evenly over the noodles. Add another layer of 4 noodles, then the remaining filling, and finish with a layer of 4 noodles.

Season the reserved béchamel sauce with the remaining salt and pepper, and pour the sauce over the lasagna, spreading evenly with a rubber spatula. Seal the pan with heavy-duty aluminum foil. At this point, the lasagna can be refrigerated or frozen and baked later.

Bake for 40 minutes, or until bubbling. Uncover and bake for 10 more minutes to lightly brown the top. Serve hot.

Béchamel Sauce

3½ tablespoons unsalted butter

2½ tablespoons all-purpose flour

2½ cups whole milk

4 large yellow onions finely chopped (about 4½ cups)

2 small cloves garlic, minced

1 tablespoon olive oil

1½ pounds baby spinach leaves, with stems

8 ounces ricotta cheese, preferably whole milk

8 ounces fresh crab claw meat, picked over for cartilage and shell fragments

½ cup finely grated Parmesan cheese, preferably Parmigiano-Reggiano

1 large egg yolk

1 teaspoon kosher salt

½ teaspoon freshly ground pepper

12 dry lasagna noodles (not the nonboil type)

Makes 6 to 8 servings

MOSCA'S CHICKEN À LA GRANDE

Roasted Potatoes

8 potatoes (about 4 pounds total weight), peeled and halved

1 tablespoon salt

1 tablespoon freshly ground pepper

1 tablespoon dried oregano

1 tablespoon dried rosemary

½ cup yellow onion, finely chopped

3 cloves garlic, crushed

½ cup olive oil

½ cup dry white wine

2 cups water

One 3-pound chicken, cut into eight serving pieces

¾ cup olive oil

1 tablespoon salt

1 tablespoon freshly ground pepper

6 to 10 unpeeled garlic cloves, crushed

1 tablespoon dried rosemary

1 tablespoon dried oregano

¼ cup dry white wine

The Huey P. Long Bridge is the bridge from New Orleans to Mosca's. It's wide enough for two horse-drawn buggies or four bicycles to pass in each direction, but it wasn't meant for cars, and definitely not for big luxury sedans. The whole time, you're looking at the Mississippi River out the car window and calculating your chances of swimming to shore if the car veers a few inches in the wrong direction. The whole time you're driving, the New Orleanians in the car will be telling you how the Mosca family came from Italy to Chicago, where one ancestor was Al Capone's personal chef. That makes you wonder if anyone was ever pushed out of the door of a moving car into the river. After you get off the bridge you have to drive another 20 minutes along a dark strip of highway that would be perfect for dumping a body. This adventure is the appetizer for a dinner at Mosca's.

When you finally get to the restaurant and talk to the family, you realize that most of what you've heard isn't true. Their ancestors came from San Benedetto del Tronto, which is probably closer to Switzerland than it is to Sicily. They did go to Chicago first, but they never worked for Al Capone. They did rent from Carlos Marcello, the man who everybody says was head of the New Orleans mafia, and he ate at the restaurant a lot. But every time I ate at Mosca's, I saw John Mosca, and he made me forget all about that mafia talk. He was truly a nice guy.

They say Mosca's serves Sicilian-Creole food, which might explain why you never see those dishes on the menu at any Italian-Italian restaurant. But even though a lot of what they say about Mosca's isn't true, when they tell you it's one of the best restaurants in a town of great restaurants, believe them. If you want Italian-Italian, order the Chicken Cacciatore or the spaghetti and meatballs. But for my money the Chicken à la Grande is the dish to get. Whatever else this guy Grande was, he must have been a helluva cook.

To make the potatoes: Preheat the oven to 450°F. Place the potatoes in a rectangular baking dish, skin-side down. Sprinkle the salt, pepper, oregano, rosemary, and onion over the potatoes, distributing them evenly. Add the crushed garlic, distributing it evenly over potatoes. Pour the olive oil, wine, and water over top of the potatoes. Cover the baking dish with foil. Place the potatoes in the oven and bake for 1 hour. Remove the foil and bake for another 30 minutes or until brown.

Place the chicken pieces in a large skillet. Pour the olive oil over the chicken, making certain the pieces are well-coated. Season the chicken with salt and pepper, making certain the seasoning is evenly spread. Over medium-high heat, brown the chicken on all sides, about 25 minutes, turning as needed. Add the garlic, rosemary, and oregano, distributing them evenly on the chicken pieces. Remove the skillet from the heat. Pour the white wine over the chicken. Return the skillet to the stove, reduce the heat to medium-low, and simmer uncovered until the wine is reduced by half, about 10 to 15 minutes.

Serve the chicken hot with the pan juices and the roasted potatoes.

Makes 4 servings

COUSIN KAMI'S CARNE GUISADA

"Guisada" means stew. So carne guisada is just beef stew. They have it all over Latin America. Some people cook the meat until it's in shreds; some people cut it up into chunks so you still have tender, intact pieces when you eat it. It's all good, if you season it right and let it cook long enough. I asked my grandmother for this recipe a dozen times. Each time she had an excuse. Finally she said she'd teach it to my wife once I got married. I couldn't wait that long. So this is my cousin Kami's version. She's not my grandmother, but the girl can really cook.

Serve the Carne Guisada warm, wrapped in flour tortillas, alongside beans and rice, over scrambled eggs for breakfast, with fried tortilla chips, or just in a bowl by itself.

4 pounds beef chuck roast, cut into 1-inch cubes

1 tablespoon kosher salt

2 teaspoons freshly ground pepper

⅓ cup vegetable oil

2 yellow onions, chopped

2 jalapeño chiles, seeds intact, chopped

2 serrano chiles, seeds intact, chopped

2 pasilla chiles, chopped

5 large cloves garlic, sliced

½ cup chopped fresh cilantro stems, plus ¾ cup chopped fresh cilantro leaves

1 tablespoon cumin seed

1 tablespoon chili powder

2 teaspoons dried oregano

1 bay leaf

One 14-ounce can petite diced tomatoes, with juice

1 cup Basic Chicken Stock (page 230) or store-bought chicken broth

1 cup water

Season the beef all over with the salt and pepper.

In a Dutch oven over medium-high heat, heat the vegetable oil. When the oil is hot, add about one-third of the beef and cook until nicely browned on all sides, 5 to 8 minutes. Remove the browned beef with a slotted spoon and set aside. Repeat with the remaining beef.

When all the beef has been browned, add the onions, chiles, garlic, cilantro stems, cumin seed, chile powder, oregano, and bay leaf to the pot and cook, stirring as needed until the vegetables are softened, about 5 minutes. Return the beef to the pot and add the tomatoes, chicken stock, and water. Stir to combine, bring the beef to a simmer, cover, and reduce the heat to low.

Simmer the beef for 5 hours until tender, stirring occasionally. Stir in the cilantro leaves, ladle into bowls, and serve at once.

Makes 8 to 10 servings

New Orleans Cuisine: Caribbean or Southern?

"When the United States took possession of the Louisiana Purchase in 1803, the city was an urban crossroads of languages, both spoken and musical, with a complex Afro-Louisianan culture already in existence. . . . [By 1812] New Orleans was a hub of commerce and communication that connected the Mississippi watershed, the Gulf Rim, the Atlantic seaboard, the Caribbean Rim, Western Europe (especially France and Spain), and various areas of West and central Africa. . . . "
—Ned Sublette, *The World that Made New Orleans*

Standing in New Orleans looking north, the food can seem strange. It's not that all of our foods and ingredients are unheard of in other places. You can go to grocery stores in Atlanta or Philadelphia or pretty much anywhere and find red kidney beans. But where else in the continental United States are red beans eaten so often? Where else are mirlitons not in the Latin section of the supermarket? Where else are grillades and gumbo such staples? And, compared to the rest of the South, where else is barbecue such a minor player in the food culture?

With its rum drinks and rice fixation, New Orleans is not exactly Southern.

In Haiti and eastern Cuba, Jamaica, and other parts of the Caribbean, red beans and Creole tomato sauces are as common as rum drinks and seafood-centric menus. But you're not going to find biscuits or black-eyed peas or bourbon as staples down there. Pecan pie, cornbread, pound cake? Forget about it.

This is why you have to understand New Orleans as its own entity. It's a port city that decades ago attracted immigrants from all over the world, but especially from the Caribbean, Latin America, Europe, and Africa. New Orleans attracted migrants from other parts of the United States as well. The foods of these people have been incorporated into New Orleans Creole cuisine to such an extent that you can't easily decipher the national, ethnic, or regional origin of any major New Orleans dish.

If you say you want "soul food" in New Orleans, that usually means you want to go to a black restaurant. If you analyze the menus at places like Two Sisters or Dunbar's or Li'l Dizzy's, you'll find that almost all of the food can be divided into two categories: Creole dishes that you'd find versions of in many white-tablecloth places in town, and "soul food" dishes that you'd find on the steam tables at meat-and-three restaurants all over the South. Whether you're in New Orleans or in the South proper, you can't separate black food from white food dish by dish.

Maybe that's yet another reason why this place and this food are so special. Because people from very different parts of the world can see their reflection on the plate and taste their own heritage in the food. Or maybe New Orleans strikes an inviting balance. It's just exotic enough to be interesting and familiar enough to feel comfortable.

Besh Steakhouse's Cowboy Steak with Wild Mushrooms, Root Vegetables, and Bordelaise Sauce

In Texas Hill Country, they have these places alongside the road that sell humongous steaks. They say if you can eat a whole one, it's free. They're like *72 ounces*. I've never *ever* tried to eat one by myself. But once, after a lucky night at the craps table, I was feeling Texas-proud, so I moseyed on in to Besh Steakhouse, where Chef Jared Tees has a cowboy rib-eye on the menu. It's a big mother, no doubt about it. It's not Texas big, but it is Texas good. If you've had a hot streak at the casino, you might be excited enough to eat this whole thing by yourself. But this version has been adjusted to serve 4 at home.

To make the sauce: In a saucepan over medium heat, heat the olive oil. Add the onion, shallots, carrot, celery, and garlic and sauté until the vegetables are soft, about 5 minutes. Add the bay leaf, thyme sprig, wine, and Port. Bring to a boil, then reduce to a simmer and cook until reduced by three-fourths, about 40 minutes. You should have about ½ cup liquid remaining. Stir in the demi-glace and continue to simmer until the sauce reaches a consistency that coats the back of a spoon, about 40 minutes longer. Strain the sauce through a fine-mesh sieve into a bowl and discard the solids. Season with salt and pepper. Set aside until ready to serve.

To make the mushroom sauté: In a large sauté pan over medium-high heat, melt the butter with the olive oil. When the butter has melted, add the shallots, garlic, and mushrooms to the pan and sauté, stirring often, until the mushrooms are nicely browned and all the moisture has evaporated, 10 to 15 minutes. Remove from the heat, season to taste with salt and pepper, then set aside and cover to keep warm until ready to serve.

To begin the vegetables: Fill a large bowl with water and ice cubes to make an ice water bath. In a large saucepan, bring the water to a boil over high heat and stir in the salt. Add the turnips, squash, and radishes and blanch just until tender-crisp, 2 to 3 minutes, checking them every 30 seconds. Immediately transfer with a slotted spoon to the ice bath. Repeat the same process with the beets,

blanching them last so they don't discolor the other vegetables. While the beets are cooking, transfer the other vegetables from the ice bath to a colander to drain. Once the beets are done, transfer them to the ice bath and then the colander.

Preheat the oven to 400°F.

Season both sides of the steak generously with kosher salt and pepper. Place a cast-iron skillet just large enough to hold the steak and the protruding bone over high heat. When the pan is hot, place the steak in the pan and sear until nicely browned, about 5 minutes per side. Place the pan in the oven and bake until the steak registers 145°F on an instant-read thermometer. Transfer the steak to a cutting board, tent with aluminum foil, and let rest for 20 minutes.

Gently rewarm the sauce over low heat.

In a small skillet over medium heat, melt the 3 tablespoons butter and stir in the herbs. When the butter is just starting to bubble, add the turnips, squash, radishes, and beets. Stir so that the vegetables are all coated in the butter and warmed through, about 1 minute.

Divide the vegetables among four dinner plates, fanning them attractively. Slice the steak and divide among the plates. Spoon the sautéed mushrooms over the meat. Spoon the sauce over the top of the steak and vegetables and serve at once.

Makes 4 servings

Bordelaise Sauce

1 tablespoon olive oil

½ yellow onion, thinly sliced

3 shallots, thinly sliced

1 carrot, peeled and coarsely chopped

1 celery stalk, coarsely chopped

1 clove garlic, crushed

1 small bay leaf

1 thyme sprig

1 cup dry red wine

1 cup Port

1 cup veal demi-glace

Salt and freshly ground pepper

Wild Mushroom Sauté

2 tablespoons unsalted butter

1 tablespoon olive oil

2 shallots, minced

3 cloves garlic, chopped

4 cups mixed chanterelle, shiitake, and other wild mushrooms, stemmed and halved

Salt and freshly ground pepper

Root Vegetables

2 quarts water

1 teaspoon salt

2 medium turnips, peeled and cut into ¼-inch-thick slices

2 medium pattypan squash, cut into ¼-inch-thick slices

4 radishes, cut into ¼-inch-thick slices

2 medium beets, peeled and cut into ¼-inch-thick slices

One 38-ounce cowboy steak (bone-in choice rib-eye steak, "frenched" by your butcher)

Kosher salt and freshly ground black pepper

3 tablespoons unsalted butter

2½ tablespoons chopped fresh tarragon

2½ tablespoons chopped fresh thyme

2½ tablespoons chopped fresh parsley

AUNT MIMI

When it comes to the kitchen, Ella Brennan said it best: "Paint it white and close the door." Ella owns Commander's Palace, so saying that might have been her sneaky way of getting people to abandon cooking at home and eat at her restaurant instead. If that's what Ella's offering, I say "Deal! Where do I sign?"

I intended to maintain a nonaggression pact with the kitchen. My mother insisted on starting a war. She told me that the only way I could ever hope to land a really good husband was to learn to cook. Naturally, I asked her what I should do if I wanted to land a really bad husband.

Mother never got my jokes, especially the serious ones.

Even when I was a young woman, I knew I'd rather be single than commit to a life of culinary servitude. Some people cook well and they enjoy it. Far be it from me to stand in their way. I drink well. I should be allowed to do that.

Fortunately, I came of drinking age after the famous "storming of the Sazerac" incident. The name would suggest that this was some violent, revolutionary, feminist act. In fact, it was a publicity stunt thought up by a man. My friend Russ Bergeron, who works at the Sazerac Bar today, let me in on this open secret: In 1949, Seymour Weiss, the owner of the Roosevelt Hotel, came up with a brilliant idea. He bought the Sazerac Bar up the street from his hotel, shut it down, then reopened a bar of the same name in his hotel. With all the subtlety of a stage whisper, he let it be known that the bar would serve women every day instead of just on Mardi Gras, as had been the rule. Just in case anyone missed the point, he went to Godchaux's Department Store on Canal Street and recruited the ladies from the makeup department to come "storm" the bar. These are the ladies that appear in the iconic pictures.

By the time I was ready for a drink, I didn't have to wait until Carnival to get it. Or, I suppose I should say, I didn't have to keep some secret flask in my purse to nip at in case some downtown bar deigned to decline the pleasure of my company.

There are a few basic things I look for in a bar. It has to do the traditional stuff well: Sazeracs, Ramos Gin Fizzes, Martinis. And it has to be able to do these standards without looking them up in a book. Any bartender who can't make a Sazerac from memory is too young to be tending bar.

The music should be soft enough so you don't have to shout and loud enough so the people at the next table can't hear you. It should be warm enough for you to feel like you're at home, but special enough for you to feel like you're out. And they have to pass the Flip Wilson test—they have to have a few booths, in the back in the corner in the dark, just in case whispering is too loud for what you have to say.

When I heard Janette was creating this book of New Orleans recipes, I volunteered myself to spearhead the libation section. New Orleans has some of the world's greatest bars. Not that Bourbon Street drinks-as-big-as-your-head silliness. I'm talking about real bars for people who take their drinking seriously. I've included some interesting libations from the bartenders around here who really know what they're doing. Most of these are new recipes, not formulas for the standards. Other than the Sazerac recipe, you can find a lot of the classics in any cocktail book. I like my classic drinks, Martinis especially, but I don't like to dwell in the past. The drinks in this chapter are the ones people are drinking now. And, every now and then, when I get a wild hair, I stray from the tried and true into untested territory. If you're going there, these are the bartenders to take you where you want to be.

BRANDY CRUSTA

CHRIS HANNAH

1½ ounces **Cognac**

½ ounce **fresh lemon juice**

½ ounce **orange curaçao**

¼ ounce **Maraschino Originale Luxardo liqueur**

2 dashes of **Angostura bitters**

Ice

Lemon twist for garnish

Chris Hannah is an old-school bartender and an old-school gentleman. He can be seen sporting self-tied bow ties even when he's not at his professional perch, the French 75 Bar at Arnaud's Restaurant. How does he fit into the New Orleans scene? He says it best: "I've been tending bar for fourteen years, eight of which have been right here in New Orleans. Coming to New Orleans was enlightening on many levels and it helped lead to my decision to bartend. I thought I knew jazz before moving to New Orleans, but I didn't know Danny Barker. I also thought I knew cocktails before moving to New Orleans, but I didn't know the Vieux Carré (see page 216). Choosing bartending as a profession became an easy decision after realizing I'm both part of the great culture of New Orleans, as well as helping to preserve it."

The Brandy Crusta was the first sugar-rimmed cocktail. It was invented in the 1840s by Joseph Santini at the New Orleans City Exchange Cafe and bar.

Combine the first five ingredients in a cocktail shaker. Fill the shaker with ice and shake vigorously. Strain into a sugar-rimmed rocks glass, garnish with the lemon peel, and serve.

Makes 1 serving

FRENCH 75

1¼ ounces **Cognac**

¼ ounce fresh **lemon juice**

¼ ounce **simple syrup** (see **Note**)

Ice

3 ounces chilled **Champagne** or other **sparkling wine**

The French 75 pays homage to the French 75 artillery weapon from World War I. When the French and American fighter pilots came back from their raids successfully, they drank this cocktail in honor of the artillery weapon's design.

Combine the first three ingredients in a cocktail shaker. Fill the shaker with ice and shake vigorously. Strain into a chilled champagne flute. Top with the Champagne and garnish with the lemon twist. Serve.

Note: Simple syrup could not be simpler. In a small saucepan, combine 1 cup sugar with 1 cup water and heat over medium heat, stirring to dissolve the sugar. Do not let boil. Remove from the heat and let cool. Store the simple syrup in a tightly sealed bottle in the refrigerator for up to 3 weeks.

Makes 1 serving

ABSINTHE SUISSESSE

¾ ounce **absinthe**

¾ ounce **Herbsaint**

½ ounce white **crème de menthe**

¼ ounce **orgeat**

1 **egg white**

1¼ ounces cold **half-and-half**

Mint leaf for garnish

This cocktail may be even older than the Ramos Gin Fizz. The French named it after the Swiss ladies who were visiting and moving to the city.

Combine all the ingredients in a cocktail shaker. Shake vigorously, strain into a chilled glass, and garnish with the mint leaf. Serve.

Makes 1 serving

SAZERAC

CHRIS McMILLIAN

1 sugar cube

2 or 3 dashes of Peychaud's bitters

½ ounce water

2 ounces rye whiskey

2 dashes of Herbsaint or Legendre

Lemon twist for garnish

Chris McMillian is a walking history of damn near everything, and certainly everything cocktail-related. A simple question about a particular spirit or cocktail might occasion a wild verbal ride through the backroads of French colonial trading patterns, American agriculture and French Quarter architecture. A co-founder of the Museum of the American Cocktail, he's an inspiration to young bartenders in this increasingly mixology obsessed town. *Imbibe* magazine places Chris on its list of the 25 Most Influential Cocktail Personalities of the Past Century.

As for the Sazerac, in 2008 it was named the official state cocktail of Louisiana. Some folks argue that the original Sazerac was made with brandy. If you'd prefer, substitute brandy for the rye. Chris prefers to use a sugar cube rather than simple syrup; that way he can adjust the sweetness without diluting the beverage.

Fill a double old-fashioned glass with ice water and let chill. Put a sugar cube in a second double old-fashioned glass and saturate it with the bitters. Add the ½ ounce water and muddle until the sugar, water, and bitters are completely dissolved. Add the rye. Discard the contents of the first glass. Add the Herbsaint to the chilled glass and spin the glass to coat the interior. Discard any excess. Strain the contents of the second glass into the first glass. Garnish with the lemon twist and serve.

Makes 1 serving

2 ounces Hayman's Old Tom gin
(see Note)

¾ ounce fresh lime juice

¾ ounce fresh lemon juice

¾ ounce Demerara syrup (see
page 222; follow the instructions
for Demerara and Lemongrass
Syrup, but omit the lemongrass)

1 egg white

1½ ounces cold heavy (whipping)
cream

8 drops of orange flower water

Ice

Chilled soda water

Named by the Beverage Network as one of the 10 Mixologists to Watch, Lucinda Weed works at Sylvain, a French Quarter restaurant of recent vintage.

If drinks can be said to have cousins, then the lemon and lime juice in this drink make it cousin to the daiquiri, the margarita, and the other members of the "sours" family of cocktails. This is a New Orleans original, invented here by Henry C. Ramos in 1888.

In a cocktail shaker, combine all the ingredients and shake briefly, then add a little ice and shake very hard for a long time. Fill a Collins glass one-fourth full with soda water, then strain the shaker contents on top of the soda. Serve.

Note: Old Tom gin is sweeter than its cousin, London Dry gin.

Makes 1 serving

Vieux Carré

Ice

¾ ounce Benedictine

¾ ounce Cognac

¾ ounce sweet vermouth

1 ounce rye whiskey

2 dashes of Angostura bitters

2 dashes of Peychaud's bitters

Lemon twist for garnish

Marvin was managing restaurants for years when he realized that he'd much rather abandon those higher order headaches and spend his time making drinks and enjoying the company of his bar customers. He made that decision twenty years ago. For the past ten years, he's been a steady presence at the rotating Carousel Bar in the Monteleone Hotel.

Walter Bergeron, a bartender at the Monteleone Hotel, created this drink in 1938. This is the peacemaker of New Orleans cocktails. It contains tributes to many of the peoples who have populated and defined New Orleans culturally. The Haitians are represented by the Peychaud's bitters, the French by the Cognac and Benedictine, the Americans by the rye, and the Italians by the sweet vermouth. This is the version Marvin Allen serves up at the Carousel Bar.

In an ice-filled old-fashioned glass, build the drink in the order of ingredients given. Garnish with the lemon twist and serve.

Makes 1 serving

HURRICANE

RHIANNON ENLIL

It is possible to make a good Hurricane, despite all the watered-down, high-on-alcohol, low-on-flavor versions you get on Bourbon Street. This drink was invented at Pat O'Brien's on St. Peter Street, a half block off Bourbon Street. As the story goes, at a point in the 1940s when whiskey was in short supply, bars were forced to buy a large quantity of rum, which was plentiful, whenever they ordered whiskey. So the folks at Pat O'Brien's invented a cocktail specifically to use up all their rum. The original recipe called for only the first three of these ingredients.

Rhiannon is the perfect bartender to create this drink. She was behind the bar at Cure, the craft cocktail lounge, when it opened. She's still there, but she also works regularly in the less rarified air of Erin Rose, a bar just off Bourbon Street in the French Quarter.

You can buy the grenadine and passion fruit syrups from anywhere that has a full range of mixology products, such as a well-stocked liquor store.

1½ ounces aged rum

1 ounce fresh lime juice

1 ounce passion fruit syrup

¾ ounce fresh orange juice

¼ ounce grenadine syrup

Ice

¼ ounce dark rum

Orange slice for garnish

Fresh or brandied cherry for garnish

Combine the first five ingredients in a cocktail shaker. Fill the shaker with ice and shake vigorously. Strain into a hurricane glass filled with ice. Float the dark rum on top. Garnish with the orange slice and cherry and serve.

Makes 1 serving

The Casserole Cocktail

Sweet Potato Syrup

½ cup sugar

½ cup water

½ cup roasted sweet potato liquid (see **Note**)

2 tablespoons roasted sweet potato purée (see **Note**)

½ teaspoon freshly grated nutmeg

¼ teaspoon ground cloves

2 ounces bourbon

¼ ounce orange curaçao

¼ ounce fresh lemon juice

Ice

Freshly grated nutmeg for garnish

Lu Brow is known as the "bar chef" at Café Adelaide. Such is the esteem they have for the drinking arts in general and Chef Lu in particular. Café Adelaide is owned by the same family that owns Commander's Palace, so this would be the perfect way to start Thanksgiving if you're cooking the recipes from Commander's Palace (see pages 102–104).

To make the syrup: In a small saucepan over low heat, combine the sugar, water, roasted sweet potato liquid, roasted sweet potato purée, nutmeg, and cloves. Bring to a slow simmer, stirring occasionally to keep it from sticking or burning. Simmer, stirring, until the sugar is completely dissolved and the sweet potatoes have dissolved into the syrup, about 5 minutes. Remove from the heat and let cool.

In a mixing glass, combine 1 ounce of the sweet potato syrup, the bourbon, the curaçao, and the lemon juice. Add ice and stir, then strain into a rocks glass and add a large chunk of ice. Garnish with a grating of nutmeg and serve. (Store the remaining syrup in a tightly sealed bottle in the refrigerator for up to 3 weeks.)

Note: To make the sweet potato liquid and purée, preheat the oven to 375°F. Place 1 large unpeeled whole sweet potato in a small baking dish and bake until very tender, about 1 hour. Let cool, then remove the potato skin and discard. Pour the liquid from the baking dish into a glass bowl and set aside; you should have about ½ cup. Put the sweet potato flesh in a food processor and process to a smooth purée. Save any remaining cooked sweet potato for another use.

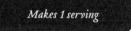

Makes 1 serving

Congo Square Cooler

KIMBERLY PATTON BRAGG

Mint Simple Syrup

2 cups water

A big handful of fresh mint leaves

2 cups sugar

1 ounce orange marmalade

2 ounces bourbon

3 ounces fresh-brewed or sun-brewed iced tea

Ice

Before she moved to New Orleans, Kimberly did much of her mixing at Blue Smoke, a New York barbecue restaurant. They serve a lot of iced tea there. She's also worked the bar for several demanding New Orleans chefs, including John Besh and Dominique Macquet. Here, she joins ice tea with another Southern beverage icon, the mint julep, to create a most perfect union.

To make the mint syrup: In a small saucepan, heat the water over medium-high heat until hot but not boiling. Reserve 1 mint leaf for garnish. Add the rest of the mint leaves to the hot water and steep, like a tea, for about 10 minutes. Strain into another small saucepan and discard the mint. Add the sugar to the infused water and place over low heat, stirring to dissolve the sugar. Remove from the heat and let cool.

In a small bowl, stir ½ ounce of the mint syrup into marmalade, stirring until the jam loosens. Transfer the mixture to a cocktail shaker. Add the bourbon and iced tea, fill the shaker with ice, and shake vigorously. Pour into an iced tea glass. Garnish with the reserved mint leaf and serve. (Store the remaining syrup in a tightly sealed bottle in the refrigerator for up to 3 weeks.)

Makes 1 serving

GINGER–PEACH JULEP

WAYNE CURTIS

Ginger Simple Syrup

4 ounces fresh ginger, chopped (no need to peel) (about 1 cup)

1 cup sugar

1 cup water

3 or 4 peppercorns

2 or 3 cloves

1 ripe peach slice

8 to 10 fresh mint sprigs

2½ ounces top-shelf sippin' bourbon

Ice

There's an old sign painted on the side of a building on Decatur Street advertising Emerson's Ginger-Mint Julep, "the new drink." That drink is nowhere else in evidence now. But here's a version of what it might have tasted like had it been a cocktail and not a tonic or soft drink. Wayne Curtis is the author of *And a Bottle of Rum: A History of the New World in Ten Cocktails*. He moved to New Orleans a few months before Hurricane Katrina and the ensuing federal levee failures. He didn't let a little water drive him away.

To make the ginger syrup: In a small saucepan, combine the ginger, sugar, and water. Bring to a boil over medium-high heat, stirring to dissolve the sugar. Add the spices, remove from the heat, and let cool. Strain into a bottle. Put the peach slice in a mixing glass. Reserve 1 mint sprig for garnish and put the rest in the mixing glass. Add the bourbon and ½ ounce of the ginger syrup. Muddle gently, crushing the peach and bruising (but not tearing) the mint leaves.

Set the mixing glass aside to let the contents macerate for 2 to 3 minutes while you prepare the ice: Place 8 to 10 ice cubes in a sturdy cloth or plastic bag and pound with a large mallet until finely crushed. Remove and discard any unsightly lumps.

Pack a chilled julep cup with the pulverized ice; insert a straw extending no more than 2 inches above the rim. Slowly strain the contents of the mixing glass into the ice-packed julep cup. Garnish with the reserved mint sprig and serve. (Store the remaining syrup, tightly sealed, in the refrigerator for up to 3 weeks.)

Makes 1 serving

THE NEUTRAL GROUND

RHIANNON ENLIL

2 ounces rye whiskey

½ ounce Benedictine

½ ounce amontillado sherry

2 dashes of orange bitters

Ice

Thin orange slice for garnish

Named for the median on Canal Street that historically separated the American district from the Spanish/French district (now the French Quarter), this cocktail contains spirits from each country.

In a mixing glass, combine the first four ingredients. Fill the glass with ice, stir, and strain into a chilled martini glass. Garnish with the orange slice and serve.

Makes 1 serving

Bittersweet Sour

Demerara and Lemongrass Syrup

1 stalk **lemongrass**, roughly chopped into 3-inch pieces

1 cup **Demerara sugar**

1 cup **water**

1 ounce **Domaine de Canton ginger liqueur**

¾ ounce **Angostura bitters**

½ ounce **fresh lemon juice**

½ ounce **fresh lime juice**

¼ ounce **fresh orange juice**

¼ ounce **lemongrass syrup**

Ice

1¾ ounces **chilled soda water**

Bitters aren't really "bitter," per se. Nonetheless, they tend to be used sparingly in cocktails. In this drink, the bitters are second only to the ginger liqueur in prominence.

To make the lemongrass syrup: In a small saucepan, combine the lemongrass, sugar, and water. Bring to a boil over medium-high heat, stirring to dissolve the sugar. Remove from the heat and let cool. When cool, strain into a bottle.

In a cocktail shaker, combine the ginger liqueur, bitters, citrus juices, and ¼ ounce of the lemongrass syrup. Shake vigorously. Pour into a Collins glass filled with ice. Top with the soda water and serve. (Store the remaining syrup, tightly sealed, in the refrigerator for up to 3 weeks.)

Makes 1 serving

SECOND LINE SWIZZLER

2 ounces **citrus vodka**

1 ounce **black raspberry liqueur** such as Chambord

1 ounce **fresh lemon juice**

1 **egg white**

½ ounce **Simple Syrup** (see Note, page 214)

1 cup **crushed ice**

Thin lemon slice for garnish

Here the Ramos Gin Fizz (page 216) gets a vodka update.

In a cocktail shaker, combine the first five ingredients and shake until frothy. Add the ice to the shaker and shake again to chill. Strain into a chilled martini glass. Garnish with the lemon slice and serve.

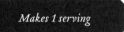

Makes 1 serving

N'awlins Nectar

STAR HODGSON

The N'awlins Nectar was inspired by the farmers' market in New Orleans and the simplicity of letting quality ingredients shine. Local grapefruit is at its peak all through winter, and our extraordinarily long growing season produces flowers that create a mecca for busy bees. The zest from the grapefruit makes for an aromatic sensory experience with each sip.

Honey Simple Syrup

1 cup local honey

1 cup water

2 ounces dry bourbon such as Bulleit

2 ounces fresh grapefruit juice

Ice

Grapefruit twist for garnish

To make the honey syrup: In a small saucepan, combine the honey and water and heat over medium heat, stirring to dissolve the honey. Do not let boil. Remove from the heat and let cool.

In a cocktail shaker, combine the bourbon, the grapefruit juice, and ½ ounce of the honey syrup. Fill the shaker with ice and shake vigorously. Strain into a rocks glass. Garnish with the grapefruit twist and serve. (Store the remaining syrup in a tightly sealed bottle in the refrigerator for up to 3 weeks.)

Makes 1 serving

CREOLE SNO-BALL

STAR HODGSON

The Creole Sno-Ball was inspired by an early arrival of spring one year: Star Hodgson's backyard garden was in full bloom with mint and Meyer lemons. The Creole bitters add a nice depth to the drink. Serve over crushed ice on a warm day like a traditional New Orleans snowball.

Paw Paw's Honey-Ginger Simple Syrup

½ cup local honey

½ cup hot water

2 tablespoons fresh ginger juice, juiced from about 4 ounces fresh ginger

8 fresh mint leaves

2 ounces bourbon

½ ounce fresh Meyer lemon juice

2 dashes of Creole bitters

Ice

To make the honey-ginger syrup: In a small saucepan, combine the honey and water and heat over medium heat, stirring to dissolve the honey. Do not let boil. Remove from the heat and stir in the ginger juice. Let cool.

Reserve 1 mint leaf for garnish. In a cocktail shaker, combine the rest of the mint, ½ ounce of the honey-ginger syrup, the bourbon, the lemon juice, and the bitters. Fill the shaker with ice cubes and shake vigorously. Strain into a rocks glass filled with crushed ice and garnish with the reserved mint leaf. Serve with a small spoon. (Store the remaining syrup in a tightly sealed bottle in the refrigerator for up to 3 weeks.)

Makes 1 serving

The Marsaw

Crushed ice

2 ounces Maker's Mark bourbon

1 ounce Angostura Lemon, Lime & Bitters

½ ounce strawberry syrup

½ ounce almond syrup

Orange slice for garnish

Maraschino cherry for garnish

For thirty-four years, Martin worked the bar at the Rib Room in the Omni Royal Orleans Hotel. When each hotel in the chain was asked to choose a drink to represent Omni in a book they were putting together, Sawyer bested all the other bartenders at the Royal Orleans with this drink. He uses Monin premium brand for the syrups.

Fill a highball glass halfway with crushed ice. Pour all the ingredients over the ice, stir, and garnish with the orange slice and a cherry. Serve.

Makes 1 serving

McMillian

5 fresh mint leaves

2 ounces Rittenhouse rye

½ ounce orange curaçao

¼ ounce Benedictine

½ ounce orgeat syrup

¾ ounce fresh lime juice

1 dash of Angostura bitters

Ice

Chris McMillian is an inspiration, a giant among bartenders. His specialty is nineteenth-century cocktails. But, as David Wondrich, a cocktail historian, told Wayne Curtis, a rum historian, in *Imbibe* magazine, "Chris is not just doing historical recreations. Chris is a nineteenth-century bartender." Chris happened into Geoffrey Wilson's bar one year on his birthday. That event was the inspiration. McMillian was the result.

Geoff describes himself as the "assistant trainee to the barback at Loa Bar and International House Hotel." If he keeps making drinks like this, he may well be a senior trainee.

Reserve 1 mint leaf for garnish. Combine the remaining mint and all the other ingredients in a cocktail shaker. Fill the shaker with ice and shake vigorously. Double-strain with a cocktail strainer and then a tea strainer into a martini glass. Float the reserved mint leaf on top and serve.

Makes 1 serving

HOT-OR-COLD HENDRICK'S #1

IAN JULIAN

Ian Julian moved to New Orleans hoping to find something more exciting than retail or an office job. Here, he fell in love with mixology. "I love to cook, and I learned that being a bartender is like being a chef except instead of using solids you use liquids."

This moody drink can be served hot or cold, depending . . .

Cucumber Simple Syrup

1 large cucumber, peeled

½ cup sugar

2 ounces Hendrick's gin

¼ cup (heavy) whipping cream (optional)

4 drops rose water (optional)

2 ounces hot or cold Earl Grey tea

Thin slice of cucumber for garnish (optional)

To make the cucumber syrup: Juice the cucumber; you should get about ½ cup. Transfer the juice to a small saucepan. Add the sugar and bring to a boil over medium-high heat, stirring to dissolve the sugar. Remove from the heat and let cool.

To make the hot Hendrick's #1: In a mug, stir together the gin and ½ ounce of the cucumber syrup. Combine the whipping cream and rose water in a bowl and beat with an electric mixer until soft peaks form. Brew the tea and add to the mug while hot. Spoon a dollop of the whipped cream on top and serve.

To make the cold Hendrick's #1: In a mixing glass, combine the gin and ½ ounce of the cucumber syrup. Brew the tea and chill over ice, then strain into the mixing glass. Stir to mix, then transfer to a lowball glass, garnish with the cucumber slice, and serve.

(Store the remaining syrup in a tightly sealed bottle in the refrigerator for up to 3 weeks. You'll probably be making a few of these to use up that whipped cream . . . or use your imagination.)

Makes 1 serving

New Orleans and the Invention of the Cocktail

The story of how the cocktail was invented in New Orleans is a great one. Antoine (a.k.a. Amédée Peychaud), the immigrant from Saint-Domingue who created Peychaud's bitters, owned an apothecary. Bitters were supposed to be good for upset stomachs, so people would buy them at the drugstore, or apothecary. Peychaud noticed that by mixing a few dashes of his bitters, some sugar, and some brandy, he could create a drink that would be at least as tasty as it was medicinal. He used a double-ended egg cup, or coquetier, as a measuring tool, and from thence the word "cocktail" is thought to have derived. The problem is, the word "cocktail" had been in use a couple of decades before 1838, when Peychaud made his brandy-and-bitters concoction.

Tuesday, May 6, 1806 is the day the word "cocktail" made its first known appearance in print. It happened in Claverack, New York, but the story sounds like it could have come out of Louisiana political history. The loser of an election presented an itemized list of his gains and losses in the campaign. In the loss column, he listed:

720 rum-grogs

17 [dozen] brandy

32 gin-slings

411 glasses bitter

25 [dozen] cock tail

My election

In the gains column, he listed only one word, in all caps: "NOTHING."

Fortunately for history, a reader sent in a letter the next week asking what a "cock tail" was. The editor of the newspaper responded with a definition that tells us as much about drinking as it does about democracy:

"Cock tail then is a stimulating liquor, composed of spirits of any kind, sugar, water, and bitters . . . it is vulgarly called a bittered sling, and is supposed to be an

excellent electioneering potion inasmuch as it renders the heart stout and bold, at the same time that it fuddles the head. It is said also to be of great use to a democratic candidate: because, a person having swallowed a glass of it, is ready to swallow anything else."

Even though New Orleans didn't invent the cocktail, we are home to both theorists and practitioners of the drinking arts. If you want to learn about drinking, go to the Museum of the American Cocktail and have Chris McMillian tell you little-known facts about things you never knew you wanted to know. If you want to drink, we have Bourbon Street for the undiscriminating. For the serious drinker, there are a dozen or so bars with bartenders who can talk and mix a good cocktail.

There are many reasons that this city has been an important drinking town for a couple of hundred years. Wayne Curtis, the author of *And a Bottle of Rum: A History of the World in 10 Cocktails*, moved to New Orleans shortly after the federal levees failed. He says that New Orleans was the perfect drinking town in the 1800s because its proximity to the Mississippi River meant that the best whiskey from Kentucky and Tennessee could easily make its way down. The best bitters from the West Indies could easily make their way up. And the best Cognac could easily makes its way in on any of the many ships traveling between New Orleans and France.

"New Orleans was the place where you came to get rich," McMillian explains. "If you were a young person, an adventurer, a fortune seeker, New Orleans was the last place you would have gone before going to California for the gold rush. It was the last gateway of civilization before California. In the 1830s, the population of the city tripled—from 30,000 to 100,000—because of this influx." In addition to new citizens, there were thousands of transient capitalists coming to the city around harvest time to make deals. To accommodate the needs of these travelers, the city developed hotels and restaurants. When it was built in 1829, the Tremont House in Boston set a new standard with innovations like running water, indoor plumbing, and free soap. Astor House in New York followed seven years later. The St. Charles Hotel in New Orleans on St. Charles Avenue and the St. Louis Hotel came shortly after that.

Of all the important things that took place around then at the St. Louis Hotel, none was more important than the drinking. In those days, the drink crossing everyone's lips was the mint julep. In his 1854 book, *Health Trip to the Tropics*, Nathaniel Parker Willis dedicates a chapter to New Orleans and nearly half a page to the sensual pleasure of juleps at the St. Louis bar: "A marble counter extends around one-half of its circular area, and so vast is the interior, that the half-moon of busy bar-keepers, seen from the opposite gallery as they stand and manipulate behind their twinkling wilderness of decanters, looks like a julep-orama, performed by dwarfs, the murmur of the gliding ice amid the aroma of fragrant mint betraying their occupation."

These days, New Orleans isn't a craft cocktail capital like New York or San Francisco. We don't have a bunch of bars making their own bitters and combing the history books for lost recipes. But we have a lot of professional bartenders who know what they're doing. These guys are trying to make you a good drink, not audition for a role in your next movie.

Basic Creole Seasoning Blend

1½ tablespoons table salt

½ tablespoon kosher salt

1½ tablespoons ground cayenne

2 tablespoons coarsely ground black pepper

1 tablespoon ground white pepper

2½ tablespoons sweet paprika

2 tablespoons granulated garlic

2 tablespoons granulated onion

1 tablespoon dried thyme

1 teaspoon dried oregano

1 teaspoon dried basil

1 teaspoon celery seed

Combine all the ingredients in a blender or food processor and process until thoroughly mixed. Use immediately, or store in an airtight container for up to 4 weeks.

Note: Creole seasoning mix is a classic blend from the area, generally of onion and garlic powders, celery seed, a few kinds of pepper, some dried herbs, and salt. You can make your own or buy one of the excellent versions in the market, such as Tony Chachere's, Zatarain's, or Chef Paul Prudhomme's Magic Seasoning Blend.

Makes about 1 cup

Fish Stock

4 pounds fish bones with heads (gills removed) from (about 6 pounds) whole, firm white fish, such as drum, snapper, redfish, or bass

Cold water for rinsing the bones and heads, plus 3 quarts

1 tablespoon vegetable oil

1 cup chopped carrot

1 cup chopped celery

2 cups chopped onion

2 large cloves garlic, smashed

1 bay leaf

Several sprigs parsley or thyme

⅛ teaspoon whole black peppercorns

If necessary, cut the bones in half so they will fit into a large stockpot. Thoroughly rinse them and then place them in a bowl filled with cold water and soak for 30 minutes.

Heat the oil in the stockpot over medium-high heat. Add the carrot, celery, onion, and garlic, and sauté for 1 minute. Transfer the fish bones and heads from the soaking water to the stockpot. Add to the pot with the vegetables along with the bay leaf, parsley, peppercorns and 3 quarts cold water. Bring to a boil, then immediately reduce heat to low and simmer for at least 30 minutes and up to 45 minutes until the broth is flavorful.

Remove from the heat. Strain the stock through a fine-mesh strainer into a heat-proof bowl. Discard the solids. Let the stock cool completely, then transfer to an airtight container. Store in the refrigerator for up to 3 days or in the freezer for up to 1 month.

Makes about 2 quarts

Shrimp Stock

In a soup pot or small stockpot over high heat, heat the tablespoon of oil. Add the shrimp shells and onion and cook stirring constantly, until the shells of the shrimp are thoroughly pink and the onion is starting to brown, about 5 minutes.

Add the celery, allspice, bay leaf, tomato paste (if using), and water and bring to a boil, then immediately reduce the heat to low and simmer for 20 minutes. Strain the stock through a fine-mesh strainer into a heatproof bowl. Discard the solids. Let the stock cool completely, then transfer to an airtight container. Store in the refrigerator for up to 3 days or in the freezer for up to 1 month.

Makes about 4 quarts

1 tablespoon canola oil

Shells and heads from 1 pound shrimp

1 medium yellow onion, unpeeled, cut into quarters

2 stalks celery

2 whole allspice berries, crushed

1 bay leaf

1 tablespoon tomato paste (optional)

5 quarts water

Rich Shrimp Stock

In a wide and shallow heavy-bottomed pot, heat the canola oil until hot but not smoking. Add the shrimp and sear until most of the shells are bright orange, about 2 minutes. Add the onion, carrot, and celery and cook until the vegetables become tender, about 5 minutes. Add the tomato paste and mix in well with a wooden spoon. Cook, stirring constantly so the mixture does not scorch, until the tomato paste has changed color, from red to orange, and the tomato flavor has cooked out, about 10 minutes. Add the water to the pot and bring to a boil. Remove the pot from the heat and carefully transfer the mixture to a blender or food processor. Process until the shrimp is coursely chopped. Return the stock to the heat and bring it to a simmer, then remove it from the heat again and let it sit for 10 minutes to let the flavors infuse.

Strain the stock through a fine-mesh strainer and then through a chinois, pressing on the mixture with the back of the spoon to extract as much liquid as possible from the shells. Transfer to an airtight container and refrigerate to cool and until ready to use. Store in refrigerator for up to 3 days or in the freezer for up to 1 month.

Makes 1 quart

1½ teaspoons canola oil

1 pound whole shrimp (41/50)

½ onion, diced

1 carrot, diced

1 stalk celery

One 8-ounce can tomato paste

5 cups cold water

Basic Chicken Stock

3 large onions, unpeeled, coarsely chopped

3 ribs celery with leaves, coarsely sliced

3 large carrots, unpeeled, coarsely sliced

½ head garlic, cut in quarters

3 pounds chicken or other poultry necks, wings, and/or backs

About 6 quarts cool water

Place all the vegetables and chicken in a large stockpot. Add the water and bring to a strong simmer, uncovered, over high heat. Lower heat to maintain a gentle simmer and cook for at least 3 hours or up to 8 hours. While the stock cooks, replenish water as needed to keep about the same amount of water covering the vegetables and chicken, and occasionally skim the fat off the surface.

Once the stock has finished cooking, remove it from the heat, and let cool completely. Strain the stock through a fine-mesh strainer. Discard the solids. Transfer the stock to an airtight container. Store in the refrigerator for up to 3 days or in the freezer for up to 1 month.

To make a rich chicken stock, use well-browned chicken backs (roasted in the oven at 350°F for 45 minutes) to make the basic stock, then strain and skim as directed for the basic stock and reduce by half over low heat, approximately 4 hours.

Makes about 4 quarts

Veal Stock

5 pounds veal bones, cut into 3- to 4-inch pieces (by the butcher)

2 tablespoons olive oil

1 large leek, rinsed clean and chopped

1 large onion, chopped

8 ounces carrots, peeled and chopped

5 ribs celery, chopped

1 head garlic, cut in half

5 quarts, plus 1 pint of water

2 tablespoons tomato paste

1 cup dry red wine

4 sprigs fresh thyme or 1 teaspoon dried

1 bunch parsley

2 bay leaves

12 black peppercorns

4 whole cloves

Preheat your oven to 350°F. Rinse the bones. Toss the bones in 1 tablespoon of the olive oil until well-coated. Put the bones in a large roasting pan. Roast for 30 minutes. Toss the leek, onion, carrots, celery, and garlic in the remaining 1 tablespoon olive oil. Add them to the roasting pan. Continue roasting the bones and the vegetables for 45 minutes longer, or until well browned, but not burned.

Using tongs, remove the bones and vegetables from the roasting pan and place in the stockpot. Pour off the fat and discard. Put the roasting pan on the stovetop and add 1 pint of water and the tomato paste. Bring it to a simmer over medium-high heat. Scrape any brown bits from the bottom of the pan and stir until the tomato paste is well incorporated. Pour the water and drippings into the stockpot. Add the 5 quarts of water and 1 cup red wine to

the stockpot. Add the thyme, parsley, bay leaves, peppercorns, and cloves. Bring the stock to a boil over medium-high heat. Reduce heat to medium low. Simmer the stock for 6 to 8 hours, skimming off foam that accumulates on the surface.

Using a slotted spoon, remove and discard the solids. Allow the stock to cool for at least 1 hour. Put 8 to 10 ice cubes in the stock, which will cause the fat in the stock to congeal on the surface. Using a slotted spoon, remove the fat. Strain the stock through a fine-mesh strainer or a cheesecloth. Transfer the stock to an airtight container. Store in the refrigerator for up to 3 days or in the freezer for up to 1 month.

Makes about 4 quarts

POSTSCRIPT

And then, there's the cookbook . . .

In the spring of 2008, David Simon phoned with news that *Treme*, the series that he and Eric Overmyer created, had been green-lighted by HBO. On the basis of their script, HBO would fund the production of the first episode, after which they would decide whether to order an entire season. That meant I would be returning to New Orleans, a city I had visited previously as a tourist. The wonderful thing about filming on location is the opportunity to meet people and experience places in a way that casual visitors never can. In order to start imagining what the show might look like, I had to walk those streets—to smell, taste, and hear New Orleans. And we needed to assemble a team of experts, both local and not, to help interpret the material and answer the many questions that would help to define the characters. David and Eric described the music, the collective energy of the second-line parades, the taste and smell of the food, the rhythm of the city, the decadence, the spontaneity and unapologetic joy with which people live, the fearless devotion to preserving traditions—these were just a few of the details that we needed to convey from the script to the screen.

When faced with such a daunting task, I've always found it's best to just get started. So I called Wendell Pierce, who had graciously accepted the role David had written for him—Antoine Batiste, an itinerant musician living in exile in Jefferson Parish. I asked him to meet me at the Louisiana Music Exchange, a used instrument store. With advice offered by Keith Hart, who became our brass instrument teacher, and later played the role of band director Darren LeCoeur in the show, I made my first official *Treme* purchase, a used trombone appropriate for Antoine Batiste. The need for instruments was obvious. Understanding what we would need to know and acquire with regard to New Orleans cuisine was more complex.

There is a unique way that people who cook speak about food. For the character of chef Janette Desautel, we knew we needed a skilled actor to master not only the practical skills of a chef—chopping, sautéing, plating—but the passionate, slow, deliberate way that people who love food describe ingredients, flavors, and presentation. I sent our top casting auditions to Anthony Bourdain and a few other chef friends, to see which of the actresses selected by casting director Alexa Fogel could fool the pros. We hired Kim Dickens and never looked back. Tom Colicchio made his kitchen at Craft in Los Angeles available for Kim's initial training, and then later Susan Spicer's Bayona became the place where both Kim and Ntare Mwine (Jacques) could

observe the rhythm of the kitchen, and also practice the specific skills necessary for each episode.

I was beginning to discover that not only is the food different here, but the attitude toward it as well. Whether from the kitchens of Susan Spicer, Leah Chase, or Donald Link, or from Bingo's sidewalk grill outside of Bullets Sports Bar, there is unparalleled pride in culinary creation. When someone in New Orleans serves you a plate of food and says, "Hope you like it," they mean it. It is truly important to them that you enjoy their food. In his book *Hungry Town*, Tom Fitzmorris describes New Orleans as the city where food is almost everything. Requests from readers of his online newsletter, nomenu.com, led him to start compiling a daily list of restaurants that had opened or reopened after Katrina. He soon realized that New Orleanians saw the growing list as a symbol of hope that their city was coming back, that they might one day return to something familiar. Similarly, Desautel is determined to keep her restaurant afloat after the storm in New Orleans, as a source of not only sustenance for her clientele, but a sign that all is not lost.

We filmed a total of eleven episodes that first season, and HBO ordered a second season almost immediately.

As we prepared for *that* season, we met with heads of various HBO departments, as well as the creative executives, to present the major themes and character arcs for the year. During this annual ritual, we try to create as much enthusiasm as possible, since the attendees all work on other HBO projects, and we wanted ours to be a priority. Just as David and Eric finished describing another exciting series of adventures for our characters in the upcoming season, someone asked what additional products we had in mind. We had a soundtrack featuring music from the season . . . "and . . . of course, there's the cookbook!" I said spontaneously, knowing the Desautel storyline had been popular among the HBO execs. I hadn't a clue how to actually produce a cookbook.

Within a week I had calls from three different people at HBO wanting to hear more about the cookbook. I quickly contacted Lolis Eric Elie, story editor on *Treme* and established food writer, and confessed my impulsive act. Thankfully, he agreed to write the book. Lolis's book agent, Claudia Menza, offered expert guidance and determination, and Lorena Jones at Chronicle Books shared our vision and enthusiasm for the project.

As Desautel, Kim Dickens does a masterful job of capturing the frustration and weariness, the joys and passions of a chef who ultimately makes the decision to move to New York and just cook without the burden of owning a restaurant in a broken city. For Season 2, the writers sent Desautel on a journey to three New York kitchens. The first was the fictitious Brulard, which we built in a warehouse in New Orleans on the west bank of the Mississippi River. The second was the real life kitchen at Le Bernardin, Eric Ripert's restaurant par excellence. He graciously agreed not only to play himself on camera, but to allow our actress to work in his kitchen, preparing tuna tartar alongside his entire kitchen staff on their day off. Gracious does not even begin to describe the level of hospitality afforded to our film crew, and on more than one occasion. The third restaurant was Lucky Peach, production designer Chester Kaczenski's rendition of a David Chang restaurant. David played himself and generously shared his recipes. Gradually he became accustomed to the repetition of words and actions that is a regular part of the filming day. By putting Janette Desautel in the same space as real chefs and by serving real food created by food artist Soa Davies, our character became credible within the real culinary universe as well as the fictional world of *Treme*. At one point, there was discussion about using plastic food to cut down on waste, but we never could bring ourselves to do it. (And so cast and crew happily enjoyed leftovers and we were able to make substantial food donations to the local homeless shelter, Ozanam Inn.)

For Season 3, we brought Desautel back to New Orleans, seduced by an offer from an investor who not only seemed to share our chef's passion for food, but who was also willing to take on much of the operational and financial burden. This new restaurant required a much larger set, one in which we could feature both the dining room and kitchen. We had to learn the choreography of the new space, both to discover the best camera angles and to figure out

the way the cooks/actors would move around each other. If we were going to sell the idea that there was chemistry among the kitchen staff, this had to be a well-practiced dance. Bourdain offered a series of obstacles for Desautel to encounter, illuminating both the trials of opening a new restaurant and the tension between art and commerce. What would seriously slow the kitchen down? An unexpectedly popular pasta dish. What dish would challenge the skills of the waitstaff? *Rentier de cochon*, pork backbone stew, plated tableside. What else can we throw at her? Kitchen injuries. A live cooking demo. Brunch service.

What makes *Treme* unique is the way our characters live credibly in the real world: Antoine Batiste playing a gig with trumpeter Kermit Ruffins; chef Janette Desautel seeking the advice of her colleague, Emeril Lagasse; Big Chief Albert Lambreaux encountering Big Chief Donald Harrison Jr. in the street. And the food is treated no differently. Much care is given to ensure that each of the characters cook and eat appropriately for the real life New Orleanians they represent—our holiday episodes especially might feature four or five different menus depending upon who's doing the cooking. So it makes sense that LaDonna's red beans and rice be included alongside Donald Link's shrimp risotto. In this spirit we bring you this cookbook—a culinary journey through New Orleans with the characters of *Treme*.

Nina Kostroff Noble
Executive Producer, HBO's *Treme*

ACKNOWLEDGMENTS

Long before there was this book, there was the television show. For that I have to thank David Simon and Eric Overmyer, the creators, and Nina Noble the third executive producer of the triumvirate. In conceiving the show, they wanted all the key aspects of the culture of New Orleans—the music, architecture, and food—to be integral to the story. In order to bring this idea of culture-as-character to fruition, it took a lot of support and vision from the people at HBO.

The cookbook was Nina Noble's idea, but our agent, Claudia Menza, and our editor, Lorena Jones, helped shape it and spent many long hours and endured many revised revisions.

Much of what is written here is based on the scripts of the writers: George Pelecanos, Tom Piazza, Mari Kornhauser, Chris Offutt, Jen Ralston, Chris Yakaitis, and the late David Mills. Whatever accuracy this book can lay claim to is in part the result of the work of those in the writers' office: Lyndsey Beaulieu, Molly Reid, and Jordan Hirsch.

The main job of the *Treme* crew was to produce a television show, not a cookbook. So I owe a great debt to all of people who found the time to contribute to this book in addition to handling their production duties: Laura Schweigman, Kate Evans, Karen Thorson, Chester Kaczenski, Beau Harrison, and Luci Leary. And a special thanks to Kim Dickens for her thoughtful crafting of Janette Desautel.

Thanks to all the chefs who appeared on the show, especially Susan Spicer, for sharing their worlds with us. And thanks to Anthony Bourdain, a master craftsman of kitchen stories who helped us bring that world to the screen. Thanks also to our on-set food stylists, Ann Churchill and Chris Lynch.

Recipes don't count for much unless they actually work. Paulette Rittenberg, our meticulous recipe tester, and her team, Murray Pitts, Susie DeRussy, and Annette Hinds made sure these recipes do indeed work.

And a hearty thank you to our family and friends who made suggestions, tested recipes, wrote recipes and shared their own tips, especially Gerri Elie (whose recipes and inspiration pepper these pages), David Noble (whose appreciation of food helped inspire the book itself), Poppy Tooker, (teacher, chef, friend), Sue Ceravolo, (a generous chef whose kitchen is always open), Jackie Blanchard, Kamili Hemphill (both speakers of multiple culinary languages), Jessica B. Harris (a walking culinary encyclopedia), Judy Walker (host of testing parties), Ben Gersh (who knows every bartender in town), and Pableaux Johnson (culinary and technical consultant). Also, thank you to Soa Davies, Chef Anne Kearney, Chef André Daguin, Chef Aaron Burgau, Chef Dana Logsdon, Chef Alon Shaya, Chef Anne Churchill, Chef Donald Link, Chef Myung Hee Lee, Chef John Besh, Chefs Allison Vines-Rushing and Slade Rushing, Chef Greg Sonnier, Chef Sue Zemanick, the family of Dutch Morial, Althea Pierce, Phyllis Montana-LeBlanc, Kermit Ruffins, Chef Ken Smith, Chef Tory McPhail, Chef Frank Brigtsen, Chef Austin Leslie, Carmen Owens, Chef Darin Nesbit, Chef Nathaniel Zimet, Chef Joe Segreto, Chef Wayne Baquet, Prejean's Restaurant, Chef Frances Chauvin, Chef Christina Quackenbush, Chef Scott Boswell, Chef Philipe La Mancusa, Chef Ruth Fertel, Chef Alfred Singleton, Chef Tenney Flynn, Chef Stephen Stryjewski, Ralph Brennan, Chef Mary Jo Mosca, Chef Jared Tees, Chris Hannah, Chris McMillian, Lucinda Weed, Marvin Allen, Rhiannon Enlil, Lu Brow, Kimberly Patton Bragg, Wayne Curtis, Star Hodgson, Martin Sawyer, Geoffrey Wilson, and Ian Julian.

Thank you to series photographer Paul Schiraldi. Thanks to our food photographer Ed Anderson and the great food styling team he put together: Christine Wolheim, Lillian Kang, and Amanda Anselmino.

And thanks to all the folks at Chronicle Books: Doug Ogan, Claire Fletcher, Marie Oishi, Alice Chau, Tera Killip, David Hawk, Peter Perez, Elizabeth Yarborough, Kate Willsky, Carrie Neves, Ellen Wheat, and Ken DellaPenta. You'd never know from their enthusiasm that they'd published many, many cookbooks before this one.

And finally, thanks to the viewers, the fans of *Treme* whose support of this unusual show allowed us to produce four seasons and a cookbook.

—Lolis Eric Elie

INDEX

A

Absinthe Suissesse, 214
Ajan Étouffée, 34–35
Alcott, William, 168
Allen, Marvin, 216, 222
Almonds, Gautreau's Citrus–Olive Oil Cake with Kumquat Marmalade and, 70
Amato, Henry, 188
Anderson, Brett, 130
Antoine's, 10, 13
Apples
    Appeltaart (Dutch Apple Pie), 185
    Rodekool met Appels (Braised Red Cabbage with Apples), 181
Armstrong, Louis, 32, 78
Arnaud's Restaurant, 13, 213
Asian-Cajun Red Pepper Glaze, 65
Asian Slaw, 172

B

Bachemin's meat market, 122, 145
Bacon
    Bacon-Wrapped Pork Loin with Smothered Greens, Butternut Squash, and Cane Syrup Jus, 67
    Boucherie's Collard Greens with French Fried Grits, 138
    Cochon's Braised Pig with Stewed Turnips and Cabbage, 197
    Creole Crab-and-Corn Bisque, 28–29
    Pork and Beans with Bacon and Onions, 199
    Smothered Cabbage with Onion and Bacon, 85
    Yaka Mein, 32–33
Bagna Cauda Drizzle, 18
Baker, Josephine, 179
Bananas
    Brigtsen's Banana Bread Pudding, 106
    Chunky Peanut Butter and Chocolaty Banana Cake, 105
Baquet, Wayne, 142
Barker, Danny, 78, 213
Barrow's, 145
Batiste, Antoine, 78, 81, 83, 88, 231, 232
Batiste-Williams, LaDonna, 10, 120, 232
Bayona, 13, 38, 40, 73, 114
Beans
    Black Beans and Rum à la Austin Leslie, 113
    Creole Crab-and-Corn Bisque, 28–29
    Creole Succotash, 87
    Fricassee of Peas, Fava Beans, and Morel Mushrooms, 53
    Kermit Ruffins's Butter Beans, 88
    Pork and Beans with Bacon and Onions, 199
    Red Beans and Rice with Smoked Turkey Wings, 198
    White Beans and Shrimp, 89
Béchamel Sauce, 205
Beef
    Besh Steakhouse's Cowboy Steak with Wild Mushrooms, Root Vegetables, and Bordelaise Sauce, 209
    Bun (Vietnamese Vermicelli Salad with Beef), 183

Cousin Kami's Carne Guisada, 207
Dooky Chase's Gumbo Z'herbes, 156–57
Dutch Morial's Oyster Dressing, 82
Eleven 79's Pasta Bolognese, 140
Hachee met Leffe Bier (Beef Onion Stew with Dark Beer), 182
Peppered Hanger Steak with Crispy Rice Cakes, 68
Bégué, Elizabeth Kettenring Dutrey and Hypolite, 184
Beignets, 163, 168, 171
Belle, Lula, 91
Bell Peppers, Creole Stuffed, 84
Benedictine
    McMillian, 224
    The Neutral Ground, 221
    Vieux Carré, 216
Bergeron, Russ, 211
Bernette, Creighton, 93, 94, 102, 103, 106
Bernette, Toni, 93, 94, 96, 98, 99, 101, 102, 105, 106
Berry Parfaits, Oatmeal and, with Chantilly Cream, 111
Besh, John, 7, 10, 28, 39, 58, 220
Besh Steakhouse, 209
Binder, Alois J., 150
Bingo's, 231
Biscuits, La Spiga's Buttermilk, 160–62
Bittersweet Sour, 222
Blanchard, Jacqueline, 28
Blount, Roy, 93
Blue Hill, 28
Blue Smoke, 220
Bob's Smokehouse, 203
Bordelaise Sauce, 209
Boswell, Scott, 68, 172
Boucherie, 138
Bouis, Catherine, 119
Bouley, David, 7
Bourbon
    Bourbon-Molasses Sauce, 114–15
    The Casserole Cocktail, 218
    Congo Square Cooler, 220
    Creole Sno-Ball, 223
    Ginger-Peach Julep, 221
    The Marsaw, 224
    N'awlins Nectar, 223
Bourbon House, 137
Bourdain, Anthony, 6–7, 231, 232
Bragg, Kimberly Patton, 220
Brandy Crusta, 213
Bread. See also Bread pudding; Cornbread; Po-boys
    Bayona's Sweet Potato Brioche, 38
    Creole Stuffed Bell Peppers, 84
    Dutch Morial's Oyster Dressing, 82
    French, New Orleans–style, 150–51
    Trout Farci, 99
Bread pudding
    Brigtsen's Banana Bread Pudding, 106
    history of, 107
    Shrimp and Mirliton Bread Pudding, 103
Brennan, Ella, 211

Brennan, Ralph, 105, 205
Brennan's, 10, 109, 205
Bridges, David, 98
Brigtsen, Frank, 93, 106, 118, 131, 134, 163
Brigtsen, Marna, 106
Brigtsen's Restaurant, 13, 106, 150
Brioche, Bayona's Sweet Potato, 38
Brooks, Odella, 10
Broussard, Joe, 140
Broussard's, 140
Brow, Lu, 218
Brulard, Enrico, 10, 50, 53
Brulard's, 39, 53, 130, 232
Brunch, history of, 184
Bultman, Bethany, 88
Bun (Vietnamese Vermicelli Salad with Beef), 183
Burgau, Aaron, 30

C

Cabbage
    Asian Slaw, 172
    Cochon's Braised Pig with Stewed Turnips and Cabbage, 197
    Dooky Chase's Gumbo Z'herbes, 156–57
    Emeril's Tuna and Butter Lettuce Wraps, 18–19
    Green Garlic Coleslaw, 40
    Marinated Red Cabbage, 18
    Rodekool met Appels (Braised Red Cabbage with Apples), 181
    Smothered Cabbage with Onion and Bacon, 85
Café Adelaide, 218
Café au Lait Pots de Crème with Mudslide Cookies, Bayona's, 73–74
Café du Monde, 10, 163, 168, 171
Cajun vs. Creole cuisine, 130–31
Cakes
    Chunky Peanut Butter and Chocolaty Banana Cake, 105
    Gautreau's Citrus–Olive Oil Cake with Kumquat Marmalade and Almonds, 70
    Pound Cake Paul Trevigne, 119
Calas
    characteristics of, 163
    Crawfish Calas with Green Garlic Mayonnaise, 96
    history of, 163
    Yeast Calas, 127
Capone, Al, 206
Captain Sal's, 134
Carne Guisada, Cousin Kami's, 207
Carrot Casserole, 146
Carter, Julia, 160
Cashion, Ann, 150–51
Cashion's Eat Place, 150
The Casserole Cocktail, 218
Caviar
    Bourbon House Trio of Oyster Shooters, 137
    Momofuku's Poached Eggs with Caviar, 42–44
Champagne Mignonette, 137
Chang, David, 6, 7, 10, 27, 32, 33, 42, 68, 232
Chantilly Cream, 111

Chase, Leah, 156, 231

Chauvin, Frances, 155

Chayotes. *See* Mirlitons

Cheese
  Dickie Brennan's Steakhouse Tomato Napoleon, 191
  French Fried Grits, 138
  Grandmother Besh's Braised Rabbit with Cavatelli, 58–59
  Ralph's on the Park's Crabmeat Lasagna, 205

Chez Panisse, 13, 163

Chicken
  Basic Chicken Stock, 230
  Chicken Adobo, 167
  Chicken Étouffée, 175
  Mosca's Chicken à la Grande, 206
  Paper-Skin Chicken and Rice-Flour Waffles with Asian-Cajun Red Pepper Syrup, 65–66

Chicken Deluxe, 145

Chicory Coffee–Glazed Quail with Swiss Chard and Creamy Grits, MiLa's, 60–61

Chiles
  Chile–Sweet Soy Glaze, 68
  Cousin Kami's Carne Guisada, 207
  Habanero-Laced Lamb Shanks with Spiced Couscous, 116
  Jalapeño Cornbread, 126
  Nuoc Mam, 183

Chocolate
  Chunky Peanut Butter and Chocolaty Banana Cake, 105
  Ganache, 105
  Mudslide Cookies, 73
  Pound Cake Paul Trevigne, 119

Christian's, 99

Churchill, Anne, 40

Cilantro Purée, 194

Citrus fruits. *See also* individual fruits
  Citrus-Chile Oil, 194
  Citrus–Olive Oil Cake with Kumquat Marmalade and Almonds, Gautreau's, 70
  Citrus Salad, 137

Clancy's, 15

Clemenceau'd Shrimp, 49

Clevenger, JoAnn, 93, 98

Cochon, 130, 141, 197

Cocktails
  Absinthe Suissese, 214
  Bittersweet Sour, 222
  Brandy Crusta, 213
  The Casserole Cocktail, 218
  Congo Square Cooler, 220
  Creole Sno-Ball, 223
  French 75, 214
  Ginger-Peach Julep, 221
  history of, 226–27
  Hot-or-Cold Hendrick's #1, 225
  Hurricane, 217
  The Marsaw, 224
  McMillian, 224
  Muscadine Wine Lemonade, 188
  N'awlins Nectar, 223
  The Neutral Ground, 221
  Ramos Gin Fizz, 216
  Sazerac, 215

Second Line Swizzler, 222
  Vieux Carré, 216

Coffee
  Bayona's Café au Lait Pots de Crème with Mudslide Cookies, 73–74
  Chicory Coffee–Glazed Quail with Swiss Chard and Creamy Grits, MiLa's, 60–61

Cognac
  Brandy Crusta, 213
  French 75, 214
  Vieux Carré, 216

Colicchio, Tom, 6

Collard greens
  Boucherie's Collard Greens with French Fried Grits, 138
  Dooky Chase's Gumbo Z'herbes, 156–57

Colson, Terry, 168

Commander's Palace, 102–4, 131, 150, 174, 205, 211, 218

Congo Square Cooler, 220

Cookies, Mudslide, 73

Coop's, 158

Coquette, 163

Corn. *See also* Cornbread
  Creole Crab-and-Corn Bisque, 28–29
  Creole Succotash, 87
  Roasted Corn Coulis, 50

Cornbread
  Cornbread–French Bread Dressing, 149
  Jalapeño Cornbread, 126
  Lambreaux's Cornbread, 148

Cortese, Sam, 76

Couscous, Spiced, 116

Crab
  Blue Crab Fritters, 194
  Creole Crab-and-Corn Bisque, 28–29
  Creole Gumbo, 122–24
  Li'l Dizzy's Trout Baquet, 142
  Peristyle's Jumbo Lump Crabmeat and Herb Salad over Chilled Roasted Beets and Pickled Onions, 20–22
  Ralph's on the Park's Crabmeat Lasagna, 205
  Trout Farci, 99
  Uptown Egg and Rice, 112

Crawfish
  Ajan Étouffée, 34–35
  Crawfish Calas with Green Garlic Mayonnaise, 96
  Crawfish Ravioli with Sea Urchin Butter Sauce and Mississippi Paddlefish Roe, 47

Crème de menthe
  Absinthe Suissese, 214

Creole Crab-and-Corn Bisque, 28–29

Creole Gumbo, 122–24

Creole Roasted Turkey, 102

Creole seasoning mixes
  Basic Creole Seasoning Blend, 228
  Commander's Creole Seasoning, 103

Creole Sno-Ball, 223

Creole Stuffed Bell Peppers, 84

Creole Succotash, 87

Creole vs. Cajun cuisine, 130–31

Crescent City Steak House, 91, 176

Cucumbers
  Bun (Vietnamese Vermicelli Salad with Beef), 183

Cucumber and Tobiko Salad, 137
  Cucumber Simple Syrup, 225

Culinary Institute of America (CIA), 13

Curaçao
  Brandy Crusta, 213
  The Casserole Cocktail, 218
  McMillian, 224

Cure, 217

Curtis, Wayne, 221, 224, 226

Cushaw Pie, 155

D

Daguin, André and Ariane, 13, 24

D'Artagnan, 13, 24

Davies, Soa, 7, 45, 232

Demerara and Lemongrass Syrup, 222

Desautel, Janette, 6, 10, 13, 15, 109, 168, 231, 232

Desautel's, 15, 30, 67, 70

Desdunes, Rodolphe, 136

Desiree, 78, 81, 82, 84, 85, 87, 89

Desserts
  Appeltaart (Dutch Apple Pie), 185
  Bayona's Café au Lait Pots de Crème with Mudslide Cookies, 73–74
  Chunky Peanut Butter and Chocolaty Banana Cake, 105
  Cushaw Pie, 155
  Gautreau's Citrus–Olive Oil Cake with Kumquat Marmalade and Almonds, 70
  Microwave Pralines, 133
  Oatmeal and Fresh Berry Parfaits with Chantilly Cream, 111
  Pie Four Nuts, 118
  Pound Cake Paul Trevigne, 119
  Thyme-Satsuma–Black Pepper Ice, 75

Dickens, Kim, 231

Dickie Brennan's Steakhouse, 191, 205

Dixie Tavern Uptown, 120

Domenica, 39

Dominique's, 13

Domino, Fats, 78, 179

Dong Phuong, 13

Dooky Chase, 13, 49, 89, 156

Dorignac's, 145

Doughnuts, 168. *See also* Beignets

Drago's, 176

Dressing
  Cornbread–French Bread Dressing, 149
  Dutch Morial's Oyster Dressing, 82

Drinks. *See* Cocktails

Duck
  Bayona's Roasted Duck with Bourbon-Molasses Sauce and Sweet Potato Fries, 114–15
  Gabrielle's Slow-Roasted Duck with Cracklin' Skin, 62–63
  Seared Duck Breast on Green Onion Pancakes with Daikon Salad, 27

Dufresne, Wylie, 6

Dutrey, Louis, 184

E

Edge, John T., 168

Egerton, John, 184

Eggs
  Momofuku's Poached Eggs with Caviar, 42–44

Uptown Egg and Rice, 112

Yaka Mein, 32–33

Eleven 79, 140, 158

Emeril's, 13, 15, 18, 91, 118

Encalade, Byron, 176–77

Enlil, Rhiannon, 217, 221

Erin Rose, 217

Escoffier, Auguste, 107

F

Fay's Honey Whip Donuts, 134

Fennelly, Beth Ann, 93

Fertel, Randy, 189

Fertel, Ruth, 176, 189

Fish

Crawfish Ravioli with Sea Urchin Butter Sauce and Mississippi Paddlefish Roe, 47

Emeril's Tuna and Butter Lettuce Wraps, 18–19

Fish Stock, 228

Genghis Khan's Whole Fried Fish, 56–57

GW Fin's Grilled Lemon Fish with Thai-Style Mirliton Slaw, Blue Crab Fritters, and Chile Oil, 194–96

Kitchen Witch's Hot and Cold Redfish Salad, 174

Le Bernardin's Pounded Tuna with Foie Gras, 54–55

Li'l Dizzy's Trout Baquet, 142

Listen-to-Your-Fish Fish, 53

Patois Oyster Stew with Pan-Fried Grouper and Fried Parsnips, 30–31

Trout Farci, 99

Fitzmorris, Tom, 231

Flowers, Johnnie, 120

Flynn, Tenney, 194

Fogel, Alexa, 231

Foie gras

Le Bernardin's Pounded Tuna with Foie Gras, 54–55

L'Hôtel de France's Foie Gras in a Pumpkin Terrine, 24–25

Folse, John, 28, 184

Franklin, Tom, 93

Frasca, 28

French Laundry, 28

French 75, 214

Fritters, Blue Crab, 194

G

Gabrielle Restaurant, 13, 15, 62, 109

Galatoire's, 10, 49, 109, 189

Gamay, 15, 109

Ganache, 105

Gautreau's, 70

Gendusa, John, 151

Genghis Khan, 56

Gigi's, 120

Gin

Hot-or-Cold Hendrick's #1, 225

Ramos Gin Fizz, 216

Ginger

Ginger-Peach Julep, 221

Ginger Sauce, 56–57

Ginger Simple Syrup, 221

Paw Paw's Honey-Ginger Simple Syrup, 223

Ginger liqueur

Bittersweet Sour, 222

Glazes

Asian-Cajun Red Pepper Glaze, 65

Chile–Sweet Soy Glaze, 68

Grapefruit

Citrus Salad, 137

N'awlins Nectar, 223

Green, Linda, 32

Greens

Boucherie's Collard Greens with French Fried Grits, 138

Dooky Chase's Gumbo Z'herbes, 156–57

Vegetarian Mustard Greens, 147

Grits

French Fried Grits, 138

MiLa's Chicory Coffee–Glazed Quail with Swiss Chard and Creamy Grits, 60–61

Grouper, Pan-Fried, Patois Oyster Stew with Fried Parsnips and, 30–31

Gumbo

Creole Gumbo, 122–24

Dooky Chase's Gumbo Z'herbes, 156–57

history of, 117

Prejean's Pheasant-Quail-Andouille Gumbo, 143

GW Fins, 194

H

Hachee met Leffe Bier (Beef Onion Stew with Dark Beer), 182

Hall, Gwendolyn Midlo, 131

Ham

Creole Stuffed Bell Peppers, 84

Creole Succotash, 87

Dooky Chase's Gumbo Z'herbes, 156–57

Shrimp and Mirliton Bread Pudding, 103

Hannah, Chris, 213, 214

Harris, Jessica, 93, 156, 163

Harrison, Donald, 232

Hart, Keith, 231

Hemphill, Kamili, 15

Herbsaint (liqueur)

Absinthe Suissesse, 214

Sazerac, 215

Herbsaint (restaurant), 46, 130

Hidalgo, Nelson, 203

Highlands Bar and Grill, 13

Hill, Lance, 200

Hodgson, Star, 223

Honey

Honey Simple Syrup, 223

Paw Paw's Honey-Ginger Simple Syrup, 223

Hot-or-Cold Hendrick's #1, 225

Howell, Mary, 93

Hubig's, 36

Hurricane, 217

I

Ice, Thyme-Satsuma–Black Pepper, 75

Irene's Cuisine, 158

J

Jack's Luxury Oyster Bar, 60

Jackson's Bar & Oven, 163

Jhoni, Jacques, 15, 109

Johnnie's Half Shell, 150–51

Julian, Ian, 225

K

Kaczenski, Chester, 232

Kale

Bacon-Wrapped Pork Loin with Smothered Greens, Butternut Squash, and Cane Syrup Jus, 67

Domenica's Crispy Kale, 39

Karma Kitchen, 40

Kearney, Anne, 13, 15, 20

Kimball, Narvin, 78

Kim Son, 13

Kitchen Witch, 174

Koch, Felix, 184

Kotteman, Ron, 76

K-Paul's, 13, 15, 62, 131

Kumquat Marmalade, 70

L

Lafon, Thomy, 136

Lagasse, Emeril, 18, 131, 232

La Mancusa, Philipe, 174

Lambreaux, Albert, 145, 148, 232

Lambreaux, Davina, 153, 155, 156

Lambreaux, Delmond, 186

Lamb Shanks, Habanero-Laced, with Spiced Couscous, 116

Lasagna, Ralph's on the Park's Crabmeat, 205

La Spiga, 13, 36, 158, 160

Le Bernardin, 6, 7, 45, 53, 54, 232

LeCoeur, Darren, 231

Lee, Henry, 56

Lee, Myung Hee, 56

Leidenheimer, George, 150

Leidenheimer's, 150, 151

Lemons

Citrus-Chile Oil, 194

GW Fin's Grilled Lemon Fish with Thai-Style Mirliton Slaw, Blue Crab Fritters, and Chile Oil, 194–96

Muscadine Wine Lemonade, 188

Leslie, Austin, 7, 113

Lettuce

Bun (Vietnamese Vermicelli Salad with Beef), 183

Dickie Brennan's Steakhouse Tomato Napoleon, 191

Dooky Chase's Gumbo Z'herbes, 156–57

Emeril's Tuna and Butter Lettuce Wraps, 18–19

Kitchen Witch's Hot and Cold Redfish Salad, 174

Ruth's Garlicky White Shrimp Remoulade, 189

Salad without Papers, 164

Levitt, Sally, 168

L'Hôtel de France, 13, 24

Li'l Dizzy's Cafe, 142

Link, Donald, 7, 10, 46, 130, 231, 232

Listen-to-Your-Fish Fish, 53

Lobsters, Peppy, 50–51

Logsdon, Dana, 36, 160

Logsdon, Joe, 150
Lonzo, Freddie, 78
Lou, Mr., 118
Lucky Peach, 65, 68, 232

M

MacGowan, Shane, 8
Macquet, Dominique, 220
Magee, Kamili, 15
Mandich's Restaurant, 98
Marcello, Carlos, 206
Marisol, 116
Marmalade, Kumquat, 70
Marsalis, Ellis, 10, 78
The Marsaw, 224
Martin, Bennie and Clovis, 141
Martin Brothers' Coffee Stand and Restaurant, 141
Maximo's, 91
Maylie's Restaurant, 93
Mayonnaise, Green Garlic, 96
McAlary, Davis, 134, 158, 164, 166
McCusker, John, 78
McMillian, 224
McMillian, Chris, 215, 224, 226
McPhail, Tory, 102
Mike's, 13
MiLa, 60
Mimi, Aunt, 211
Mint Simple Syrup, 220
Mirlitons, 200–201
    Mirliton Slaw, 194
    Shrimp and Mirliton Bread Pudding, 103
    Stuffed Mirliton, 153–54
Mr. B's Bistro, 150, 205
Mizell-Nelson, Michael, 150
The Modern, 163
Momofuku, 7, 27, 42
Morial, Dutch, 82
Mosca, John, 206
Mosca's, 206
Mudslide Cookies, 73
Muffalettas, 141
Mulé's, 145
Mullins, Paul R., 168
Muscadine Wine Lemonade, 188
Mushrooms
    Besh Steakhouse's Cowboy Steak with Wild Mushrooms, Root Vegetables, and Bordelaise Sauce, 209
    Clemenceau'd Shrimp, 49
    Fricassee of Peas, Fava Beans, and Morel Mushrooms, 53
    Gabrielle's Slow-Roasted Duck with Cracklin' Skin, 62–63
    Grandmother Besh's Braised Rabbit with Cavatelli, 58–59
    Karma Kitchen's Husk-Wrapped Mushroom Boudin Tamales, 40–41
    Pickled Chanterelle Salad, 50
Mustard-Butter Sauce, 53
Mustard greens
    Dooky Chase's Gumbo Z'herbes, 156–57
    Vegetarian Mustard Greens, 147

N

Napoleon House, 141
Nardo's Trattoria, 15
N'awlins Nectar, 223
Neal, John, 15
Nelson, Danny, 78, 81
Nesbit, Darin, 137
The Neutral Ground, 221
New Orleans City Exchange Cafe, 213
New Orleans cuisine, influences on, 130–31, 208
Nine Roses, 13
Noble, Nina Kostroff, 232
NOLA Cake Cafe, 158
Noodles. *See* Pasta and noodles
Nott, John, 107
Nuoc Mam, 183
Nuts. *See also individual nuts*
    Pie Four Nuts, 118

O

Oatmeal and Fresh Berry Parfaits with Chantilly Cream, 111
Oil, Citrus-Chile, 194
Okra
    Creole Gumbo, 122–24
    Creole Succotash, 87
    Tee's Smothered Okra, 83
Okra, Mr., 76, 127
Olney, Richard, 13
Omni Royal Orleans Hotel, 224
Onions
    Green Onion Pancakes, 27
    Hachee met Leffe Bier (Beef Onion Stew with Dark Beer), 182
    Onion Soubise, 42
    Pickled Red Onions, 20
Oranges
    Citrus-Chile Oil, 194
    Citrus Salad, 137
    Gautreau's Citrus–Olive Oil Cake with Kumquat Marmalade and Almonds, 70
Ory, Kid, 78
Overmyer, Eric, 8, 231
Oysters
    Bourbon House Trio of Oyster Shooters, 137
    Dutch Morial's Oyster Dressing, 82
    farming, 176–77
    Oysters on the Half Shell with Yuzu Mignonette, 17
    Patois Oyster Stew with Pan-Fried Grouper and Fried Parsnips, 30–31
    Upperline's Oysters St. Claude, 98

P

Palace Café, 13, 111, 150
Palladin, Jean-Louis, 105
Pancakes
    Green Onion Pancakes, 27
    Pancakes Lafon, 136
    Pecan Pancakes, 94
P&J Oysters, 176
Parasol's, 13
Parfaits, Oatmeal and Fresh Berry, with Chantilly Cream, 111
Parsnips, Fried, 30

Pascal's Manale Restaurant, 18
Pasta and noodles
    Bun (Vietnamese Vermicelli Salad with Beef), 183
    Crawfish Ravioli with Sea Urchin Butter Sauce and Mississippi Paddlefish Roe, 47
    Eleven 79's Pasta Bolognese, 140
    Gabrielle's Slow-Roasted Duck with Cracklin' Skin, 62–63
    Grandmother Besh's Braised Rabbit with Cavatelli, 58–59
    Pasta with Shrimp, Garlic, and Parsley, 101
    Ralph's on the Park's Crabmeat Lasagna, 205
    Yaka Mein, 32–33
Pat O'Brien's, 217
Patois, 30
Paulsen, Eric, 81
Peach Julep, Ginger-, 221
Peanut Butter, Chunky, and Chocolaty Banana Cake, 105
Peas
    Clemenceau'd Shrimp, 49
    Fricassee of Peas, Fava Beans, and Morel Mushrooms, 53
Pecan Grove Dairy, 145
Pecans
    Microwave Pralines, 133
    Pecan Pancakes, 94
    Pie Four Nuts, 118
    Pound Cake Paul Trevigne, 119
Pelecanos, George, 7
Peristyle, 15, 20, 174
Peychaud, Antoine Amédée, 226
Pheasant-Quail-Andouille Gumbo, Prejean's, 143
Pho Tau Bay, 13
Piazza, Tom, 93
Pierce, Althea, 83
Pierce, Wendell, 231
Pies
    Appeltaart (Dutch Apple Pie), 185
    Cushaw Pie, 155
    Pie Four Nuts, 118
Po-boys (poor boys)
    bread for, 141, 150–51
    characteristics of, 141
    history of, 141
    Restaurant Stanley's Chili-Prawn Po-boy with Asian Slaw, 172
Pork. *See also* Bacon; Ham; Sausage
    Bacon-Wrapped Pork Loin with Smothered Greens, Butternut Squash, and Cane Syrup Jus, 67
    Cochon's Braised Pig with Stewed Turnips and Cabbage, 197
    Eleven 79's Pasta Bolognese, 140
    Kermit Ruffins's Butter Beans, 88
    Pork and Beans with Bacon and Onions, 199
Potatoes
    Clemenceau'd Shrimp, 49
    Creole Crab-and-Corn Bisque, 28–29
    Fingerling Potato Chips, 42
    Potato Salad, 128
    Roasted Potatoes, 206
Pots de Crème, Bayona's Café au Lait, with Mudslide Cookies, 73–74

Pound Cake Paul Trevigne, 119

Pralines, Microwave, 133

Prejean's, 143

Prima, Louis, 140

Prudence, Milton, 109

Prudhomme, Paul, 62, 105, 131

Pudding. See Bread pudding

Pumpkin Terrine, L'Hôtel de France's Foie Gras in a, 24–25

Q

Quackenbush, Christina, 167

Quail

MiLa's Chicory Coffee–Glazed Quail with Swiss Chard and Creamy Grits, 60–61

Prejean's Pheasant-Quail-Andouille Gumbo, 143

R

Rabbit, Grandmother Besh's Braised, with Cavatelli, 58–59

Ralph's on the Park, 205

Ramos, Henry C., 216

Ramos Gin Fizz, 216

Randolph, Lazone, 109

Raspberry liqueur

Second Line Swizzler, 222

Ravioli, Crawfish, with Sea Urchin Butter Sauce and Mississippi Paddlefish Roe, 47

Redfish

GW Fin's Grilled Lemon Fish with Thai-Style Mirliton Slaw, Blue Crab Fritters, and Chile Oil, 194–96

Kitchen Witch's Hot and Cold Redfish Salad, 174

Reggio, Greg, 81

Reising, George, 150

Remoulade

Garlicky White Remoulade, 189

Remoulade Sauce, 191

Restaurant August, 28

Restaurant One, 158

Restaurant Stanley, 172

Rice

Crawfish Calas with Green Garlic Mayonnaise, 96

Herbsaint's Shrimp and Louisiana Brown Rice Risotto, 46

Karma Kitchen's Husk-Wrapped Mushroom Boudin Tamales, 40–41

Peppered Hanger Steak with Crispy Rice Cakes, 68

Red Beans and Rice with Smoked Turkey Wings, 198

Sesame Rice Cakes, 34

Smothered Turnip Soup, 125

Uptown Egg and Rice, 112

Yeast Calas, 127

Richman, Alan, 130

Riomar, 167

Ripert, Eric, 6–7, 10, 45, 54, 232

Risotto, Herbsaint's Shrimp and Louisiana Brown Rice, 46

Rittenberg, Paulette and Bill, 105

Roahen, Sara, 32

Roberts, Sally-Ann, 81

Robinson, Arthur "Mr. Okra," 76

Rodekool met Appels (Braised Red Cabbage with Apples), 181

Roe, Mississippi Paddlefish, Crawfish Ravioli with Sea Urchin Butter Sauce and, 47

Roker, Al, 34

Roman Candy Man, 76

Ruffins, Kermit, 7, 10, 78, 88, 90–91, 232

Rum

Black Beans and Rum à la Austin Leslie, 113

Hurricane, 217

Rushing, Slade, 60

Ruth's Chris Steak House, 91, 176, 189, 194

Rye whiskey

McMillian, 224

The Neutral Ground, 221

Sazerac, 215

Vieux Carré, 216

S

St. Charles Hotel, 226

St. Claude Sauce, 98

St. Louis Hotel, 227

Salads. See also Slaws

Bun (Vietnamese Vermicelli Salad with Beef), 183

Citrus Salad, 137

Cucumber and Tobiko Salad, 137

Dickie Brennan's Steakhouse Tomato Napoleon, 191

Kitchen Witch's Hot and Cold Redfish Salad, 174

Pickled Chanterelle Salad, 50

Potato Salad, 128

Salad without Papers, 164

Salmon

Listen-to-Your-Fish Fish, 53

Sammy's Deli, 91

Santini, Joseph, 213

Satsumas, 75

Gautreau's Citrus–Olive Oil Cake with Kumquat Marmalade and Almonds, 70

Roasted Satsuma–Sweet Potatoes in Satsuma Cups, 104

Thyme-Satsuma–Black Pepper Ice, 75

Sauces

Béchamel Sauce, 205

Bordelaise Sauce, 209

Bourbon-Molasses Sauce, 114–15

Champagne Mignonette, 137

Garlicky White Remoulade, 189

Ginger Sauce, 56–57

Mustard-Butter Sauce, 53

Nuoc Mam, 183

Remoulade Sauce, 191

Roasted Corn Coulis, 50

St. Claude Sauce, 98

Sausage

Creole Gumbo, 122–24

Creole Succotash, 87

Dooky Chase's Gumbo Z'herbes, 156–57

Eleven 79's Pasta Bolognese, 140

Kermit Ruffins's Butter Beans, 88

Prejean's Pheasant-Quail-Andouille Gumbo, 143

Tee's Smothered Okra, 83

Sawyer, Martin, 224

Sazerac, 215

Sazerac Bar, 211

Schilder, Sonny, 158, 160, 179

Seasoning mixes

Basic Creole Seasoning Blend, 228

Commander's Creole Seasoning, 103

Second Line Swizzler, 222

Segreto, Joe, 140

Sesame Rice Cakes, 34

Shaya, Alon, 39

Shorty, Trombone, 81

Shrimp

Clemenceau'd Shrimp, 49

Crawfish Ravioli with Sea Urchin Butter Sauce and Mississippi Paddlefish Roe, 47

Creole Crab-and-Corn Bisque, 28–29

Creole Gumbo, 122–24

Creole Stuffed Bell Peppers, 84

Creole Succotash, 87

Herbsaint's Shrimp and Louisiana Brown Rice Risotto, 46

Pasta with Shrimp, Garlic, and Parsley, 101

Restaurant Stanley's Chili-Prawn Po-boy with Asian Slaw, 172

Rich Shrimp Stock, 229

Ruth's Garlicky White Shrimp Remoulade, 189

Salad without Papers, 164

Shrimp and Mirliton Bread Pudding, 103

Shrimp Bisque, 166

Shrimp Stock, 229

Stuffed Mirliton, 153–54

Tee's Smothered Okra, 83

Trout Farci, 99

White Beans and Shrimp, 89

Yaka Mein, 32–33

Zucchini and Shrimp Semplice, 192

Simon, David, 7, 8–9, 231

Simple Syrup, 214

Singleton, Alfred, 191

Singley, Patrick, 70

Slaws

Asian Slaw, 172

Green Garlic Coleslaw, 40

Mirliton Slaw, 194

Smith, Alverda, 119

Smith, Ken, 93, 98

Sonnier, Greg and Mary, 15, 62, 109, 131

Soups. See also Gumbo

Creole Crab-and-Corn Bisque, 28–29

Shrimp Bisque, 166

Smothered Turnip Soup, 125

Spicer, Susan, 7, 10, 13, 15, 38, 73, 114, 231

Spinach

Dooky Chase's Gumbo Z'herbes, 156–57

Patois Oyster Stew with Pan-Fried Grouper and Fried Parsnips, 30–31

Peppered Hanger Steak with Crispy Rice Cakes, 68

Ralph's on the Park's Crabmeat Lasagna, 205

Squash. See also Mirlitons

Bacon-Wrapped Pork Loin with Smothered Greens, Butternut Squash, and Cane Syrup Jus, 67

Besh Steakhouse's Cowboy Steak with Wild Mushrooms, Root Vegetables, and Bordelaise Sauce, 209
Cushaw Pie, 155
Herbsaint's Shrimp and Louisiana Brown Rice Risotto, 46
Soa's Garden Vegetable "Fettucini" with Fresh Tomato Sauce, 45
Zucchini and Shrimp Semplice, 192
Stabler, Ken, 13
Stanley, 172
Stella!, 68
Steve's, 91
Steve's Poultry House, 145
Stitt, Frank, 13, 36
Stitt, Pardis, 13
Stocks
Basic Chicken Stock, 230
Fish Stock, 228
Rich Shrimp Stock, 229
Shrimp Stock, 229
Turkey Stock, 149
Veal Stock, 230
Street vendors, 76–77
Stryjewski, Stephen, 197
Sublette, Ned, 208
Succotash, Creole, 87
Sweet potatoes, 104
Bayona's Sweet Potato Brioche, 38
The Casserole Cocktail, 218
La Spiga's Sweet Potato Turnovers, 36–37
Roasted Satsuma–Sweet Potatoes in Satsuma Cups, 104
Sweet Potato Fries, 114–15
Sweet Potato Syrup, 218
Swiss Chard, MiLa's Chicory Coffee–Glazed Quail with Creamy Grits and, 60–61
Sylvain, 216
Syrups
Cucumber Simple Syrup, 225
Demerara and Lemongrass Syrup, 222
Ginger Simple Syrup, 221
Honey Simple Syrup, 223
Mint Simple Syrup, 220
Paw Paw's Honey-Ginger Simple Syrup, 223
Simple Syrup, 214
Sweet Potato Syrup, 218

T

Talarico, Annie, 158, 179
Tamales, Karma Kitchen's Husk-Wrapped Mushroom Boudin, 40–41
Taormina family, 76, 134
Tea
Congo Square Cooler, 220
Hot-or-Cold Hendrick's #1, 225
Tees, Jared, 209
Thyme-Satsuma–Black Pepper Ice, 75
Tofu
Karma Kitchen's Husk-Wrapped Mushroom Boudin Tamales, 40–41
Tomatoes
Bun (Vietnamese Vermicelli Salad with Beef), 183
Cousin Kami's Carne Guisada, 207

Creole Crab-and-Corn Bisque, 28–29
Creole Succotash, 87
Dickie Brennan's Steakhouse Tomato Napoleon, 191
Eleven 79's Pasta Bolognese, 140
Grandmother Besh's Braised Rabbit with Cavatelli, 58–59
Kitchen Witch's Hot and Cold Redfish Salad, 174
Salad without Papers, 164
Shrimp Bisque, 166
Soa's Garden Vegetable "Fettucini" with Fresh Tomato Sauce, 45
Tee's Smothered Okra, 83
Tommy's Cuisine, 158
Tooker, Poppy, 96, 99, 163, 175
Tortillas
Emeril's Tuna and Butter Lettuce Wraps, 18–19
Trevigne, Paul, 119
Trout
Genghis Khan's Whole Fried Fish, 56–57
Li'l Dizzy's Trout Baquet, 142
Trout Farci, 99
Tucker, Susan, 107
Tuna
Emeril's Tuna and Butter Lettuce Wraps, 18–19
Le Bernardin's Pounded Tuna with Foie Gras, 54–55
Turkey
Creole Roasted Turkey, 102
Oven-Braised Turkey Necks, 129
Red Beans and Rice with Smoked Turkey Wings, 198
Turkey Stock, 149
Turnips
Besh Steakhouse's Cowboy Steak with Wild Mushrooms, Root Vegetables, and Bordelaise Sauce, 209
Cochon's Braised Pig with Stewed Turnips and Cabbage, 197
Smothered Turnip Soup, 125
Turnovers, La Spiga's Sweet Potato, 36–37

U

Uddo family, 76, 134
Uglesich's, 13, 176
Unkel, Kurt and Karen, 46
Upperline Restaurant, 93, 98, 150
Uptown Egg and Rice, 112

V

Vaucresson, 145
Vazquez, Pete and Janis, 116
Veal
Eleven 79's Pasta Bolognese, 140
Veal Stock, 230
Vermouth
Vieux Carré, 216
Verti Mart, 158
Vietnamese Vermicelli Salad with Beef (Bun), 183
Vieux Carré, 216
Vines-Rushing, Allison, 60
Vizard's, 158

Vodka
Citrus Salad, 137
Second Line Swizzler, 222
Vujnovich, Milos, 176
Vujnovich, Pete, 176

W

Waffles
Paper-Skin Chicken and Rice-Flour Waffles with Asian-Cajun Red Pepper Syrup, 65–66
Waffles Lafon, 136
Walker, Judy, 200
Walnuts
Mudslide Cookies, 73
Warren, Frank, 13
Weed, Lucinda, 216, 222
Weiss, Seymour, 211
Whann, Sandy, 38, 150
Whiskey. *See* Bourbon; Rye whiskey
White, Alice, 153
White, Willie, 93
WildFlour Breads, 38
Willie Mae's, 13, 91
Willis, Nathaniel Parker, 227
Wilson, Geoffrey, 224
Wine
Bordelaise Sauce, 209
French 75, 214
Muscadine Wine Lemonade, 188
Wondrich, David, 224
Wraps, Emeril's Tuna and Butter Lettuce, 18–19

Y

Yaka Mein, 32–33
Yeast Calas, 127

Z

Zea's, 81
Zemanick, Sue, 70
Zimet, Nathaniel, 138
Zonneveld, Dirk-Jan, 181, 182, 185
Zucchini
Soa's Garden Vegetable "Fettucini" with Fresh Tomato Sauce, 45
Zucchini and Shrimp Semplice, 192

TABLE OF EQUIVALENTS

The exact equivalents in the following tables have been rounded for convenience.

Liquid/Dry Measurements

U.S.	Metric
¼ teaspoon	1.25 milliliters
½ teaspoon	2.5 milliliters
1 teaspoon	5 milliliters
1 tablespoon (3 teaspoons)	15 milliliters
1 fluid ounce (2 tablespoons)	30 milliliters
¼ cup	60 milliliters
⅓ cup	80 milliliters
½ cup	120 milliliters
1 cup	240 milliliters
1 pint (2 cups)	480 milliliters
1 quart (4 cups, 32 ounces)	960 milliliters
1 gallon (4 quarts)	3.84 liters
1 ounce (by weight)	28 grams
1 pound	448 grams
2.2 pounds	1 kilogram

Oven Temperature

Fahrenheit	Celsius	Gas
250	120	½
275	140	1
300	150	2
325	160	3
350	180	4
375	190	5
400	200	6
425	220	7
450	230	8
475	240	9
500	260	10

Lengths

U.S.	Metric
⅛ inch	3 millimeters
¼ inch	6 millimeters
½ inch	12 millimeters
1 inch	2.5 centimeters